UNDERSTANDING
CHARLES JOHNSON

Understanding Contemporary American Literature
Matthew J. Bruccoli, Series Editor

Volumes on

Edward Albee • Nicholson Baker • John Barth • Donald Barthelme
The Beats • The Black Mountain Poets • Robert Bly
Raymond Carver • Fred Chappell • Chicano Literature
Contemporary American Drama
Contemporary American Horror Fiction
Contemporary American Literary Theory
Contemporary American Science Fiction
Contemporary Chicana Literature
Robert Coover • James Dickey • E. L. Doctorow • John Gardner
George Garrett • John Hawkes • Joseph Heller • Lillian Hellman
John Irving • Randall Jarrell • Charles Johnson • William Kennedy
Jack Kerouac • Ursula K. Le Guin • Denise Levertov
Bernard Malamud • Bobbie Ann Mason • Jill McCorkle
Carson McCullers • W. S. Merwin • Arthur Miller
Toni Morrison's Fiction • Vladimir Nabokov • Gloria Naylor
Joyce Carol Oates • Tim O'Brien • Flannery O'Connor • Cynthia Ozick
Walker Percy • Katherine Anne Porter • Richard Powers
Reynolds Price • Annie Proulx • Thomas Pynchon
Theodore Roethke • Philip Roth • May Sarton • Hubert Selby, Jr.
Mary Lee Settle • Neil Simon • Isaac Bashevis Singer
Jane Smiley • Gary Snyder • William Stafford • Robert Stone
Anne Tyler • Kurt Vonnegut • David Foster Wallace
Robert Penn Warren • James Welch • Eudora Welty
Tennessee Williams • August Wilson

UNDERSTANDING
CHARLES
JOHNSON

Gary Storhoff

University of South Carolina Press

© 2004 University of South Carolina

Published in Columbia, South Carolina, by the
University of South Carolina Press

Manufactured in the United States of America

08   07   06   05   04   5   4   3   2   1

Library of Congress Cataloging-in-Publication Data

Storhoff, Gary, 1947–
  Understanding Charles Johnson / Gary Storhoff.
      p. cm. — (Understanding contemporary American literature)
  Includes bibliographical references (p.   ) and index.
  ISBN 1-57003-562-8 (alk. paper)
  1. Johnson, Charles Richard, 1948– —Criticism and interpretation.
2. African Americans in literature. I. Title. II. Series.
  PS3560.O3735Z86 2004
  813'.54—dc22

2004012287

In ongoing love for my mother,
and in memory of my beloved father

Contents

Series Editor's Preface

The volumes of *Understanding Contemporary American Literature* have been planned as guides or companions for students as well as good nonacademic readers. The editor and publisher perceive a need for these volumes because much of the influential contemporary literature makes special demands. Uninitiated readers encounter difficulty in approaching works that depart from the traditional forms and techniques of prose and poetry. Literature relies on conventions, but the conventions keep evolving; new writers form their own conventions—which in time may become familiar. Put simply, *UCAL* provides instruction in how to read certain contemporary writers—identifying and explicating their material, themes, use of language, point of view, structures, symbolism, and responses to experience.

The word *understanding* in the titles was deliberately chosen. Many willing readers lack an adequate understanding of how contemporary literature works; that is, what the author is attempting to express and the means by which it is conveyed. Although the criticism and analysis in the series have been aimed at a level of general accessibility, these introductory volumes are meant to be applied in conjunction with the works they cover. They do not provide a substitute for the works and authors they introduce, but rather prepare the reader for more profitable literary experiences.

M. J. B.

Acknowledgments

As a Buddhist fellow traveler, I know that the doctrine of dependent origination applies especially to projects like this one, since this book could not have been written without the goodwill, help, encouragement, and knowledge of countless people.

Nevertheless, specific thanks are in order. I am most grateful to Charles Johnson, whose friendly encouragement and kindness were essential to me. I am indebted to Professor Vera Kutzinski for introducing me to Johnson's work. Professor John Whalen-Bridge acted as my resource in Eastern philosophy, and his friendly e-mails were constantly welcome. My colleague Professor Susan Anderson, who read a portion of the book, was an unfailing help in my wrestling with Western epistemology and ethics. I have very much appreciated the professionalism, efficiency, courtesy, and friendliness of the staff at the University of South Carolina Press, especially the efforts of Barry Blose and Karen Beidel.

I stand in awe of the Interlibrary Loan Office at the University of Connecticut's Homer Babbidge Library. Their efficiency and willingness to search the globe for requested articles and books were essential. I especially appreciated Nancy Romanello's collegiality, friendliness, and eagerness to help me at the University of Connecticut's Jeremy Richard Library at Stamford.

Finally, I enjoyed as always the support and understanding of my family as I worked. A special thank you goes to my daughter, Danielle, who carefully proofread the entire manuscript for me.

To all, *Pranam* (I bow to you).

UNDERSTANDING
CHARLES JOHNSON

CHAPTER 1

Understanding Charles Johnson
Singing the World

> Were it not for the Buddhadharma, I'm convinced that, as a black American and an artist, I would not have been able to successfully negotiate my last half century of life in this country.
>
> Charles Johnson, *Turning the Wheel*

For Charles Richard Johnson, the unexamined *and* unchanging life is not worth living. Johnson is a leading African American artist, and his work has been deeply influenced by his childhood in an integrated, northern community, by his lifelong interest in graphic arts, by his background in philosophy, and by his practice of the martial arts, which led him to Buddhism. Johnson's Buddhist perspective is a linchpin in his work. Raised in the African Methodist Episcopalian Church, Johnson became a Buddhist in 1967 at the age of nineteen. As an extraordinarily flexible artist and thinker, he finds it impossible to locate himself in only one religious tradition, and his work reflects his openness to religious dialogue. Thus, his Christian background enriches and expands his Buddhist themes with imagery and allusion, while the liberating aspects of his Buddhist convictions give his Judeo-Christian sensibility a provocative intensity that spiritually challenges his reader.

Johnson, who earned a doctorate in philosophy and who also has written philosophical texts, writes fiction to express a fundamentally philosophical vision. As Johnson told an interviewer, "The subjects that interest me are the ones that require philosophical archaeology."[1] Philosophical discourse tends to be formidable, even forbidding, reaching conclusions as finished products and often offered with clenched minds. Yet Johnson's fiction is wonderfully accessible to lay readers interested in philosophical reflection. They will find at the center of his rigorously intellectual work his celebration of the ordinary, prosaic, typical activities of life. But his work is not simply a salute to the way things already are, a simple acceptance of the status quo. Instead, his work stresses the need for transformation of ordinary experience. Johnson's uniqueness as a contemporary writer lies in his profound understanding of the ordinary, and in the very ordinariness of his profound understanding. Johnson's aesthetics may be justly described as an exaltation of the ordinary. To use Stanley Cavell's felicitous phrasing, Johnson wants us to regain "an intimacy with existence." To Johnson, "the everyday, the ordinary, is not a given but a task."[2]

Johnson was born on April 23, 1948, in Evanston, Illinois, the only child of Benny Lee and Ruby Elizabeth (Jackson) Johnson at Community Hospital, an all-black facility.[3] His childhood showed him at an early age that apparent opposites can unite harmoniously. Johnson writes that his parents "seemed as different as two people could be" but nevertheless "complemented and completed each other."[4] His father remains his model of steadfast masculinity. A conservative Republican, he never went to high school, and he often worked three jobs at once to support his family. Johnson's mother also worked at several jobs, including that of a cleaning woman. She was a liberal Democrat intensely interested in the arts and literature, bringing home discarded books from her cleaning jobs. As a child, Johnson absorbed her artistic and literary interests and intended to become a commercial artist. Although his father was at first skeptical of art as a possible career, Johnson wrote to a professional artist, Lawrence Lariar, who encouraged Charles and disagreed with his father's bleak assessment. Charles's father relented and paid for a two-year correspondence art course with Lariar. Johnson remembers his father's faith in him and his financial sacrifice for his art lessons as a demonstration of the nature of authentic love.

Lariar proved to be seminal in Johnson's early life, and he helped Johnson begin his career as a cartoonist in 1965. Johnson thereafter published his cartoons regularly in the *Chicago Tribune* and the *St. Louis Proud*. His career as an artist continued while he was in college, and he created his own fifty-two-part how-to-draw television series for the Public Broadcasting Service (*Charlie's Pad,* 1970). It was later distributed nationally. He also oversaw the publication of two collections of his cartoons: *Black Humor* (1970) and *Half-Past Nation Time* (1972). In his current fiction writing, Johnson occasionally sketches his characters so he can more vividly imagine them.[5]

Johnson learned his habits of hard work and persistence from his father. As he writes in *Black Men Speaking,* "He taught me, I truly believe, *how* to work—indeed, to see whatever I did, regardless of how humble the labor, as being a portrait of myself. And never to stop until my goal was realized. Never!"[6] His sense of indebtedness to his father is matched by his acknowledgment of his mother's influence. Johnson attributes his career in fiction primarily to his mother. She filled her house with books and joined book clubs, leading Johnson as a teenager to organize his own book club in science fiction. As an only child, Johnson made books his best friend. Attending an integrated school in Evanston—Johnson calls it "the number-one high school in the nation in the 1960s"—Johnson disciplined himself to read one book a week.[7] Mrs. Johnson motivated him to write when she gave him a diary, though he was later disturbed to discover she was reading his entries. Johnson has kept a journal throughout his life. As Johnson said in an interview, "There is nothing more beautiful—more suggestive of unlimited possibility—than a blank page or canvas."[8]

In the summer evenings of 1967, he began to practice Chinese martial arts at a monastery, where students were expected to say a prayer before practice. Johnson began to study Buddhism and to meditate, and these factors have continued to play major roles in his art. Currently, Johnson is a contributing editor to the Buddhist journal *Tricycle*.

Johnson enrolled at Southern Illinois University in 1966, where he began as a journalism major. He received his bachelor's degree from SIU in 1971, and a master of arts in philosophy in 1973. In June 1970, he married Joan New, a student at National College of Education in Evanston. While in SIU's graduate program, he met John Gardner, whom Johnson describes as his "literary father."[9] Writing under the influence of Richard Wright, James Baldwin, and John A. Williams, Johnson had already completed six novels before he began working with Gardner, though Johnson has suppressed these novels as products of his apprenticeship. Gardner led Johnson to realize the extraordinary versatility of form in African American literature. As Johnson writes in *Being and Race*, "The modern short story or novel may assume the form of [realism or fantasy] or . . . any other narrative form people have employed—diaries, slave narratives, hymns, sermons, interlocking business documents—to clarify their experiences."[10] Johnson's appropriation of this diversity of literary forms has thereafter distinguished his career, establishing him as one of America's most unpredictably imaginative writers. Johnson also credits Gardner's *On Moral Fiction* with providing him with the sense of writing as an ethical commitment.

Under Gardner's guidance, Johnson published *Faith and the Good Thing* in 1974, while he was also studying for a doctoral degree in philosophy at State University of New York at Stony Brook. As a graduate student at Stony Brook, he taught classes in literary theory and radical philosophy, such as Radical Thought, Third World Literature, and The Black Aesthetic. Pressed to provide financially for his family, Johnson left SUNY to accept a teaching position in creative writing at the University of Washington in 1976. His dissertation, on phenomenology and literary aesthetics, entitled *Being and Race: Black Writing since 1970,* was published in 1988. *Being* provides the reader with an understanding of how Johnson's literary work implicates race, but also escapes the political constrictions imposed by black cultural nationalism. Because he left for the University of Washington, he did not complete his degree at SUNY in the allotted time; however, Johnson was awarded both an honorary and an earned doctorate from SUNY–Stony Brook in 1999. The awarding committee backdated his doctorate to 1988, when *Being and Race* was published.

Besides working on his novels, Johnson continued his affiliation with PBS, writing docudramas, including *Charlie Smith and the Fritter Tree* (1978), about the oldest African American cowboy, and *Booker* (1984), a program on Booker T. Washington, which received the Writer's Guild Award. His association with PBS includes an appearance on Bill Moyer's series *Genesis* (1996) and his collaboration with Patricia Smith and others in the production *Africans in America: America's Journey through Slavery* (1998). Johnson contributed twelve short stories to the series, which was later published as a history book. Johnson also published his stories as a volume entitled *Soulcatcher* (2001).

While studying philosophy and teaching at the University of Washington, Johnson began an ambitious manuscript, *Oxherding Tale,* published in 1982. This novel was followed by *The Sorcerer's Apprentice* (1986), his collection of short stories previously published during the 1970s and early 1980s. *The Sorcerer's Apprentice* was nominated for the PEN/Faulkner Award, PEN American Center. In 1990, Johnson published *Middle Passage,* which won the National Book Award; Johnson was the first African American male to win this prize since Ralph Ellison in 1953. *Dreamer: A Novel,* Johnson's first book on Martin Luther King Jr., was published in 1998. *Turning the Wheel: Essays on Buddhism and Writing,* a book discussing Buddhism and his theories of writing, was published in 2003. Johnson received the MacArthur Foundation "Genius" Grant in 1998. He was elected to the American Academy of Arts and Sciences in 2003. He is currently the S. Wilson and Grace M. Pollock Professor of Creative Writing at the University of Washington. He has received honorary degrees from SUNY, Northwestern University, Whittier College, and Southern Illinois University, which also administers the Charles Johnson Award for Fiction and Poetry, a nationwide competition in creative writing for college students.[11]

Johnson's Buddhism has led him to reject a prevailing impulse to discover meaning in an abstract, concealed, metaphysical order: a unifying, all-encompassing system that is repressed, deferred, or buried. But Johnson also rejects the contemporary axiom that meaning is a mere chimera, that it is impossible to demonstrate any truth whatsoever. For Johnson, a contemporary oscillation between an absolutist system and nihilism can be avoided by the reader willing to cultivate an appreciation for the ordinary, unexceptional moments of life—with all their unrealized opportunities and wasteful carelessness. Johnson, however, does not employ Buddhist principles in a reductive, one-on-one relationship between his text and the Buddhist "sources."[12] Indeed, Johnson explicitly avoids dogmatic and reductive formulations, and (like many Buddhist writers) imbues his work with rich humor. Johnson's reader should always be prepared to laugh. His fiction points to how a person will be transformed by a close, directed attention to everyday experience—defined by Buddhists as mindfulness (sati). For Johnson, liberated, mindful persons attend to the work before them with all the power of mind and heart; they are not distracted by momentary desires and wishes for things outside the moment. At the same time, Johnson's fiction directs a powerful critique of everyday life.

In this sense, Johnson's Buddhism is very different from Beat Zen writers like Jack Kerouac and Allen Ginsberg. Their work also advocates a kind of human excellence, since they reject an otherworldly perfection as a goal and concentrate on earthly, sensual gratification. Their vision could be fairly summarized as an acceptance of what is—whatever we do, so long as it brings voluptuous delight, is a satisfactory way to live. But their emphasis on sexuality, narcotics, and alcohol would for Johnson only masquerade as a celebration of the present moment. From Johnson's perspective, this acquiescence to sensuality and self-indulgence would lead to a distinctly unenlightened form of life, for immersion in sensual pleasure is a toxic life. For Johnson, the problem with immediate gratification of personal desire is that gratification creates an emotional attachment to the object of desire, but if this gratification were not available, disappointment and chagrin would immediately follow. The "attached" person, attached to his or her own desire, is vulnerable to suffering. Further, gratification is inevitably fleeting, to be replaced by boredom as the satisfaction wears off, or by greater craving for more extravagant pleasures. Addiction is inevitable with this way of life. Thus, Johnson's fiction features different categories of addiction—including substance abuse (alcoholism and drug addiction), the "process addictions" of contemporary psychology (sexual addiction, thrill-seeking), and other forms of compulsive-obsessive dysfunctions (hoarding, fruitless writing, kleptomania, compulsive lying, and so forth). Although not primarily a psychological novelist, Johnson evinces in his work a subtle understanding of personality disorders.

Johnson's called-for transformation of the ordinary moment requires the reader's release from the narrowness of self-centered activity and focus on the self, and a transcendence of an exclusive and static identification with the reader's gender, race, and historical time. His use of the anachronism in his fiction simultaneously criticizes the social formations of the past that promoted racism and oppression and calls for a transformation of the contemporary legacy of the past's mistakes. He condemns contemporary repressive social structures without relieving the individual of responsibility for creating those same structures.[13] His work promotes a radical contextualization of one's era in relation to a larger, more expansive history—the greater totality of being human. Johnson's literary aim is to place an individual into a greater and more coherent spiritual perspective than contemporary literature usually offers.

Johnson's philosophical vision is similar to that of Thich Nhat Hanh, the Vietnamese Buddhist nominated by Martin Luther King Jr. for the Nobel Peace Prize. Like Johnson, Nhat Hanh is committed to bringing people together by promoting interreligious dialogue. Nhat Hanh believes in spiritual commitment leading to a sense of unity. In his book *Living Buddha, Living Christ,* he makes this point poetically clear with a metaphor of a flower. Scientifically, the flower is composed of elements such as carbon dioxide, water, and minerals that in no way resemble the flower itself. What we know as a stable (and ordinary) object is a manifestation of invisible or microscopic natural processes, a miraculous mutuality of diverse elements. What "seems to be" a flower is, in fact, "made entirely of non-flower elements; it has no independent, individual existence." We are, Nhat Hanh asserts, "like the flower, like the natural world. It 'inter-is' with everything else in the universe." Nhat Hanh uses the term "interbeing," an infinite interrelatedness, to describe the spiritual connection between human beings. The term "interbeing" can thus also be applied to Buddhism and Christianity, usually considered entirely distinct religions. He writes: "Just as a flower is made only of non-flower elements, Buddhism is made only of non-Buddhist elements, including Christian ones, and Christianity is made of non-Christian elements, including Buddhist ones." To illustrate this point, he returns to his vegetative metaphor:

It is good that an orange is an orange and a mango is a mango. The colors, smells, and the tastes are different, but looking deeply, we see that they are both authentic fruits. Looking more deeply, we can see the sunshine, the rain, the minerals, and the earth in both of them. Only their manifestations are

different. . . . Buddhism is made of non-Buddhist elements.
Buddhism has no separate self. When you are a truly happy
Christian, you are also a Buddhist. And vice versa.

For Nhat Hanh this recognition is crucial to one who wishes to
progress beyond an unquestioning acceptance of religion's often
dogmatic truths and subjective sense of personal identity. He
writes, "When you are able to get out of the shell of your small
self, you will see that you are interrelated to everyone and everything, that your every act is linked with the whole of human
kind and the whole cosmos."[14]

It is Nhat Hanh's sense of cosmic interrelatedness—interbeing—that Johnson intends to impart to his reader in his fiction. In a world tragically torn apart by tribalism, sectionalism,
and the other varieties of factionalism, Johnson's vision of interbeing offers a bracing alternative. But Johnson also refuses to
offer or permit the false consolations of sentimentality or messages of unearned sympathy or love. Johnson's positive protagonists are not always nice people; often, they are grumpy,
irritable folks. For both the Judeo-Christian and Buddhist traditions, genuine compassion comes only as our suffering grows
worse and we are driven to our enlightenment and salvation. So
it is that Johnson's work, despite its often uproarious comedy, is
replete with images of sickness, physical decay, despair, suicide,
torture, and murder. Paradoxically for this comic writer, his
most vividly memorable image is the human body disintegrating at the moment of death, or shortly after death. Johnson's
emphasis on death, pain, and physical putrescence awakens us
from our sleepy routines to become someone wiser, more mindful, more compassionate, and more flexibly attuned to the world
than we have formerly been.

It is understandable, then, that Johnson as a philosopher would choose art rather than discursive philosophical prose for his purpose. But he would dismiss the distinction between philosophy and literature as one more misleading dualism, for he believes the ultimate purpose of great literature is intrinsically philosophical. To be a great writer is to engage in the philosophical debate that has been carried on for millennia. In *Being and Race,* Johnson asserts that philosophy and literature are "sister disciplines . . . and unless a critic realizes this, his position is simply untenable." Johnson writes that the purpose of all great art is beyond conventional morality; its purpose is to challenge the fundamental ways we see our world, our metaphysics: "Our perception—or way of seeing—has been shaken, if one is talking about great art."[15]

Johnson shakes our "way of seeing" because philosophically, he is a metaphysical antirealist, his position similar to that of many Eastern religions (such as Buddhism and Taoism). In Johnson's fiction, a subtle and interesting metaphysics of antirealism always lurks on the page, often concealed by the humor of the self-mocking narrator. Antirealists like Johnson do not dismiss the external world. (He is not a solipsist, nor does he recommend ontological solipsism.) Instead, antirealists like Johnson oppose the claim that any definitive statement about reality can entirely or even adequately mirror the empirical world. Whatever picture of the world we may have, alternative pictures, different from ours, can be arrived at by other people (living in other places and other times) and cannot be summarily dismissed. Our interpretation of experience may change tomorrow; we may upon reflection improve our interpretation, or evidence discovered subsequently may lead us to reject it entirely. There is, then, no final truth, no exhaustively "correct" account of reality. Instead there is a multitude of perspectives, some of which may be more effective in explaining our lives at the present moment than others, but which are nevertheless themselves not conclusive or terminal. Johnson's antirealism teaches readers the folly of thinking that we can understand reality properly with judgments, categories, or vast systems that explain "hidden" meanings.

As a metaphysical antirealist, Johnson's great American predecessor is Ralph Waldo Emerson. Johnson has acknowledged Emerson as a "spiritual brother" in an interview, and explains, "I'm deeply thankful for the presence of Transcendentalism in nineteenth-century literature—as a first groping toward the vision of the Dharma [that is, the Way, the Law]."[16] The discovery of divinity within humanity—the point of Emerson's "The Divinity School Address" (1838)—redounds throughout Johnson's work. Perhaps the best example of Emersonian enlightenment (shared by Johnson's work) appears in the notorious passage from Emerson's *Nature:*

> Standing on the bare ground,—my head bathed by the blithe air and uplifted into infinite space,—all mean egotism vanishes. I become a transparent eyeball; I am nothing; I see all; the currents of the Universal Being circulate through me; I am part or particle of God.[17]

It is as if this passage is seminal to Johnson's *corpus.* In order to "see all," the self becomes "nothing," emptied of "all mean egotism." This is the goal of Johnson's protagonists, though they seldom know it at the beginning of their narratives; instead, they are infected with an intense desire to affirm a self (that in actuality is not there). Self-emptying occurs, however, not with the exercise of one's will, but with a cultivated passivity, an opening of oneself to the world in all its immensity. Emerson's image of the eyeball's transparency is a passive purgation, for everything passes through and nothing is retained or grasped; the boundary between the person and the world is suddenly permeable. In this moment of passivity, however, is an experienced power, the "currents of the Universal Being." Concomitant with the power is the identification of divinity—what Johnson's protagonists discover at the end of their plots. But in that discovery, they return to what they were in the first place, in the ordinary world, "standing on the bare ground." Perhaps this last, unnoticed point of this much-discussed passage is most important for an understanding of Johnson's work: one never leaves the unadorned, simple, mundane bare ground. Johnson thus answers the famous challenge of Emerson's "The American Scholar" (1837), for a writer to illuminate the wondrous possibilities of the mundane and the ordinary: "What would we really know the meaning of? The meal in the firkin; the milk in the pan; the ballad in the street; the news of the boat; the glance of the eye; the form and the gait of the body."[18]

Charles Johnson's Syncretistic Self

In his book *Religion in the Making*, the philosopher Alfred North Whitehead writes:

> The decay of Christianity and Buddhism, as determinative influences in modern thought, is partly due to the fact that each religion has unduly sheltered itself from the other. The self-sufficient pedantry of learning and the confidence of ignorant zealots have combined to shut up each religion in its

own forms of thought. Instead of looking to each other for
deeper meanings, they have remained self-satisfied and unfer-
tilized.[19]

Though Whitehead writes here of just Christianity, his passage
is equally descriptive of the entire Judeo-Christian tradition.
Johnson's work cross-fertilizes Buddhism and Judeo-Christian
traditions, as Whitehead believes is needed, to make them
"determinative influences in modern thought." Though not necessarily with a specific, deliberate intent to respond to Whitehead's book, Johnson answers Whitehead's call for a highly
complex, syncretistic synthesis of Buddhist and Judeo-Christian
traditions. Johnson's central goal is to create a religious, "syncretistic self." For Johnson, a syncretistic sensibility would "find
it the most natural thing, as Merleau-Ponty was fond of saying,
to go about 'singing the world.'"[20]

The word *syncretism* is used advisedly. While for most social
scientists *syncretism* is of relatively neutral value, for many theo-
logians the word stipulates an awkward and imprecise religious
yoking. In contrast, Whitehead and Johnson see that religion
itself should be the ultimate syncretism. As Johnson writes in his
novel *Dreamer,* "'religion' derives from the Latin *religare,* 'to
bind,' or to bring together those things broken, torn asunder."[21]
To locate oneself in only one religious tradition is ultimately,
for Johnson, too limiting. Thus, to have a religious faith is
inevitably to become a "syncretistic self," the product of a
process of selective appropriation of spiritual truths drawn
from vastly varied religions. Johnson's characters are religious
amalgams, assemblages of pluralistic spiritual elements,
brought together out of Johnson's conviction of the need for
religious cross-fertilization. His fictive goal is to create a dialogic

interaction between those elements that have usually been thought of as exclusive to very diverse traditions.

Johnson writes his novels to provide a transcultural experience for the reader, leading to a mutually creative transformation of each religious tradition. Johnson's purpose is to create a "Christianized Buddhism and a Buddhized Christianity."[22] This concern for religious transformation manifests consistently from *Faith and the Good Thing* through *Dreamer.* As his work matures, Johnson becomes more confident and daring in his religious exploration. *Faith* is Johnson's *Pilgrim's Progress,* an elaborate exploration of the contemporary world by a questing African American Everywoman. Her journey through urban America is an allegorical disclosure of how people justify their lives with metaphysical theories—each of which is inadequate. The resolution of her quest is decidedly non-Christian, but it points toward the Buddhist direction of Johnson's later work.

Johnson's religious imagination is not enslaved by conventionality. His characters construct the concept of God along the lines of neither a mythical narrative like the Bible nor a metaphysics like fundamentalist Christianity that insists on a unified, static, substantialist deity. Instead, he uses the idea of God as a pointer (a common Buddhist image) to direct the reader's attention to the realm of the spirit as lived out in ordinary life. Although religious thinking deals necessarily with the mysterious and ineffable, Johnson's dramatizes ways that make religious thought relevant to the reader's day-to-day living. Johnson progressively explores the ethical dimensions of his antirealist philosophical position. If a supreme being is dismissed, if there can be no ultimate truth (moral or otherwise) in a world of flux, if alternative pictures of reality are incommensurable, then how can a person discover an ethical basis? How can this ethical position be enacted in the social world? Johnson fully engages these questions in his most recent novel, *Dreamer*. In *Dreamer*, Johnson proposes a dramatic expansion from individualized, personal liberation that preoccupies his earlier work to a concern for a religio-philosophical understanding of life's political dimensions. Martin Luther King Jr. embodies ethical action. Though characters cannot match King's fame and world renown, his ethical model is accessible to all human beings.

Current Western philosophy treats ethics as primarily the moral evaluation of actions. However, such an approach is insufficient for a novelist, so Johnson's interest is in the evaluation of the whole person, in evaluating character traits that make an individual good and that lead to a worthwhile life.[23] Johnson's vision is broadly ecological and melioristic, directed toward enlightenment and wisdom. American pragmatism is one philosophical branch that becomes a thematic structure in Johnson's work, though as is typical for Johnson, pragmatism is treated with subtlety and qualification. Pragmatism does not connote ethical relativism; instead, contemporary pragmatists (for example, Cornel West) conjoin humanist ethics with democratic liberalism and an Old Testament sense of justice. West calls this philosophical amalgam "prophetic pragmatism," an ethical commitment that emerges especially in *Dreamer*. Since change occurs inevitably, and since we must continually work together to reconstruct our values in response to change, it is best to discover ethical models (like King) to assist us. Because the individual lives within communities and institutions that undergo continual evaluation and occasional transformation, Johnson's goal is to help build a better world by guiding *spiritual* evaluation and transformation.

Johnson's literary intention is similar to Buddhism's transformational purpose. The word *Buddha* is a title, meaning "someone who is awake," and Johnson's purpose is to awaken the reader.[24] Johnson's work is based on the Buddhist recognition of universal, pervasive, unrelenting, and radical human unhappiness. For both Johnson and Buddha, at the root of human suffering is our ignorance of and enslavement to existential reality—termed "samsara" by Buddhists. Individuals suffer from a deluded vision of life that is inherently and inescapably sorrowful, for although they think they are pursuing pleasures in their activities, they are in fact fleeing suffering in a futile attempt to deny the world's inescapable impermanence. Pain, of course, is unavoidable in life; but Buddhists make a distinction between pain and suffering, the latter connoting an emotional attachment to or intemperate craving for the things we desire. For an unenlightened person, the desired thing is somehow essential to living a worthwhile life, and when this desired object is not acquired or experienced, disappointment, frustration, and unhappiness must be the emotional consequence. This hopeless pursuit produces unrelieved spiritual suffering (dukkha).

For Buddhists, the world that we perceive is a delusion, an emptiness colored by our human craving. This craving (tanha) informs human action universally and is the source of our suffering. That which is chased only evaporates, and that which one craves disappears even as it is experienced. This misery is increased by the immense desire to believe that what we wish for is stationary and consistent; in reality, it is instead fleeting, dissolving, and evanescent. Thus, human beings suffer as the consequence of their cognition, a mental process operating within their very being. At the root of this process is humanity's ignorance of reality (avidya).

Johnson's work revolves around Buddhism's central doctrine: All things are in constant flux. Buddhism's radical, thoroughgoing transience has enormous implications for Johnson's fiction. The seminal Buddhist concept of dependent origination (partitya samutpada) explains how things are transient, and how things eventually become what they fleetingly are. According to this concept, all people, thoughts, and objects are incessantly changing because they depend, at the very moment they come into existence and from that point thereafter, on other things, which are also changing because they too are dependent on other things, and so on ad infinitum. All things are what they are at any given moment not because it is their essential nature to be such, but because other things (also changing) have influenced, shaped, or partially determined whatever exactly they are at the present moment. Because of dependent origination, all things exist in a relational matrix throughout history. No one thing has an essential nature, nor is any thing self-determining; but any thing depends on a complex of relations with other evolving things to derive its evolving identity.

A good example of Johnson's symbolic representation of dependent origination occurs early in Johnson's first novel, *Faith and the Good Thing*. Lavidia, Faith's mother, has just died, and in her bereavement Faith enters the kitchen. Her mother's death has transformed this simple room:

> Without her the kitchen, the house, the world beyond fell apart. Fruit cabinets on the wall still held sweet jellies preserved in the odd-shaped bottles Lavidia salvaged like a scavenger from house and yard and rummage sales; her stiff mops and silver pail still rested in the corner by brooms she'd assembled by hand. Then what had changed? Certainly not the things themselves. Studying Lavidia's dresses heaped in a wash-tub by the door, her pipes in their dusty rack on the kitchen table, and dry lifeless wigs, Faith felt her answer

emerge from the contours of these objects: none of them was for her; they belonged, related to no one. Even Lavidia, perhaps, had not made them her own, because—with her death—they seemed suddenly freed to be as they were. Empty things, cold, without quality, distant.[25]

Mops, brooms, pails, jelly jars, dirty clothes in a washtub—these mundane, ordinary things are momentously transformed in Faith's perception at the moment of her mother's death. Suddenly, these simple things become "as they were." Significantly, the meaning of these objects emerge from their "contours," their form; the distinct form of objects is essential to Johnson for an understanding of their interconnection. Despite their separate forms, Faith suddenly sees that these simple objects lack any independent, autonomous, or self-determining status. Before this epiphanic moment, Faith had known these things within the single, monolithic context of her mother—her character (her parsimoniousness) and her activity (her cooking, cleaning, smoking, and scavenging). But with her mother's death, these objects are released from their familiar monistic context, passing at this moment into other contexts. Their meanings had not been final after all, and Faith "lets go" of her earlier cognition. Faith understands that not even Lavidia with all her industriousness had "made them her own"—these things resist Lavidia's (the owner's) imposition of definitive, static, and absolute meaning. With her death, they were "freed to be as they were." Thus, not even a jelly jar can be known without a context that itself depends on other contexts; all things become utterly relational and contextualized for Faith as she meditates on her mother's death. They are, in Johnson's words, "empty things."

Emptiness (sunyata) is perhaps the key concept in understanding Johnson's work. He ceaselessly repeats imagery and themes of emptiness, though often ironically and perversely, throughout his fiction. As the philosopher Dale S. Wright writes, "the concept 'emptiness' derives from, and eventually encompasses, the key elements in Buddhist contemplative practice: impermanence, dependent origination, and no self. . . . For something to be 'empty' means that, because the entity 'originates dependent' upon other entities, and is transformed in accordance with changes in these external conditions, the entity therefore lacks 'own-being' . . . or 'self-nature.'" For Johnson, an experiential understanding of emptiness leads to a release from the desires for things in the world around us, even a desire for a unique identity. As protagonists are freed from desire in Johnson's fiction, they are liberated from the hold things have over them, including the hold of their own individuality. "Emptiness" in this context does not imply a complete negation of existence, the opposite of being or "somethingness" in general. Nor does emptiness point to nihilism, a complete negation of meaning itself.[26]

Johnson, in contrast, sees the acceptance of emptiness as redemptive. All things are empty; "emptiness" is a universal descriptor. Its sense is similar to the "nothingness" in Jean-Paul Sartre's *Being and Nothingness,* representing an openness and radical indeterminacy, a rejection of an entirely definite or self-enclosed nature. Emptiness in this context may be imagined as Emerson's "transparent eyeball." A specific thing is empty because it originates dependent on other things, but that thing also constantly changes in correlation with all those other changing things. All things—objects, ideas, and sentient beings too—derive their character from the infinite number of factors

that precipitate their beginnings and partially shape their trans-
figurations, which in turn derive their attributes from other factors or contexts throughout history. Thus, no one thing has its
own unique identity; no one thing becomes what it is because
of its essential nature or its will, its own self-determining drive
for actualization. Each thing depends utterly on an infinitely
complex network of correlated and interdependent entities.
Emptiness is in essence what Nhat Hanh means by "interbeing"
—reality is composed of interpenetrating and contingent elements brought together in an instant of time, only to slide
immediately into a slightly different configuration. Interbeing
points Johnson, like Emerson, meditatively to the Oneness of
the world.

It is no exaggeration to say that Johnson's work moves
relentlessly toward the concept of emptiness. For Johnson,
emptiness has a profound meaning for the individual's concept
of self. Even the self—conceived as a ghostly, unchanging
essence of an individual usually defined in terms of an individual's societal roles, or (in religious terms) as the soul—cannot
exist as an independent entity, but is regarded as only a bundle
of swiftly changing, complementary, and conditional states.
Nothing in the world, whether mental or physical, has any dis-
tinctive identity without its mutual relationships to other elements. Consequently, no one individual can be considered as
isolated and unique but is instead an aggregate of experiences
shared with others, with the past, and with the earth itself. The
idea of "no-self" (anatman) is perhaps the most familiar Buddhist doctrine, but the idea is often misunderstood. Individuals
certainly exist, with qualities and traits different from other
individuals. Yet the self is also empty. Like the world itself, the
self has no permanent identity, neither an enduring essence nor

a self-determining nature immune from the shaping power of the external world.

For Johnson as an African American author, interbeing or emptiness has obviously profound racial implications. Insofar as Johnson engages the issue of race, he dramatizes its illusory nature (its emptiness), and his disavowal of identity politics in his fiction is perhaps his most controversial aspect. For example, in *Middle Passage,* he writes that "the (black) self was the greatest of all fictions"; for many reviewers, his dismissal of race as a category is shocking, even flatly wrong. Molly Abel Travis, for example, argues that Johnson's "transcendence" of race is unrealistic and politically implausible. It is possible, however, to disagree with Travis's negative assessment and understand Johnson positive assertions within a more generous, religious context. The Buddhist rejection of a permanent personal identity illuminates Johnson's concept of race. Racial identity, like everything else, cannot be self-determining but is also contingent. Because the African American is embedded in the world, immersed in America and American history, America and the African American exist in infinite interconnection—expressed succinctly as interbeing. It is for this reason that Johnson so vehemently opposes essentialism, separatism, and black cultural nationalism. For Johnson, the only way to liberate oneself from essentialism is to accept the illusory nature of the race and rejoice in its emptiness.[27]

Johnson is highly optimistic that human beings can overcome racism by acknowledging emptiness. Invoking this Buddhist concept alien to his Western readership, Johnson is empiricist and pragmatic. To free oneself, one must know the world as it is: empty. But in knowing emptiness, one paradoxically knows the world's fullness, its wondrous mutuality. The objective world is ultimately a product of our patterns of knowing. For Johnson, this is not entirely an ontological assertion (that is, objects do not exist), but instead is an antirealist, epistemological insight: the perceived world is in fact an altered and transformed construction, formulated from the sensory projections of our own desires and emotional needs. We know the world only as it is formulated in our minds, as we emotionally need it to be. As Johnson writes in *Being and Race,* "the world we live in is, first and foremost, one shaped by the mind."[28] Johnson's Buddhist outlook is the acknowledgment that reality, including our most earnestly embraced ideas, is a temporary, delusive, perceptual amalgam, created by our language and our emotions.

This problem of the mind is reflected in the first two verses of *The Dhammapada,* an early collection of sayings attributed to the historical Buddha:

> All that we are is the result of what we have thought: it is founded on our thoughts, it is made up of our thoughts. If a man speaks or acts with an evil thought, pain follows him, as the wheel follows the foot of the ox that draws the carriage. . . . If a man speaks or acts with pure thought, happiness follows him, like a shadow that never leaves him.[29]

Johnson asserts one can change one's thoughts, and the entirety of his work calls for the reader's paradigm shift. In his basically comic vision, human problems and deficiencies, including racism, are always susceptible to reform and correction. It is possible to awaken from illusion; the notion of an egocentric but limited self can be abandoned by an enlightened person. Awakening from the material realm offers complete freedom and utter tranquility (nirvana). Nirvana for Johnson has nothing to do with the Christian belief of life after death; instead, it consists of seeing the world with clarity, apart from how we would shape it to conform to our desire.

Liberation (awakening), then, depends on a realization of the world as empty. In Johnson's fiction, this startling recognition almost always occurs with a character's experiential understanding of his or her mortality. Johnson typically organizes his narratives to embody a technique that is classical in both Buddhist and Judeo-Christian traditions, the memento mori pattern, or a mental focus on the imminence of one's own death. His fully realized characters finally face their own extinction with equanimity, becoming more focused on each moment. This focus fosters detachment from sensory things and purges unconscious terrors; his characters are ultimately awakened to their freedom. Although he is a comic novelist, his meditation on death is his salient narrative rhythm, for it prompts his protagonists to relinquish the grasping, clinging ego of the character to accept a cosmic order that is impersonal, universal, but infinitely benevolent. This moment of acceptance of a larger reality occurs in *Oxherding Tale,* and Johnson uses the Hindu term *moksha* to define this awakening. In this awakening, each Johnsonian protagonist discovers the actual meaning of freedom: not to do simply what one wishes, but to deal mindfully with whatever problem is closest at hand, what pragmatically needs to be done first.

The attainment of freedom for Johnson is the consummate paradox. Though each plot is designed as a quest for freedom, the questing character always possesses the potentiality for freedom, from the beginning of the plot to the end. Spiritual freedom, even for Johnson's fictive slaves, is a dimension of life the protagonist always possesses, a quality from which a person has never been divided, except by his or her own delusions. This is not to say that the character's quest is entirely irrelevant; each character through the quest discovers important aspects of the world unknown or misunderstood previously. But Johnson dissuades the reader from looking for seminal or definitive moments, or for heroes. For Johnson, neither the transcendent moments nor the extraordinary character exists. Instead, each instant is merely part of an ongoing process, folded back into a multitude of events that constitute the past—countless, ordinary, daily actions, whose cumulative operation in its totality a human being cannot possibly understand. In those seemingly unimportant actions lies our karmic destiny, but we often do not heed the importance of those minute choices. In this way, Johnson challenges the literary tradition of the heroic. There are no heroes, no larger-than-life characters performing superhuman feats. Even in *Dreamer*, Johnson is not interested in depicting the historical Martin Luther King Jr. as heroic, but as a person struggling with the existential cares and woes that all people experience. Johnson wants to shift our attention to the multitudes of people who day by day make history: each person growing toward a more nearly perfect realization of emptiness. In Johnson's work, it is they who go about "singing the world."

CHAPTER 2

Faith and the Good Thing

> Joshu asked Nansen: "What is the path?"
> Nansen said: "Everyday life is the path."
> Joshu asked: "Can it be studied?"
> Nansen said: "If you try to study, you will be far away
> from it."
>
> *Zen Flesh, Zen Bones*

In *Faith and the Good Thing*, Charles Johnson sets forth the fundamental themes that he will develop throughout the rest of his career. When he wrote *Faith*, his first published novel, in nine months, he saw it as "fun," but also as a tour de force of the "artistic strategies [he] would employ later—genre crossing, folklore, comedy, western philosophy from the pre-Socratics to Sartre, the strongest possible narrative voice, poetically layered prose lines."[1] Interestingly, Johnson does not mention in his commentary Indic philosophy, especially Buddhism, though the novel experiments with Buddhist principles as a complement to Western philosophy.

Johnson dramatizes the Buddhist theory of human cognition, which posits craving as the basis of human misery. As the novel's title implies, knowing the world necessarily involves our craving for "good things," a craving that depends on our memory—the internalized, collective body of love-hate experiences in our consciousness. The basic problem of humanity for Johnson is that our memory projects a dualistic vision of ordinary life that separates the "good" and "bad" things, an arbitrary division that for the enlightened person does not truly exist. In a dualistic approach to ordinary life, human beings create anguish for themselves and others. This problem has its roots in an epistemological mistake, in a misguided understanding of the world. A refusal to accept the empty nature of all things leads to an enslavement to desire: "Either you were brand new at each instant, innocent and undetermined and, therefore, free, or you were a bent-back drudge hauling all of world history on your shoulders across the landscape of your life" (59).

Johnson's prescription for the world's ache is a Buddhist recognition of the world's emptiness, the recognition that our deluded assumptions regarding "good things" are mind-marshaled. The true good thing is an acceptance of the idea of emptiness and the renunciation of the distinction between "good" and "bad" things. Faith Cross embarks on this philosophical quest toward emptiness, though her initial goal is to discover an emotional and financial security that her mother Lavidia recommends to Faith on her deathbed: "Girl, you get yourself a good thing" (4). The novel's thematic purpose is to define the "good thing" in wider terms than Lavidia understands.

Johnson's style makes this a complicated text. The novel evolves from a nostalgic reverie on the southern folk tradition in African American literature, complete with a run-down cabin. It then shifts to a harshly naturalistic depiction of the depredations of Chicago's urban life for Faith, an African American woman who struggles with poverty and who must turn to prostitution and then a loveless marriage. Johnson ends the narrative by employing magic realism; this style is used to communicate Faith's release from the bondage of the world of desire into a mystical union with the natural world. The novel is by turns lyrical, horrifying, humorous, and meditative.

"Exegesis of the Rose": Faith and the Insufficiency of Philosophical Systems

Faith's quest for "the good thing" is persistently frustrated by metaphysical systematizing and the philosophical need for coherence. The narrative's architecture is a series of confrontations with contrastive, parodic characters in quest of an absolute with which to organize their lives. Intersecting yet antithetical philosophical positions are embodied in these characters who meet Faith. They are, in essence, her "insufficient" teachers, each of whom attempts to provide an "exegesis of the rose, of the world" (93) with their own systems. Faith's life dramatizes that broad syntheses and grand formulas lead away from tranquility and understanding. Johnson makes his first and clearest antisystems statement of his career in *Faith*. In the Swamp Woman's words:

> When the struggle with synthetic systems has been fought out and the battle semmin'ly won, when the mind has categorized animals, vegetables, minerals, and all the rest, when the levels of reality have all been systematized, taxonimized, and bled dry in the antiseptic laboratories of a reason loosed from all restraint, *then* and only then does the mind grow weary of system—it grows blank and cool and clear and capable of conjurn' not only what the categories and tables of judgment can't contain, but also that in which the heart of men, beasts, and birds revel: love. (193)

This passage points to his theme: that revelations about how to endow life with meaning come to those who do not create an overarching philosophical system. Instead, one may find fulfillment in the prosaic life and familiar rhythms of family, friends, nature, and the community.

Faith, ironically, learns the nature of "the good thing" in the novel's beginning, during her childhood. Her first mentor is her father, Todd Cross, whose last name signifies his sacrificial, salvific role. Todd is a genuinely good man who revels in nature, storytelling, and his daughter's love. As a young man, Todd joined the circus, and he learned there the magic possibilities of life: "though he could do none of their stunts himself, he, too, felt special—as though he *could* cleave waves and fell giants if he tried hard enough" (44). This sense of magic he imparts to his daughter, Faith, promising her that she will eventually awaken to his optimistic and self-fulfilled vision of life: "he told her that someday she would awaken from a life of everyday slumbers and realize all she considered familiar were just shaows" (18). "Familiar," in this context, refers to the family's poverty (a result of racist oppression) and the vicious racist persecution they must endure.

Johnson does not sentimentalize the life of southern folk. Todd is continually humiliated by the Jim Crow rituals of the South, and his lynching at the hands of sexually perverted southern racists is an emphatic revelation of the blighted history of race in America, where deadly racial dualism harms all African Americans. Todd's Emersonian joy in nature, however, is not hampered by either his poverty or the racist violence directed against him. Like Emerson, he envisages the world as a constant song and himself as a cosmic singer. At his death, he is rewarded for his joyful celebration of life by becoming a tree, an allusion both to Ovidian metamorphosis that preserves the person's spirit when a life is destroyed unjustly and to ancient Buddhist folklore that is replete with tree spirits in an animistic vision of nature.

As an Everywoman, Faith is naturally born into society's dualistic system despite her father's exuberant rejection of it. She unthinkingly accepts the American credo that life is real because it is competitive. The metaphor of life as a contest, as a zero-sum game, is the novel's central motif. Faith is a normal child in that she also sees her life as a contest, an expression of her separate will combating other separate wills—a game to be won or lost, depending on her skill and wits. She is "always fighting with other children, always contesting her will against theirs" (70). Todd attempts to correct this false dualistic vision of the world as perpetual antagonism and self-defense when he tells her, "If you think there's ever a winner or a loser . . . you're dead wrong" (71). To replace her bondage to competition, Faith learns from him spontaneity, a joy in the ordinary, prosaic world: "Only the present was immediate and everywhere, disclosed to her as the miraculous." For Todd, joy is in the "whispering rustle of wind in the trees . . . a browning autumn leaf, in the minor miracle of an insect nature had fashioned like a twig" (12).

This romanticized vision of nature and its beauty is thematically repeated in her second revelation of the "good thing," which occurs with her boyfriend, Alpha Omega Holmes. While "spooning" with Alpha Omega, she experiences a spiritual connection to earth similar to her childhood sense of primordial unity:

> She felt herself at such times carried through the world as
> though she had wings . . . back to earth, deep within its
> strange fabric. No personalities existed in such a pure world
> of feeling, just flashes of human outlines in the quilt of cre-
> ation where plants had their place, and animals—all coexist-
> ing peacefully, lyrically, like notes in a lay. (13)

In her love-making, personal identity dissolves in "a pure world
of feeling"; the "music" she makes with her lover—humorously
denoted in the pun on "lay"—recalls Johnson's felt need of
"singing the world" in *Being and Race*.

Todd and Alpha Omega's sense of interbeing in the natural
world is opposed in the novel by those who promulgate an absolutist and transcendental system: an overly restrictive, pietistic
Christianity. Christianity as dramatized in the novel is a dualistic system that leads believers away from joy in the world to
their hope for heaven. The minister warns, "Woe unto you who
would dare to love this world" (11). The consequence of this
position is expressed primarily through Faith's mother's conventional faith, as inspired by her ministers. Lavidia, a counterpoise
to Todd's exuberant experience of mystical oneness, is taught by
Reverend Alexander Magnus, who, in a parody of Jonathan
Edwards, substantializes God as "the source of all good. You
are as dust and excrement to Him" (9). Reverend Magnus is
coupled with the evangelical Reverend Brown, who in his sermon expresses the neo-Platonic philosophical basis of Christianity: "This world we live in—it's like a shadowy cave fulla crazy
sounds if you've got nothin' to light it up. There's no sun but
the Saviour" (14). The metaphysical limitations of conventional
Christianity are revealed by the ministers themselves when the

reader learns later that they suffer the failure of their faith with the deaths of their parishioners.

For Johnson, then, conventional Christianity is an insufficient guide. The novel's narrative pattern consists of a series of guides, each seeking in his or her own way the Good Thing. The fundamental nature of the search is defined by a parable of origins, told by the Swamp Woman, which mythicizes the origin of human disharmony and unhappiness. Johnson merges myth with a neo-Platonic renunciation of the empirical in his version of Eden lost. In a primordial moment, the Swamp Woman explains, when "man's ethical life was quite in order" (28), Kujichagulia begins to question the "modes" of the Good Thing —the daily rituals, commonplace cultural practices, and ordinary events of the village that make manifest aboriginal joy in the world. Convinced that these mundane moments were merely "modular reflections" of an absolute, eternal Good Thing, Kujichagulia abandons his village to seek "the Good Thing itself" (29)—its unchanging and Ideal reality—on Mount Kilimanjaro. On his journey, he marries Imani, who, after bearing his children, urges him to abandon his quest. Kujichagulia, however, disregards her advice, abandons Imani and his children, and continues his search until he dies on top of Mount Kilimanjaro.

The Swamp Woman's parable of Kujichagulia is an admonition against discounting ordinary life in favor of a permanent, eternal Ideal. Even though Kujichagulia feels contentment with his Imani and their children, he is dissatisfied with his ordinary life and mundane circumstances, seeking instead to transcend his impermanence and relativism. Imani was right: Kujichagulia should have stayed with his family and celebrated quotidian life. What has seemed to be a transcendent (remote) goal for Kujichagulia was always—paradoxically—nearest to him, so that his act of striving in itself created the distance between him and what he sought to attain.

But even striving, for Johnson, cannot be rejected in a simple, dualistic way; and Kujichagulia's quest makes him human. Johnson implies that this quest is an aspect of what makes us human: "life on the earth without the Good Thing is marked by famine and misery" (31). All humanity embarks on this quest, in Johnson's view, but the philosophical assumption of the quest is fundamentally flawed. As the archetypal quester, Kujichagulia's story is also the narrative pattern of the novel's futile search for concretized, systematic meaning. The novel's complexity resides in its central paradox: the Good Thing as Buddhist enlightenment resides in both questing for and acceptance of the ordinary world.

Dr. Lynch, Lavidia's doctor, opposes Christian belief. Dr. Lynch represents a satire of contemporary scientific realism, where an absolute scientific truth exists independently of human knowledge. In this mechanistic, materialistic ontology of science, people are biological machines; human awareness is but an interesting epiphenomenon. The mind, however, is implemented in mechanical operations not completely different from other machines. The goal of science for Dr. Lynch is simply to observe and describe these mechanical operations as they enact immutable laws. Thus, all life can be reduced to scientific causality. Experience, for Dr. Lynch, is based on sensory data, observed in a pattern of energy that first accumulates, then expends itself in ceaseless but purposeless phenomena. Lynch's vision, where consciousness is merely an information-processing mechanism, leads Lavidia to count her breaths. Ironically, focusing on breaths is a central Buddhist meditative practice, known as in-and-out breathing (anapana sati), intended to promote calmness, self-control, and peace of mind; but for Lavidia, it only leads to her death. Lavidia comically totals her exhalations to reach her predetermined lifetime limit: 400,000,000 breaths.

Lynch's mechanistic understanding of human behavior has embedded a death obsession. If life is only a random and meaningless expression of energy, directed nowhere—what Lynch calls "tension and release" (39)—then for Lynch death is the only objective: "Life's meaning, if it had any meaning at all, was defined by death. Death alone" (40). The significance of his last name, recalling Todd's murder, implies the negative practical effect of his vision: "The truth," Lynch says, "isn't beautiful and it doesn't make me feel good" (39), since life for him is only "monotonous movement" (40) toward his suicide.

When Faith arrives in Chicago, she is again confronted with bracketing philosophical parodies. If Dr. Lynch satirizes an arid, materialist vision informed by philosophy of science, Arnold T. Tippis is a satire of the uncentered subject, the identityless ego in search of a permanent identity. Johnson's satire of careerism is represented in Tippis, who successively appears to Faith and the reader as a dentist, a peddler of medical dictionaries, a porter, an insurance salesman, and finally as a male nurse. Each of these social roles Tippis takes seriously, but only momentarily. Neither the reader nor Faith knows the real Tippis, nor does Tippis attempt to understand himself: "Tippis's changes were never from within, only catalyzed from without" (83). Tippis represents the failed transformation because he is incapable of seeing beyond the competitive, warring world. Tippis says, "*That's* what the world is really all about—subject-object antagonism. Objectifying a thing, making it no more than an object so it can be grasped, manipulated, and ruled" (58). This seemingly bold view justifies in his mind his raping Faith, then rationalizing his evil action in a parody of Emerson's poem "Brahma": "Forgive me! The victim and victor are One!" (52). The only way out of Tippis's dead-end philosophy is hinted at by Tippis himself: "There *is* no other way unless you kill off your feelings like a musty old monk or Indian Bodhisattva" (58). A bodhisattva is an enlightened Buddhist who defers entering nirvana so that he or she may remain with unenlightened people, assisting them in attaining enlightenment. Bodhisattvas are highly respected among Buddhists because of their willingness to sacrifice themselves on behalf of others.

Dr. Richard Barrett, Faith's next teacher, resembles a potential but unrealized "Indian Bodhisattva." Barrett is yet another bracketing philosophical position in the novel. While Tippis allows his social function to (momentarily) define him, Barrett completely repudiates the social world in favor of his search for the Good Thing. But like the other questers, he imagines the Good Thing as unified, static, and permanent. As he tells Faith, "we're questers for that which in all ages was the one thing denied man: absolute certainty" (93). This quest has done incalculable damage to him and those around him. In his "lust for certainty, virtue, what have you," he has abandoned his family and his career as professor of philosophy at Princeton. In this way, he has abrogated his responsibility to his social world, for a bodhisattva is expected to re-enter the world after enlightenment to help others.[2]

Barrett is on a Platonist quest—he tells Faith that he has "experimented with everything under the sun" (90)—to discover the Good Thing. But he commits the fundamental Johnson error in repudiating the quotidian world in favor of some transcendent, eternal, immutable truth: "the entire world was allegory for me. . . . It always pointed beyond, or perhaps below, itself to something more good, more real and glorious than what I could see" (93). "Oblivious to the external world" (93–94), Barrett eagerly accepts asceticism in hopes of gaining an eternal insight, becoming a kind of comic mendicant wandering around Chicago. But the paradoxical consequence of his quest is that the more he distances himself from the empirical world, the greater is his separation from the Good Thing, which lies before him though he cannot see it—in his children, his wife, his students, and finally in his surrogate daughter and eager student, Faith.

Barrett's wife, Amelia, resembles Imani, just as Barrett's behavior recalls Kujichagulia's failed quest. We learn from Barrett that unlike him, Amelia responds aesthetically and spontaneously to the natural world, as disclosed by Barrett's memory of her delight in a rose:

She was never tortured by beauty—she never looked at a rose and, by dint of reason, went beyond it to yearn for roseness. You see, the entire world was allegory for me. . . . It always pointed beyond, or perhaps below, itself to something more good, more real and glorious than what I could see. Uncovering this meaning—*that* to me was philosophy. Not only philosophy, Faith, but life's work itself—exegesis of the rose, of the world. (93)

The rose is, for Johnson as for Dante, the classic symbol of the ardor of the devotee. Yet the result of his devotion is that he becomes "moral wreckage" (93), since he deliberately separates himself from those he could awaken: students, family, and friends. Barrett's "moral wreckage" occurs because he is incapable of thinking beyond two categories, the empirical, which he disdains, and the Ideal, which he invests with total and absolute meaning. For Barrett, an Ideal (the "roseness") is meaningful but the thing itself (the rose) is empty of meaning. Barrett lacks Todd's (and Amelia's) gift for living from moment to moment, satisfied with the rose's beauty. Barrett's dualistic perspective on experience leaves his world as blank as his *Doomsday Book,* which supposedly contains his philosophical insights. Ironically, the book hints at a truth that (because it contains only blankness) neither Faith nor Barrett can read: emptiness. Barrett's book's blankness is a pointer to the revelation of the Buddhist concept of emptiness at the novel's end.

Yet Johnson writes, Barrett is "not such a fool as he seems" (95). One of Barrett's questions about ancient philosophy from beyond the grave (when he presumably understands more) is intended to point the reader toward Johnson's philosophy:

> Children, there's nothing worse than being haunted by a philosopher's spirit—waking up in the middle of the night with your heart heaving heavy strokes to hear, next to your ear, something muttering, . . . "Riddle me this, if you're so smart: Will an arrow ever strike its intended target if, before it can cross that distance, one-half of that distance must be crossed first, and one-half of *that,* and one-half of *that,* and one-half of *that*—." (98)

As William Nash correctly notes, Barrett's spirit alludes to Zeno's paradox.[3] Zeno of Elea (490–425 B.C.E.) intends to show through the arrow paradox (and a number of other paradoxes) that the material universe is ultimately a unity and that the universe is not composed of "many" objects even if the material multiplicity of our experience appears to our senses to be true.

Zeno's arrow paradox asks us to imagine an arrow traveling from point A to point B. The distance between these two points contains an infinite number of dividing points (it can be divided by two, again and again), so the arrow must reach the halfway point (between points A and B) before it can reach point B. But before it reaches the halfway mark, it must reach a point halfway to that, and so on, since we can divide the line of the arrow ad infinitum. Using this logic (that is, that the universe is infinitely divisible), one must conclude that it is impossible for the arrow even to leave the archer's bow. Zeno's paradox, then, leads to accepting either an unsupportable statement ("movement is impossible") or the conception of the universe as a single, seamless, indivisible Whole. The point of Zeno's paradox is, of course, the latter (certainly for Johnson and presumably for Zeno too). As Johnson told an interviewer, a central theme of *Faith* is the unitary nature of the universe: "everything really is one whole, one unit. I hadn't figured out, exactly, how to carve at that until *Faith and the Good Thing*."[4]

Understanding the universe as an indivisible One leads Faith to an ethical challenge. Although he has led a failed life, Barrett represents a pole of thought that Faith must necessarily confront: the necessity of interrelatedness. Throughout his life, he desired to "do a little good in this world" (92). Barrett's "moral wreckage" is a consequence of his repudiation of the world as Oneness, for he was not ethically responsible to those who depended on him, and his "discoveries" did not compensate for his withdrawal from others. Barrett's mistake is not acknowledging the world as "one whole, one unit," instead abandoning everyone to search for an Ideal apart from experience.

Johnson implies the fallacy of Barrett's distinction with Faith's reverie of the horizon:

Faith [was] . . . surfeited with the stillness of a morning so
blue that sky and water on the lake were merged without the
slightest suture. The skyscrapers were the color of deep-sea
pearls, as were the clouds, an armada passing overhead. She
longed to look upon them forever, to fix them in her mind, to
hold on to *some*thing. (93)

Johnson has in mind Emerson's *Nature,* where Emerson writes
(shortly after the eyeball passage), "I am the lover of uncon-
tained and immortal beauty. . . . In the tranquil landscape, and
especially in the distant line of the horizon, man beholds somewhat as beautiful as his own nature."[5] Like the world itself,
human beings are natural phenomena for Emerson (and Johnson), just as beautiful, mysterious, and elusive as the "distant
line of the horizon." The mutuality of the landscape and horizon move Emerson and Faith. The horizon, where heaven
touches earth and where air seems to merge with water, suggests
the permeability of the ideal and the real for both Johnson and
Emerson. The boundary between the individual and the world
seems to dissolve, the symbolic meaning of Lake Michigan mirroring Chicago. In this horizon image, Johnson emphasizes ecological complexity: how far our social relations extend, but also
how far we are from realizing the potential of our relatedness.
It is understandable that Faith, like Barrett, would like to "hold
on to *some*thing" forever, but in her "lack" the reader is given
a sense that there is a potential of fullness, if only she affirms
connection with the universe.

She does not have an opportunity to do this with her next
guide, Isaac Maxwell, another bracketing position in Faith's
quest. If Barrett represents the failed idealist, Maxwell embodies the corrupt materialist. In fact, he verges on becoming a

stereotype of the conniving, covetous, ruthless, but vacuous executive climbing the corporate ladder. His crassness is especially ironic given that, according to Faith's thinking, "Maxwell [was] after all, the good thing Lavidia told her to find" (131). He sustains the novel's metaphor of life as a competitive game, since he sees his life only as "carrying the ball across the field through dint of pure Will" (116). Maxwell goes to the extreme of prostituting Faith to gain an advantage. For him, the attainment of happiness is an economically measurable goal, just as quantifiable as a victory in a Rose Bowl game.

Perhaps the weakest creation in Johnson's career, Maxwell, as Johnson told an interviewer, was a difficult character for him to create. Because Johnson detests what Maxwell stands for —"his lack of values, his vulgar materialism"—Johnson oversimplified his character in his original drafts, making him into a straw man easy to knock down and an artistic mistake that drew a rebuke from his mentor, John Gardner. Gardner may, however, have misunderstood Johnson's artistic purpose. Maxwell is not a character in the Aristotelian sense of a convincing, plausible, mimetic depiction of human action; he is, on the contrary, a thematic variant in the novel—a purely commercialized satire of the Good Thing. Nevertheless, Johnson took Gardner's criticism to heart and revised Maxwell, trying "to understand his motivations and what things in his life hurt him and what his goals were so that we understand better why he acts the way he does in the present."[6] Johnson's rather awkward authorial intrusions attempt to explain Maxwell's behavior to the reader. "Maxwell wasn't evil," the impersonal narrator intones, "just disillusioned, not malicious, only disappointed" (131). What depth Johnson gives Maxwell is a consequence of his effort to dramatize Maxwell's disillusionment and disappointment.

One way Johnson strengthens Maxwell's character is by providing him with a quasi-philosophical foundation. Maxwell represents a satiric version of an existential will to power, an ersatz Nietzschean philosophy, which in America has devolved into a popularized rationalization of "get[ting] ahead" (105). His library is stocked with popular texts by "Horatio Alger, Colin Wilson, Norman Vincent Peale, and a slim one about a sea gull [*Jonathan Livingston Seagull,* by Richard Bach]" (116) —all icons of self-help and financial success in America. Maxwell claims that "Will Power's a self-preservative principle of evolution. . . . Superior to matter and stronger than mind" (116). Because of his commitment to this faux existential principle, he (like Tippis) transforms Faith and himself into objects to be manipulated: "He was her object, pure and simple, and she was his, and between them this twirling exchange for supremacy of wills, as he called it, built a tension or bond that she was willing to call, for want of a better word, love" (109). Though Faith senses her own "self-betrayal in contrast to her life's half-forgotten promise" (109), she is able to satisfy herself with forging a "comfortable agreement" (114) with Maxwell: a marriage to him that provides her a tenuous middle-class security in exchange for the relinquishment of her quest. "I certainly don't need the Good Thing any more" (111), she says to herself.

Johnson's second method of providing more depth to Maxwell's character is to reveal Maxwell's troubled relationship with his father, partially a cause (Maxwell thinks) of his disappointment and disillusionment. Maxwell's despairing vision of life as a clash of wills—with its consequent objectifying of others—emerges from his oedipal revolt against his working-class father. As an African American, Maxwell's father was beaten down in a racist system that never allowed him to succeed, and as a result of his victimization he lashed out at his son.

He belittled Maxwell by telling him he was weak and "couldn't do anything"; his father, Maxwell believed, "was whipped . . . somebody snuffed out the Will in him like you do a candle" (113).

The image of an extinguished candle to describe Maxwell's father's defeat has ironic Buddhist implications. The etymology of nirvana, as Heinrich Dumoulin explains, is from the Sanskrit verb *va* (to blow), with the negative prefix *nir,* denoting motionless rest, "where the fire is quenched, the light has been extinguished." Thus, nirvana is often imaged in Buddhist texts as an extinguished flame. Dumoulin writes, "The saint vanishes into nirvana, according to the Buddha's famous simile, like an oil lamp sinking in upon itself and expiring when its fuel has been consumed. Such language and images evoke the concepts of emptiness and nothingness."[7] Nirvana is a state of tranquility, a liberation from the petty wants and desires that have ensnared Maxwell and (now) Faith too.

According to Maxwell, his father did not attain this release. Instead, his father apparently slipped into a depression or a nihilistic renunciation, a symbol of the "negative" view of nirvana held in the West until recently.[8] The extinguished candle image thus makes even Maxwell's character consonant with Buddhist experience. But it is an experience that Maxwell misinterprets out of his own narrow self-interests. Maxwell's father presents Maxwell with an opportunity to show his love and understanding. But instead of feeling compassion for his father, who lacked opportunity because of racism, Maxwell gains satisfaction from symbolically defeating his father as a putative opponent. Psychologically, it is essential for Maxwell to defeat his father by writing, even though, ironically, he gains success by cheating, enlisting Faith's old boyfriend, Alpha Omega Holmes, to do his writing for him.

As an artist, Holmes, as his name implies, represents a potential guide to salvation for Faith. In his character, Johnson introduces the possibility of a return to the rural, southern folk wisdom of Faith's childhood in Georgia. In committing himself to his art, Holmes mediates the dichotomies of Platonic idealism and degraded materialism that Barrett and Maxwell respectively represent, and Holmes thereby achieves an enviable tranquility. Maxwell complains that "Holmes is too at peace with himself and the world" (146), since Maxwell believes that Holmes should feel only emotional turmoil as an African American. Holmes's connection with the southern folk is made explicit through Holmes's link with Todd, since Holmes is "a storyteller like [Todd] himself" (153). Holmes's confident complacency, however, places him outside the mainstream of African American writing, according to Maxwell. Although Maxwell had wanted Holmes to provide naturalistic anecdotes about the horror of African American life in prison—"all the rage a prisoner feels, all the frustration and bitterness" (146)—Holmes's stories express a much more hopeful view, the sense of "spirit transcending confinement" (161). Indeed, Jonathan Little and Nash both see the Holmes/Maxwell characters as Johnson's ironic criticism of the Black Aesthetic. Little writes, "Where Maxwell (and the black cultural national critic) wants realism, rage, and a kind of social determinism for his newspaper article, Holmes gives him instead a kind of dreamy fairy tale sentimentality."[9]

Holmes's affirmative and cheerful spirit is a partial reflection of his author, and Johnson's characterization of Holmes includes self-reflexive details. In a sublime mindfulness, while creating art Holmes is "freer, happier, and more whole than anyone she'd seen since she arrived in Chicago" (158). A graphic artist as well as a writer, Holmes covers his room with "preliminary charcoal sketches" and "half finished canvases" (149), a detail that reflects Johnson's tendency to sketch out his characters as he is creating them. Also like Johnson, Holmes is committed to the philosophical import of his themes—he mocks a mentor who tells him "*what* I painted wasn't as important as *how* I did hit" (158). He shares Johnson's contempt for sentimentalized and undisciplined literature, since he rejects an advisor who explains that in artistic expression "all that mattered was my puttin' alla my feelings in hit . . . and forgettin' form" (159). Most important, he rejects (again like Johnson) a cultural nationalist who tells him his "work was worthless unless hit was instrumental to his cause" (158–59). Holmes is also opposed to uncritical realism, for "the world'll never challenge your ideas—only other ideas can do that" (159). Through his art, Holmes achieves a momentary emotional liberation that Johnson says he enjoys: "he seemed to find release: the Good Thing" (158).

Although Holmes (like Johnson) repudiates black cultural nationalism, Holmes should not be considered Johnson's ideal artist.[10] For Johnson, Holmes's subject matter—the southern, rural, folkloric past—represents another kind of aesthetic enslavement for the African American writer. Even though Holmes disappoints Maxwell's anticipation that he will become the embittered black voice, Holmes embodies a tradition of African American art as stultifying as Maxwell's nationalistic mode. For Johnson, picturing an idealized agrarian past merely diverts the reader's attention from the actual problems confronting many African Americans: urban, institutionalized racism and economic struggles. Holmes creates mere diversion, a wholly pleasant (and therefore untrue) depiction of African American experience.

In his nostalgic revival of the southern folk tradition, Holmes's "reality" is outmoded, essentialist, and ahistorical. It is as if for Holmes black authenticity adheres only in an idealized southern past; he does not take seriously the possibility that African American culture undergoes transformation as black people migrate from the South to northern cities. The contemporary African American, as Faith's narrative demonstrates, is typically urban, contending (like her) with postmodern problems—racialized crime, the irrelevance of conventional religion, gender conflict, urban alienation, and the fetishization of race. In Chicago, Faith no longer has a "tradition," southern or otherwise, to rely on, for what seems fixed (the strength of folk sayings, wisdom, stories, and beliefs) is for Faith made problematic because of the site of her struggle.

The southern folk tradition, Johnson implies, may only be a fantasy anyway, perhaps to satisfy the needs of a white readership eager to "understand" an essentialist black experience, in order to relieve a nagging sense of moral responsibility for those oppressed by racism in contemporary America. Ignoring the daily humiliations of the southern black, the white reader of Maxwell's columns, Johnson implies, can vicariously enjoy through Holmes's stories an evocation of a preindustrial, carefree, overly simple, easy way of life, complemented with charming folk sayings such as, "I wouldn't bet a huckleberry to a persimmon if you ain't the only gal that ever meant somethin' to me" (153). Holmes's celebration of the folk, from Johnson's perspective, is a debilitating encrustation on the contemporary African American writer, a static and unchanging depiction that misleads the reader, white or black. Cultivation of the folk tradition—a practice typical of several writers whom Johnson objects to—both deprives African Americans of a true history (lynchings, extreme poverty, social humiliation, and daily abjection are conveniently forgotten) and implies that they have somehow escaped change and social upheaval.[11]

In contrast, Johnson employs the folk tradition in *Faith* only to critique it, as if to convey to the reader that the task of the African American artist must be to revise and refine the folk tradition. Johnson employs the oral tradition, identified with the southern folk; the setting of Hatten County, Georgia; and the Swamp Woman as conjuror, typical of the folk tradition. However, Johnson's attention is focused rather on the depredations experienced in the urban world by African Americans since the Great Migration. Especially vulnerable to bad housing, sexual exploitation, and unemployment are African American women, like Faith. Johnson dramatizes the sense of futility of those who are destroyed or seriously compromised by the contemporary urban world, but Johnson is also concerned with charting an end to that suffering.

Alpha Omega Holmes could help Faith, could become her bodhisattva, but he fails her because he does not live by his aesthetic creed of rejoicing in the present moment. He leads Faith to articulate the novel's theme: "the good things were the things of the moment, the things that had been felt and tasted and touched in the past, and might be tasted still" (157). His quest is yet another variant of Kujichagulia's, as Faith becomes a repetition of Imani's desolation. When Faith becomes pregnant with his child, Holmes ironizes his last name. Rather than accept his responsibility to Faith and his unborn child, he abandons her to her terrible fate in a Chicago fire, telling her that "my life'll be the finished work" (159). Holmes, then, exposes himself as an egotistical artist; he cannot "get his self out of the way" to create art, as Johnson personally says he attempts to do.[12] Indeed, Holmes employs his vocation as artist as a rationalization for acting irresponsibly, saying that he will "wake up in gutters or in hotels with strange women" (165).

Holmes's invocation of the Romantic artist is more akin to opera than real life.

"Who Says Ya Gotta Understand the Universe": Faith's Transformed Perception

In the novel's denouement, Johnson again shifts literary styles. On the novel's literal level, the plot's resolution horrifically ends Faith's suffering. Abandoned by both Holmes and Maxwell, Faith gives birth to her daughter in the run-down tenement building where she was raped by Tippis, then she dies with her infant in a fire. If read strictly within a naturalist tradition, her ghastly end underscores the terrible suffering of African American women trapped in poverty and discrimination.[13] Johnson proposes, even in Faith's terrible suffering, a religious resolution. Faith's transcendence, ironically, occurs only when she awakens and mysteriously returns to the South—for Johnson, a site of discredited folk wisdom no longer applicable to urban life in America. It is essential to read this scene of awakening nonliterally. At the conclusion of Faith's life, Johnson employs magic realism to express his Buddhist interpretation of the conclusion of her quest.[14] Only through magic realism can Johnson at this point in his career explore the nature of Buddhist enlightenment and spiritual release. On this level, Faith and her daughter experience resurrection (or reincarnation) by journeying back to the Swamp Woman. Like James Joyce and T. S. Eliot, Johnson exploits the symbolic possibilities of reincarnation in literature without necessarily accepting it literally.

The return of Faith and her daughter to the Swamp Woman leads to the disclosure of the Swamp Woman's identity, withheld throughout the novel: she is Imani, Kujichagulia's wife, who was left behind to care for the family when Kujichagulia went on his own quest for the Good Thing. Imani/Swamp Woman tells her own story of how she attempted to reach her husband's grave, to be buried beside him. She realized, as she stood on his bones, that the Good Thing lies in conjuring: "the best way there is for callin' up the Good Thing" (191). By "conjuring," she means a refusal to cling desperately "to the belief in certainty," to resist the temptation to accept dualism, where "every object became a thing apart from ya—ya even became a thing to y'self" (192).

Imani/Swamp Woman opposes a worldview that requires "standin' back away from the world to check it out" (192), attempting to create an all-encompassing (but necessarily incomplete) philosophy. Instead, she exults in a connection to the world as the songbirds must feel, singing "in a contest to celebrate the coming of day when dull mankind slept" (193). The birds, to use Johnson's phrase, "sing the world." The Swamp Woman announces to Faith the end of conflict and the beginning of freedom. The Swamp Woman laments "the Age of Reason—an ugly age . . . filled with disillusion, rife with conflictin' theories that bend and fold and mutilate men like a computer card to explain them completely and, through all that, deny their freedom to create. To conjure" (192). The sense of "conflictin'" ways of explaining the world, dramatized throughout the novel, encourages human beings to turn dualistically away from ordinary experience in search of a unitary, transcendent truth. For the variety of characters that Faith has encountered, principles have assumed an exaggerated importance. The Swamp Woman wants Faith to recognize philosophical principles—"conflictin' theories"—for what they are. The conflict is only illusory, since these opposing views interlock and are dependent on each other, as their close proximity in the novel has implied. As Nhat Hanh would say, these theories inter-are.

Imani/Swamp Woman urges Faith to wake up, and awaken she does, as do the birds, "singing the world":

> Light burst in thin blue beams that caused her to blink, open-
> ing and closing her eyes quickly until she could see. It was
> dawn, a time that had always taken hold of something in her
> blood; dawn, a new beginning. (193)

Buddhist imagery clarifies Faith's interaction with the Swamp Woman, for the Swamp Woman's bizarre visage is explicable in Buddhist terms. Swamp Woman's salient characteristic is her green eye: "It was horrible. *Horrible!* One tiny eye, the left one, was partially closed and had no pupil—clear it was and the color of egg yolk. The other, a disk, had a green cataract float-ing free in its center" (19). The Buddhists use the imagery of see-ing with the "wisdom eye" to distinguish the ultimate mode of apprehension from our usual mechanics of seeing. Through her one green eye the Swamp Woman sees into the true meaning of experience. At this point, Faith has also lost her one eye—her "right eye closed forever" (180)—and appears as a mirror image of the Swamp Woman, about to "see" exactly what the Swamp Woman has seen all along.

What exactly does the Swamp Woman "see"? The Swamp Woman sees emptiness in the world, the source of her enlighten-ment. The craving for "certainty" (192) in an all-comprehensive theory, argues the Swamp Woman, leads humanity inevitably away from the "good thing." The "good thing" is described as the Buddhist concept of emptiness: "it's *absolutely* nothin', but *particularly* it's everythin'" (193). Emptiness is the recognition that a sentient being—a human being especially—is not self-determining. One's existence and character depend not on one's own will, but on the multitude of elements that together, corporately, condition one's transformation: in the novel, certainly Faith's parents, her church, her lovers, her various instructors, but also the universe in its entirety. For a Buddhist, the empty person accepts complete lack of permanence. Symbolically, this transformation is expressed in the Buddhist image of fire, which burns away Faith's face—destroying her illusory sense of a unique identity, a view of herself as a separate, enduring entity.

Faith, finally in congruence with emptiness, accepts her embeddedness in the world, immersed in an infinitely interconnected context so that self and nonself interpenetrate. Faith's finally seeing this Emersonian interconnectedness (the "transparent eyeball" made literal) is expressed by Johnson with Faith's intuitive certainty: "She was certain. Certain of everything. Certain the air was cool and scented with the clean smell of dew. Certain the wind pushed on, and the birds swung into the empty sky like sleek arrows, no destination, no duty, no destiny in mind. Daylight came" (194). Her certainty resides in her connection to the world and her acceptance of a lack of permanent identity as Faith Cross; she is now the Swamp Woman too.

At this moment, Faith's "awareness made her feel like an oracle" (194). Yet Faith's career is not over. If enlightenment is achieved primarily through her own individual effort, though assisted by the Swamp Woman, she now may become a guide for others, to lead them to the enlightenment that she has achieved with such difficulty. Buddhists recognize the bodhisattva who helps others, as noted earlier by Tippis. As a bodhisattva, Faith moves out into the world compassionately.

Enlightenment necessarily involves compassion, and compassion requires a wide, social context—not the seclusion of a monastic life.

Even at the novel's beginning, Faith is intuitively aware that if she discovers the Good Thing, "everybody's bondage will end" (30). At the novel's end, she acts on that early intuition and prepares to impart her sense of enlightenment to others. She is given a choice in her purgatorial return to the South: Todd's spirit offers her eternal peace by suggesting that she become a maple tree (178). But rather than accepting this alternative, she "step[s] into the Swamp Woman's abandoned skin" (194), and becomes the new guide for lost humanity. Ironically, the first person Faith assists is the Swamp Woman, who reincarnates as Faith's dead infant girl to return to the world for yet another quest. The original Swamp Woman's return to the world is Johnson's metaphor for the unending nature of the quest. For a Buddhist, even enlightenment is empty; no thought or experience (even the concept of emptiness) is absolute, eternal, and permanent.

Faith is thus set apart, and can even be seen as the realization of the Buddha-nature herself, one who can recognize the "origin of pain in the world of living beings" (195) and envisage ways of transcending suffering through compassion. Johnson creatively varies his Buddhism, since bodhisattvas are generally conceptualized as men. Her role is finally established: "she yanked back the tarpaulin to a window and saw two timorous, barefoot children crossing a bridge" (195). It is now her obligation to become their guide, to become like Johnson, reminding us that there may be levels of metaphysical reality beyond what we can complacently perceive and to open ourselves to the possibility of embracing them. Faith as Swamp

Woman embodies for Johnson what becomes his constant theme: the nature of liberation in the modern world. As an entirely transformed character, she represents for him the possibility of true freedom, an enlightenment assisted by a guide figure or teacher. To personify this state, however, Johnson abandons the realistic mode of the novel, choosing instead magic realism. In his later work, Johnson blends innovative fiction with the realistic mode in order to clarify the philosophical nature of our illusory world and the possibility of liberation from it.

CHAPTER 3

Oxherding Tale

> I hear the song of the nightingale.
> The sun is warm, the wind is mild, willows
>   are green along the shore,
> Here no bull can hide!
> What artist can draw that massive head,
>   those majestic horns?
>
> *Zen Flesh, Zen Bones*

Johnson, in his preface to *Oxherding Tale,* hints at the novel's Buddhist inspiration. He writes that the novel is his "'platform book' (a playful reference to the Zen 'Platform Sutra of the Sixth Patriarch') meaning that everything else I attempted to do would in one way or another be based upon and refer to it" (xvii). The renowned Sixth Patriarch of the Zen tradition is Hui-neng (638–713 C.E.), who explains in his autobiography, the core of the "Platform Sutra," how he attained enlightenment in his youth.[1] Hui-neng is exceptional because he was illiterate, but in his quest for liberation he was undeterred by his lowly birth as a clerk's son in south China. Told by the Fifth Patriarch, Hung-jen, that a barbarian from south China could never be a Buddha, Hui-neng answered, "Although people from the South and people from the North differ, there is no north and south in Buddha nature."[2] For his time, Hui-neng speaks of a radical equality, where all people can become enlightened. In the same way, Johnson as an African American novelist challenges the reader to consider new ways of envisioning freedom, happiness, and enlightenment.

In Buddhism, the word *sutra* is commonly reserved for writings representing a direct transmission of Buddha's words, and as sacred texts the sutras were chanted by memory by Buddhists. Yet mere parroting of the sutra was not encouraged, as Dale S. Wright points out: "Rote memorization and mindless repetition were subjected to heavy ridicule by the great teachers."[3] The sutras were to be repeated yet revised simultaneously, a paradox that relates to Johnson's concern with form in *Oxherding Tale*. Johnson's allusion to sutras implicate his unusual understanding of literary form and his goal of originality expressed within the formal properties of conventional texts. Johnson's playful description of *Oxherding Tale* within the context of a Zen understanding of the sutra, then, hints at his formal design, for he explores the boundaries of originality in his novel. An understanding of his originality depends on the Buddhist concept of dependent origination. He calls into question its status as an imaginative text: To what extent does *Oxherding Tale* "originate dependent" on other forms? Conversely, if it *is* dependent (and as a Buddhist, Johnson would argue that it indubitably is), in what sense can it be free from those antecedent texts? How do those antecedent texts interpenetrate Johnson's own?

The aesthetic problem Johnson attempts to solve—creating an original novelistic form while simultaneously acknowledging those forms on which his originality depends—also engages the novel's central theme: the nature of personal freedom. On this level, Johnson challenges the Western notion of freedom. The Western person typically conceives of freedom in purely dualistic terms: freedom opposes constraint. Just as literary originality is considered to be antithetical to slavish imitation, freedom necessarily opposes restriction. Johnson, however, breaks down the familiar dualisms of originality/imitation and freedom/ constraint. His understanding of "freedom" and "originality" is much more nuanced and subtle, for he understands that originality can only occur when imitation is acknowledged, just as freedom can be understood only against a background of multiple constraints: alternative choices, coerced acts, and a commitment freely chosen.

For Johnson, a writer's originality is expressed within the context of literary forms that have gone before, so that originality and imitation exist in a state of interbeing. They "originate dependently." Johnson's complex and paradoxical view of originality is a standard he uses to judge other writers, especially those whom Johnson greatly respects. Evaluating the work of his teacher John Gardner, Johnson argues that Gardner's best fiction incorporates age-old forms like the epic, since "by virtue of their having been in circulation for centuries, new fictions in these forms have the authority lacking in so much 'interior' modern literature. Meaning *accumulates* in the form, infuses these fictions with dignity, affirmation, and a timeless sense of value."[4] The artist's task is to synthesize and expand past forms, making them thematically applicable to contemporary circumstances.

Just as an original aesthetic work cannot be imagined without a reliance on previous forms, so too personal freedom is always relative to some type of constraint, whether recognized or not. In *Oxherding Tale,* just as authentic originality is discovered in reworking and revising conventional forms, personal freedom depends on a context of obedience to a greater good, of service to others. One's freedom depends on a meditative realization of one's connectedness to other people and their needs, and the constraints these needs place on an individual's will. Johnson as author, in his original use of form, and Andrew Hawkins, in his discovery of freedom within a community of others, are thereby mirror images. As Johnson explains in an interview about the book, his philosophical theme is freedom:

> [*Oxherding Tale*] is a slave narrative. I did not want to deny the history of slavery, but this book is not merely about legal or political slavery. It's about other kinds of bondage: sexual, emotional, psychological, and metaphysical. The main character, Andrew Hawkins, has to work his way through all these types of bondage, some of which are even more fundamental than chattel slavery. Eastern philosophy was very useful to me in that exploration, as it is in all my books.[5]

Johnson asserts that Andrew Hawkins "was the first protagonist in black American fiction to achieve classically defined *moksha* (enlightenment)" (xvi), and Andrew's enlightenment flows from his acceptance of human contingency. Andrew discovers his autonomy within a structure of limitations, just as Johnson celebrates past literary forms as a condition of his originality. Neither Johnson nor his character Andrew rejects the concept of relationships, textual or personal, but instead they navigate within their constricting forces. They exist in a state of interbeing.

"The Wheels as They Whir beneath the Stage": The Function of Parodic Homage

In *Oxherding Tale,* Johnson parodies classic African American texts, specifically the two most famous slave narratives, Frederick

Douglass's *Narrative of the Life of Frederick Douglass* and *Up from Slavery* by Booker T. Washington.[6] He wishes to show how the slave narrative's form works; as Johnson writes, he wants the reader "to glimpse fully the wheels as they whir beneath the stage" (118). For many critics, the slave narrative is the central African American form. John Sekora writes that the slave narrative is "one of the bedrock traditions of African American literature and culture."[7] For Johnson, the slave narrative requires a literary reconceptualization to yield a contemporary meaning. Johnson avoids the sense that any form, even slave narratives, can be static or unchanging, since no form (just as no meaning) can resist change through time. From a Buddhist perspective, to venerate any form is a category of aesthetic craving, a futile grasping for illusory permanence.

Johnson's irreverent treatment of the slave narrative has drawn a rebuke from critics, especially John Haynes, who writes that Johnson makes irreverent use of African American historical forms "simply for effect." At the root of Haynes's complaint is a misunderstanding of the aesthetic purpose of *Oxherding Tale*'s parody. Haynes conceives of "respect" in a conventional, dualistic way: either one venerates older forms or one doesn't. Johnson, however, uses the literary mode of parody to release himself from Haynes's dichotomy of respect/disrespect. Parody, as Linda Hutcheon writes, is "a sophisticated genre in the demands it makes on its practitioners and its interpreters." The artist's effort is to create "repetition with difference"; the work must acknowledge its literary precedents but simultaneously denote the thematic shifts and variations to which the antecedent text is subjected. The reader must recognize the target text(s) and determine the relationship between the parodic and the parodied. Hutcheon's theory distinguishes parody from the other genres with which it has often been confused, including "burlesque, travesty, pastiche, plagiarism, quotation, and allusion." Hutcheon is correct in insisting that parody must not be understood simply as criticism, mockery, or ridicule, for it can have other literary purposes—most notably, homage. In parodic homage, the author's intention is to rework a loved and well-known text or narrative form.[8]

Homage rather than criticism is Johnson's parodic purpose in *Oxherding Tale*. At no time does Johnson imply that Douglass and Washington deserve anything less than respect for their accomplishments. Rather, Johnson tests the contemporary thematic validity of older literary works and genres to establish a sense of continuity between the present and earlier periods. Furthermore, by obviously employing the slave narrative as his master form, Johnson's book is actually self-deprecating, for his artistic choice of a parodic model subordinates his own impressive imagination to that of his literary ancestors. He as an artist shows that he derives inspiration from the resources and the achievements of others. Despite being a highly original author, he is not self-determining; instead, his novel originates dependently on the work of others.

Douglass and Washington, of course, wrote in specific historical contexts with polemical concerns unique to their situations. Their two texts approach slavery in two very different ways. Douglass published his *Narrative* in 1845 with the purpose of abolishing slavery, and he describes its evil with melodramatic detail. Washington, publishing his autobiography in serial form and then as *Up from Slavery* in 1901, describes slavery as a crucible that tested and improved the race's character. Johnson's historical situation, of course, is quite different from that of his two predecessors. Though his use of the slave narrative acknowledges that his contemporary condition as an African American has been dependent on the work of Douglass, Washington, and countless others, Johnson seeks to reinterpret their work for his contemporary audience. As Johnson himself writes, he "worries" the conventions of the form, which he justifies by arguing that the slave narrative too has "a long pedigree" (118), deriving ultimately from Saint Augustine's *Confessions* in its "movement from ignorance to wisdom, nonbeing to being." Although no form "*loses* its ancestry," its "meanings accumulate in layers of tissue" (119). His "worrying" of the form teases out these contemporary meanings.

The most important meaning revised by Johnson is the authority vested in a single (as opposed to a communal) voice. Johnson's style is intensely democratic in nature: many characters get to speak, not just one. Within the first-person narrative, Johnson "worries" the form by interpolating comments, analyses, and philosophical speculations. Both the primary text (Andrew's narrative) and the secondary texts (the numerous interruptions) are interpolated in the process: the first insofar as it has been altered by the second, and the latter because it has been inserted into the former (alteration and insertion being features of Johnson's parodic homage). Formally, the text represents a kind of narratival interbeing, a diffused linkage of various voices from sometimes competing but sometimes parallel perspectives. These alternating voices "accumulate" meanings in the text itself. These interpolated structures thus become variants of the supposedly invariant structure of the slave narrative. No form, for Johnson, is invariant.

Unlike conventional slave narratives, *Oxherding Tale* also shifts point of view. There is no question but that Douglass and Washington are the centers of consciousness in their respective narratives; it is their vision that predominates. Johnson, in contrast, makes clear through his multiple voices that any single pronouncement lacks complete authority. No one pure, univocal source of authority emerges from the novel. Johnson does not exaggerate when he claims that he "liberate[s] first-person" narration (153). The textual eruptions emphasize the world's equality with an open system where virtually anyone can interrupt and talk.

Examples of these textual diversions proliferate in the novel. Many of these interpolations are fantasy, as when Andrew imagines Bannon's murder of his father. Other stories come from the novel's minor characters. Ezekiel tells the story of his parents' murder-suicide, of Trishanka and his search for Samsara, and (through Andrew) of his disappointing visit with Karl Marx. Flo gossips about her ex-husbands, who never appear in the story. We hear Reb's story of his attempts to save his dying daughter and of his confrontation with southern white supremacists. Peggy comments extensively on Evelyn Pomeroy's career as a novelist. Andrew, apparently from a quite distant historical time frame, supplies a footnote on the civil rights movement, the life of James Travis, and Travis's twentieth-century descendants. Finally, Johnson as author intrudes twice, to offer his own disquisitions on the slave narrative's history and on the problem of first-person narration. Johnson's form conveys a sense of an ever-changing, unpredictable universe by creating a form whose multiple narrators voice their stories within a supple, flexible, changing narrative.[9] Everyone has the opportunity to present an angle, and not just the protagonist's perspective holds sway.

If the implied author seems to approve of the speaker, the text works to immediately undermine him or her. For example, the Vet, Hiram Groll, recommends to Andrew "an unshakable faith . . . that will place everything in proportion, including evil" (70). This seemingly sensible advice is undermined, however, when the Vet is revealed to be a con man, selling "a series of values that brought a man peace . . . ranked according to price" (70). Even the Buddhist concept of emptiness, fundamental to this novel, is the target of a pun: "I must confess that reading Chinese thought was a little like eating Chinese food: the more one read Lao tzu and Chaung tzu, or ate subgum chop suey, the *emptier* one's head and stomach felt hours later" (emphasis added; 13). The vagaries of narrators and the reflexive, joking style, while imparting a hybrid form to the text, ultimately point to the common wisdom that practical experience in one's world rather than systematic philosophy brings enlightenment. Individual pronouncements that aspire to the status of absolute metaphysical truths—from Ezekiel, George, Flo, the Vet, and even Reb—are insufficient.

Through the numerous disruptions in the primary narrative, then, Johnson seeks to undermine the very notion of a singular authority, always a concern for the historical slave narrative. Douglass's *Narrative* required support from "authenticating documents," prefacing letters from Wendell Phillips and William Lloyd Garrison. Phillips's and Garrison's authenticating documents are included in the *Narrative* to verify Douglass's account of his suffering; antebellum America was skeptical of slavery's horrors and required witnesses who could vouch for the escaped slave's veracity. Andrew, in contrast, shows little concern for his narrative's truthfulness, for he admits that his story is "woven partly from fact, partly from fancy" (94). In a similar way, Andrew parodies Washington's *Up from Slavery*. Washington includes within his autobiography innumerable letters, anecdotes, memos, and quotations from illustrious or important people (such as President Grover Cleveland) in order to consolidate his reputation, establish his stature, and evoke his reader's admiration. Andrew, in contrast, shows us his worst self. He suffers from addictions to sex and cocaine, he strikes women, he unheroically passes for white, and for much of the text he seems incapable of sustained work.

The "worrying" of form also locates itself in Johnson's handling of time. As Andrew says, "Memory . . . is imagination" (109). Andrew acts within the narrative, but he is also a cognitive presence outside the narrative's specific time frame. He begins the novel with his own conception in 1837, but breaks the mimetic framework by commenting on the civil rights movement in the 1940s (110), while preserving his voice. By alluding to the civil rights movement, an event that occurs almost 150 years after his birth, Andrew injects himself into the movement of history itself, where past and future are folded into the present moment. Sometimes, in fact, even unactualized possibilities may leave their mark on history. For example, the racist toll guard that Andrew and Reb meet during their escape from Leviathan condemns all African Americans as "two-faced liars and thieves, lazy and without the wit of a toadstool" (110). Nevertheless, the guard does not question them extensively and lets them pass. As Andrew relates, later the toll guard marries an African American woman and is the ancestor of civil rights activists. Andrew's interjection about the toll guard's future reminds the reader that the guard's choice to allow Reb and Andrew passage is but one possibility of many; the alternatives (for example, the toll guard becoming a civil rights advocate himself, or his capturing the two escaped slaves) leave an obscure message of future possibilities. If the guard had stopped them, for example, would he have ever made himself available to his future wife? For Johnson, the idea of past as opposed to present and future is only one more dualism to be overcome, if we open ourselves to the various possibilities of the specific moment.

For Johnson, such narratives as Douglass's and Washington's may give a false impression of history to the contemporary reader. In both Douglass's and Washington's narratives, the plot's dynamic is heroic action: the hero, through superhuman performance—Douglass's fighting Covey, or Washington's achieving wealth and renown—produces historical transformation beyond his own situation. But in *Oxherding Tale,* the record of history is quite different. Typically, the moments of life that change history are lived out on a prosaic, ordinary level, one experienced day by day. Unheroic and unexceptional acts are hidden from historical record because there is nothing dramatic or ostensibly important about them. So it is that Johnson shows Andrew overcoming his drug and sex addictions, resisting the lure of promiscuity, choosing to marry, fixing a run-down house, correcting student papers: all seemingly trivial, dull, insignificant tasks. Johnson's narrative flow implies that the greatest ethical imperative lies in maintaining the rituals of prosaic, ordinary, everyday life. No one knows what the consequences of these minute choices will be, but seemingly inconsequential actions will cumulatively have momentous effects in the future.

"Even Fools Have Their Place in the Grand Design": Johnson's Quarrel with Utilitarianism

In an excellent article, William Gleason explains how *Oxherding Tale*'s plot is roughly organized around the "Ten Ox-Herding Tales," an ancient Buddhist parable of spiritual enlightenment.

Gleason discusses how Johnson's narrative takes its allegorical shape from the "Tales," ten pictures with accompanying texts developed by Chinese monks in the eleventh century.[10] The ox-herding pictures, as Gleason explains, were intended as a commentary on the individual's search for personal identity, the ox symbolizing for the Buddhist a person's true Buddha nature from which there is no separation. Gleason shows that Johnson varies the Asian text because the ox is employed by Johnson as a symbol of both racial identity and the essential Buddha self.

This symbol of the searched-for ox, however, is multileveled in the novel, permitting more than this one interpretation. On a narrative level, the ox also represents Andrew's quest for happiness (*Oxherding Tale*'s stipulation of the "good thing"). On this level each character engages in a quest for his or her happiness. Johnson's novel may be read as a sustained speculation on Jeremy Bentham's utilitarian philosophy, which since the eighteenth century has been the comprehensive philosophical foundation for Western social, political, and economic life. As if to hint at his novel's philosophical underpinnings, Johnson mentions Bentham by name when Flo asks Andrew, "You have read Jeremy Bentham?" (38). Andrew, steeped in Eastern philosophy and American transcendentalism, has not, but Johnson assumes that his reader has.

Writing over one hundred years before Sigmund Freud, Bentham identifies the "pleasure principle," and argues that human beings invariably attempt to avoid pain and increase opportunities for pleasure:

Nature has placed mankind under the governance of two sovereign masters, *pain* and *pleasure*. . . . They govern us in all we do, in all we say, in all we think: every effort we can

make to throw off our subjection will serve but to demonstrate and confirm it. In words a man may pretend to abjure
their empire, but in reality he will remain subject to it all the
while.[11]

This observation becomes Bentham's guiding principle, asserting that it is for pleasure or pain alone "to point out what we
ought to do, as well as to determine what we shall do." All
discussion in utilitarianism originates from this individualistic
point of view. The corollary of this principle is Bentham's
famous "principle of utility": "The greatest happiness of all
those whose interest is in question" is "the only right and proper
and universally desirable end of human conduct."[12] In Bentham,
good is a synonym for *happiness,* and Johnson attempts to ana-
lyze in his novel the varieties of happiness that human beings
pursue. Johnson's objection to Bentham's thesis is Bentham's
assumption of a static, inflexible human nature and Bentham's
reduction of human action as determined by an attempt to avoid
pain and increase the chance for pleasure. The utilitarian conception of a priori human identity arbitrarily assumes socialized
adults, ignoring how they were produced, their backgrounds,
race and gender, and so forth—ignoring, in effect, "dependent
origination." From a strictly utilitarian outlook, there is no
spirit enlivening the body; nor is utilitarianism directed toward
any kind of enlightenment. Thus, Johnson objects to utilitarianism's ethics, in that it assumes as axiomatic the unfree, unenlightened, and nonevolving individual, oscillating constantly
between pleasure and pain. Further, if there is no logical termi-
nus for a quest for pleasure, there is from Johnson's Buddhist
perspective a point at which even the individual pursuing happiness can see this bondage to pleasure as absurd, disgusting,

and (worst of all) boring. Thus, Andrew is often bored with pleasures usually thought to be exquisite (sex, drugs), while his release from desire for extreme pleasure brings with it an appreciation for activities often considered boring (cleaning a house, correcting student papers).

Christianity might be imagined to oppose utilitarianism, but Johnson shows that traditional Christian eschatology is a variant form of the utilitarian worldview. Andrew's mother, Mattie, represents a Christian hope for salvation, but this perspective, embedded in Western forms of utility, has declined into an otherworldly scheme that assumes happiness as the highest value but places it beyond the grave, in the "sweet by-and-by" (90). Or, conversely, ultimate *un*happiness is associated with eternal damnation to hell. Like utilitarianism, Mattie's conventional Christian piety also expresses a confidence in an individual, substantive psychological self (the soul); the difference is that Mattie hopes for the eternal perpetuation of the self as it presently exists, even if this self ends in hell (not Mattie's goal, obviously). Thus, her desire for salvation is another form of utilitarianism in a disguised form: "'You have me, I have you,' Mattie whispered, 'and we both have Jesus'" (5). For Johnson, then, "something [is] wrong" with a religion that reflects the hedonistic culture in which it is embedded and that it should criticize.

Characters in the novel embody Bentham's point, that each person is the best authority for what makes him or her happy. They believe themselves to be self-determining, following their own schemes in the pursuit of happiness. Andrew initially believes he will discover happiness in romance. His love for Minty formally initiates the plot; prior to his discovery of Minty, Andrew thought of himself as "empty"—meaning that he lacked self-esteem: "My knowledge, my clothes, my language, even, were shamefully second-hand, made by, and perhaps for, other men. I was a living lie, that was the heart of it" (17). His fervent hope is that his love will redeem him and make him unique and exceptional. He wishes to be completely self-determining, "wholly responsible for the shape I gave myself in the future, for shirting myself handsomely with a new life that called me like a siren to possibilities that were real but forever out of reach" (17). Thus, his romantic love for Minty is in reality an attempt to affirm his own ego.

Johnson exposes the egocentric quality of his protagonist's quest for happiness through a complex linkage of Euro-American and African American literary conventions. In a satire of the Renaissance pastoral narrative, Andrew endures a series of incidents that are supposed to lead him to his lost lover. His relationship with Minty begins with a clear allusion to the English pastoral conventions. As the plantation shepherd, "herding my father's Brown Swiss calves, his Leicester sheep," he is emotionally overwhelmed by an idealized Minty, the shepherdess, dressed in "osnaburg skirt and white blouse, beneath an old Leghorn hat, with a blue satin ribbon." Struck by her beauty, Andrew tells us that "I think I saw her—*really* saw her for the first time." Andrew, however, sees not simply an individual woman, but "a Whole, where no particular facet was striking because all fused together to offer a flawed, haunting beauty." He makes Minty a solipsistic reflection of his own needs: "How much of her beauty lay in Minty, and how much in my head, was a mystery to me. Was beauty truly *in* things?" (15).

In Andrew's passion for Minty, Johnson satirizes the illusion of romantic love, for his romantic notion of love is "illusory like moonlight on pond water" (16). Barely past his adolescence,

Andrew believes that he is seized by a grand passion, a love that, as Denis de Rougement would describe, is "universally moving in European literature. . . . What stirs lyrical poets to their finest flights is neither the delight of the senses nor the fruitful contentment of the settled couple; not the satisfaction of love, but its *passion*."[13] Johnson is also satirizing the devotion to the "African spirit," for Andrew senses from looking into Minty's eyes that "she had been lifted long ago from a melancholy African landscape overrich with the colors and warm smells of autumn" (15–16).[14] Andrew displays, as romantic love does by its very nature, a refusal or an "inability to enjoy the present without imagining it as absent."[15] So it is that he imagines his relationship with Minty "forty years . . . fifty years" later (15), as if these decades will pass with no corresponding change in Minty's or Andrew's (im)permanent selves.

Johnson's satire of African American conventions is no less subtle than his reworking of the pastoral romance. Andrew's patriarchal sense of masculine dominance challenges both Douglass's and Washington's narratives. Neither Douglass nor Washington acknowledges the importance of women in their slave narratives. Even though Douglass's escape from slavery was assisted with the help of his wife, he barely mentions her or his marriage in the *Narrative*.[16] Similarly, Washington's women resemble gender stereotypes, since at various points in his life a woman is on hand to save him from involving himself in the supposed trivia of day-to-day routine. Andrew, in contrast, uses Minty's image as his inspiration for freedom. Andrew ironically enslaves himself to his self-absorbed love for Minty, and it is only because of Minty that Andrew's heart suddenly "knocked violently for manumission" (15). As Andrew says, "my urgency for freedom came from my desire to see Minty free" (101). As pastoral lover transposed to South Carolina, Andrew intends to purchase her, then "own" her and live an idealized life as freeman. Attempting to live up to an abstract idea of African American masculinity, he blithely assumes present and future responsibility for Minty's well-being. Johnson hints at Andrew's folly when he enters Polkinghorne's study and sees "a soft calf-bound set of Hawthorne" (16). As the allusion to Hawthornian themes imply, Andrew, in transforming Minty into an object to be rescued, may in fact be committing the Unpardonable Sin, treating Minty as a means to his own happiness rather than as an end.

Opium-addicted Ezekiel William Sykes-Withers, Andrew's tutor, is Andrew's ironic foil as a romantic lover, though he enters the novel having renounced love. His philosophical pedantry makes him the *philosophus gloriosus,* playing Pangloss to Andrew's Candide. Introduced as one who "knows as much about metaphysics as any man alive" (9), Ezekiel is above all a systems lover: "He could not, it was clear, live without certainty" (29). Above all, Ezekiel is an ethicist, for he intends to impart to Andrew "a perfect moral education"—significantly based on utilitarianism, the "program modeled on that of James Mill for his son John Stuart" (12). For Ezekiel, behind the seeming disorder of all events there lies a hidden moral order, which Ezekiel reduces to an all-encompassing vegetarianism: "all the violence wars slavery crime and suffering in the world had, as Ezekiel suggested, its beginning in what went into our bellies" (27). Vegetarianism does not produce happiness but creates dissension, since it leads to Andrew's alienation from George when Andrew refuses to skin a deer.

Ezekiel's commitment to an abstract, eternal, and absolutist philosophical system alienates him from other people, increasing the unhappiness he tries to avoid. Ezekiel's commitment to the "Transcendental Ego" (85) is a psychological reaction to the misery of his own grief-filled family history. His father, beaten down by the world's troubles and by poverty, murders his wife and daughter, then commits suicide. Ezekiel's only remark about his background reveals the extent of his self-delusion: he says his father "deeply loved the things of this world, he held his family and work in the highest esteem" (11). Ezekiel makes his cabin into a solipsistic hermitage, surrounding himself with mirrors to reflect his own image: he "was solipsistic; [he] was emotionally bankrupt; [he] was empty" (91). Andrew, sensing the depth of self-deception in Ezekiel, understands that he can never be an effective teacher: "all life left my studies" (13).

Ezekiel's satirical rebuke results from the visit of his hero, the greatest systematizer of the nineteenth century, Karl Marx. This fictive Marx only barely resembles the historical author of *The Communist Manifesto,* who refused job offers while his children starved and who deliberately avoided the suffering workers of Manchester's mills. On the contrary, Johnson's Marx "did not, like Ezekiel, live for ideas, political or otherwise; he was, in the old sense—the Sanskrit sense—a householder. The Marx of Ezekiel's fancy, the humorless student radical of the 1830s was—you cannot guess—a *citizen* devoted, first and foremost, to his family" (84). A "householder" in this context is a person committed to Buddhist principles but who does not enter the monastery, choosing a life of work with family and friends. Ezekiel, who reads Marx's work religiously, expects a revelation from his Master on the evil of slavery and the corruption consequent of the capitalistic system, an oracular declaration that would explain the universe and thereby justify Ezekiel's life of deprivation. But Marx has little to say about slavery—"to be sure, what he saw of American slavery made him sore"—and so Ezekiel was "badly disappointed. He thought Marx dull" (84). Ironically, Marx's dullness is a reflection of Johnson's own thematics in the novel: the necessity of accepting the mundane, the pragmatic world of everyday accommodations to one's family and community.

Johnson's fictive Marx reiterates the novel's ethical theme.[17] Ezekiel wonders, how can human beings make ethical choices in a world changing from moment to moment? Expecting a grand, theoretically consistent vision of the hidden workings of economic determinism, Ezekiel is crushed by the fictional Marx's simple reply. The greatest ethical imperative, for the *Oxherding* Marx, lies in maintaining the daily rituals of humble and ordinary life: "Everything I've vritten has been for a voman—is *one* way to view Socialism, no?" (87). Ezekiel attempts to express his own philosophy to Marx, that a dualistic contest between a permanent Self and an abstract and absolute Other is essential to maintain a substantialist identity. But Marx vehemently disagrees:

> Vhen two subjects come together, they realize in their reciprocal intersubjective life a common vorld. Yes? Compared to this, all other ways are fragmentary. Partial. Hollow. No matter how passionately you pursue them. The universal name for this final, ontological achievement, this liberation— Occidental or Oriental—in vhich each subject finds another is *love*. (86)

The critical phrase in Marx's reply is "common vorld." The fictional Marx does not correspond to the Marx known through tradition, who puts together elaborate theories to account for the world's confusion; who explains disorder with the orderly design of dialectical materialism.[18] Instead, Johnson comically demolishes that caricature to introduce an American pragmatism that insists that all theoretical systems must begin with the actual, historically concrete, temporal experience of a person living through an ordinary life. For Johnson's pragmatic Marx, what we know always flows from human experience and performance.

If there is no clear code or transcendent ethical system in an ever-evolving world, what must Ezekiel do to be saved? Marx answers in one word: "'Rejoice'" (87)—or as Johnson would put it, go forth "singing the world." Yet rejoice Ezekiel cannot do. Nevertheless, he attempts to set his life aright by following Marx's command as if he has been given yet another abstract commandment for his life. Much as Andrew thinks that happiness resides in his infatuation with Minty, Ezekiel imagines that he will discover happiness in an idealized love, especially since this method has been recommended by the fictional Marx. So Ezekiel goes looking for a "voman" to love. He meets the reprobate Moses Shem (whose last name significantly puns on *sham*), who weaves a preposterous story about his ill daughter, named Althea.[19] Ezekiel immediately falls in love, not with an actual person, but with Althea's picture, "a daguerreotype . . . an underexposed print, sfumato, smudged by fingerprints" (89), given him by Moses. Johnson emphasizes the unreality of Althea with the wrecked condition of the picture; Ezekiel, "crazy as a mouse in a milkcan" (18), falls in love (as does Andrew) with an image in his mind. To prove his supposedly self-sacrificial love, he then gives Moses his month's wages—all his actions performed in congruence with what he hopes will be a new, more ardently cultivated moral order. Ezekiel hopes to attain "a sense of right proportion, a clean asymmetry: a renunciation of the fruit of his works at Cripplegate, of reward, which created, in Ezekiel's view, no further action" (91).

Just as Andrew intends to buy Minty's freedom but enslaves himself, Ezekiel's purchase of Althea with his paycheck is his own reinscription of slavery. Ezekiel, like Andrew, attempts to possess a relationship for his own self-exultation. But in giving away his month's wages to Shem, Ezekiel feels that he has grandly acted out of charity and is absolved of the world's trouble by discovering "something to serve" (91), even if his service is meted out to an image he has created out of his own craving. In his effort to "prelive the future," he rejects any possible opportunity for relationships in the present. He wishes to "enter . . . into a life of clarity and law" (93), and he thereby repudiates a life of messiness, disorder, and confusion: in other words, relationships with real people. This point is dramatically conveyed with Ezekiel's death, when he enters Shem's (significantly) empty house. A parody of an actual household, Shem's broken-down shack is inhabited not by a family but by rats, wild hogs, and birds. Ezekiel's death from a broken heart is Johnson's commentary on the futility of his illusory, solipsistic drive for permanence and solid identity. In death, he finally achieves the household he has fled from all his life. He sobs, drops his cane, and crumples against a barrel: "his spirit changed houses, and he dropped into the solitary darkness like a stone" (94).

Ezekiel's ethereal quest for happiness is bracketed by Flo Hatfield's sensualist hedonism. Andrew, "in the service of the senses" (37), is required by Flo to study the inverse of what he learned from Ezekiel: that the "way" to happiness is through sexual gratification. He is sent to Flo Hatfield's plantation, Leviathan, a five-hundred-acre farm from whose fields she picks a slave to be her "butler"—a mocking reflection of George's role as inseminator of Mrs. Polkinghorne. Andrew is transformed by Flo into a thing, forced to be the "lover of [her] fantasy . . . husband, ravager, teacher, Galahad, eunuch, swashbuckler, student, priest, and above all else, *always there*" (61). She is the incarnation of desire from a Buddhist perspective.[20] "A fairy tale witch" (54), Flo has an endless appetite for sensual pleasures and sexual experimentation and says of herself that she really belongs on another planet where there is "a world of spoiled, pampered women, who are all geniuses of love, ravishing and forever young" (39). At this point, however, Flo is "too obsessive to be sensual" (43), and so requires "the most violent stimulants to register sensation" (43). Clearly a mockery of the "stimulants" of the 1970s—sexual liberation and the drug culture—Flo has become an addict. If there is only desire for pleasure and its satisfaction, as the utilitarian assumes, addiction is irresistible.

Despite Flo's role as Ezekiel's opposing character, she also embraces exclusionist, systematizing theories, and, like Ezekiel, subscribes to utilitarianism. That Johnson disapproves of Flo's utilitarian philosophy is borne out in his comic depiction of her. With Flo, Andrew becomes addicted to both sex and drugs, though he is initially "suspicious of pleasure as a Final Cause" (43). Andrew momentarily accepts her hedonistic philosophy, which he describes as a potential "Way." He calls her an "artist" (39), and he admits there was "something of the pursuit of truth in a good lay, an epistemological edge in exposing a woman stitch by stitch" (72). When Flo refuses to pay him for his "services," however, Andrew changes his mind and finally sees that Flo's "dead-end, wheel-spinning life of desire" ultimately disappoints, as she transforms herself into an object, a "male fantasy" that makes them both "victims enslaved to an experience

. . . that neither of [them] truly wanted" (71). He needs to get off the "wheel"—a common Buddhist symbol for the life of enslaved desire. She, like Ezekiel, is caught up in her own solipsism, as her response to Andrew's question "What do you feel when you touch me?" reveals:

"Me." Now her lips were on my fingertips. "I feel my own pulse. My own sensations." She laughed. "I have a pulse everywhere."

"That's all you feel?"

"Yes." (53)

Flo's (and Bentham's) reductive, dualistic opposition of pain and pleasure is only one more category of spiritual slavery. As Reb says, "She ain't free" (62).

If "love" in the novel can devolve into Ezekiel's and Andrew's bondage to ethereal abstraction or Flo's enslavement to sensuality, it may also be incubated in a broader, but just as illusory commitment to an abstract community. In several characters, Johnson presents a version of rule utilitarianism, as opposed to act utilitarianism followed by Flo, Andrew, and Ezekiel.[21] In the novel, rule utilitarianism is a general practice (as opposed to a specific act) whose performance is restricted for the increase of happiness for a large (but abstract) African American population. The most obvious character representing this position is Nate McKay, Minty's father, the novel's caricature of a Race Man. Nate's guiding rule simply requires reversing the slave/master relationship. As he tells George, "You gonna feel daid . . . until you back in the Big House and Master Polkinghorne is down heah—permanently" (105). Nate's racial commitment, however, takes the form of increasing his sensual pleasure, since Nate has absorbed the racist stereotype of the African American male as sexual predator. He tells George that he "should have somebody on the side." No householder like Johnson's Marx, Nate did not maintain "a pleasant household," for he beats his wife and children regularly and insists that conventional sexual morality does not apply to him: "we been treated different, so we gotta have different rules" (104).

Nate's ethical thinking has much to do with black cultural nationalism, as Little has suggested.[22] For Johnson, this nineteenth-century variant of black cultural nationalism is part of the sickness Buddhism says should be escaped. Black cultural nationalism is portrayed at greater length in George, who adopts Nate's ersatz militancy because he has nothing else to "hope for, work toward" (105).[23] After he is thrown out of "the Big House," he becomes a "flinty old Race Man" (21). He tells Andrew, "You know Africa *will* rise again someday, Hawk, with her own queens and kings and a court bigger'n anythin' in Europe?" Andrew wonders at his "obsessions with the world-historical mission of Africa" (21) and feels pressure at his father's rule that whatever promotes the advancement of African Americans must be performed: "Whatever you do, Hawk—it pushes the Race forward, or pulls us back. You know what I've always told you: If you fail, everything we been fightin' for fails with you. Be y'self" (21).

Andrew implies that George's commitment to race compensates for his own emotional deficiencies and personal disappointments—losing his job as butler, his unhappy marriage, and his uneasiness with Andrew. From Andrew's perspective, George psychologically chooses his misery, identifying racial discrimination as its sole cause. From Johnson's Buddhist perspective, his pain may be seen as a consequence of his repudiation of the "Whole":

> My father kept the pain alive. He *needed* to rekindle racial horrors, revive old pains, review disappointments like a sick man fingering his sores. Like my tutor, he *chose* misery. Grief was the grillwork—the emotional grid—through which George Hawkins sifted and sorted events, simplified a world so overrich in sense it outstripped him. (142)

But Andrew is not entirely fair to his father in his accusation of George's simplifying the world, for Andrew omits the socio-historical context of George's sifting and sorting. George has learned through bitter experience what it means to be a slave, even being told which woman to sleep with. His role required a coerced acceptance of a state of "epidermalized Being" (52) in a way Andrew, with his advantages, never was forced to endure so completely. George was entrapped by the peculiar institution to think in terms of a dualistic world of slave/master, and so the material conditions of his life partly produced both his subjection and his worldview. And that has had a suicidal effect on his spirit: according to the Soulcatcher, George had "somethin' dead or static already inside [him]—an image of [himself]—fo' a real slave catcher to latch onto . . . he was carryin' fifty-'leven pockets of death in him anyways, li'l pools of corruption that kept him so miserable he *begged* me, when Ah caught up with him in Calhoun Falls, to blow out his lights—" (174). As he did with Maxwell's father in *Faith and the Good Thing,* Johnson uses the image of the extinguished candle ironically. George did not experience nirvana but a perpetual wish for death. As with Maxwell, it is Andrew's moral failure that he has neither understood nor felt compassion for his father.

"Doing Beautifully What Needs to Be Done": Johnson's Aristotelian Hero

As we have seen, Johnson rejects moral relativism, the idea that one moral decision is neither better nor worse than another. But he also rejects both act and rule utilitarianism, with "pleasure as a Final Cause" (43). Johnson dismisses ideological principles, especially conventional Marxism and black cultural nationalism, and he finds conventional Christianity a poor institutional guide to ethical action. As ethical practice, these rejected modes originate in a fixed, deterministic conception of human nature and in an imprudent attachment to "rule ethics." In an endlessly evolving world, where human beings originate dependently on others and on the world itself, a rigorously ethical life requires a different paradigm. Additionally, utilitarianism and Mattie's version of conventional Christianity focus primarily on an action's qualities that would make it an ethical action, or on the consequences of actions for the community or the individual. For Johnson's novelistic purposes, this evaluation is not adequate because it separates the individual from the action. In contrast, Johnson is more interested in the qualities of *character* that make for a virtuous person. Living virtuously does not necessarily promote pleasure for oneself or others, nor does it from Johnson's perspective guarantee eternal life in the next world. Rather, Johnson's exploration of ethics leads to an evaluation of the whole person, and of a life that is worth living. In his exploration, the issues of happiness and ethics subtly merge in the novel.

Andrew gradually evolves into an ethical person in the novel, but this is a slow process indeed. In fact, through much of the novel, Andrew is not an especially likeable protagonist, for he is not an impulsively ethical person though he is not an entirely bad person either. He is correct when he admits, "my life was a patchwork of lies" (139). His relationships with those closest to him seem strangely unsubstantial. He says he loves his father but readily betrays George, and he has little good to say about his stepmother. He is clearly not a temperate person, and he is often in "the pursuit of truth in a good lay" (72). He pledges himself romantically to Minty, but soon after, he is easily diverted by Flo's sexual hedonism and her narcotics. He exuberantly enjoys his sensual experiences with her, even as his position as slave slowly changes to that of her sexual master. After his escape, he marries Peggy, but only when Dr. Undercliff threatens to expose his false identity. He abandons his friend Reb with no great remorse and thinks little about him thereafter. Thus, ethical behavior for Andrew does not come naturally; but ethical action has, in Johnson's fiction, little to do with one's nature or one's natural powers. Ethical conduct is instead habitual, cultivated in conscious emulation of others' actions and by deliberate choices, rationally made.

In his youth, Andrew has few ethical models and little incentive to behave ethically. At Cripplegate, he is not allowed to forget his slave position, despite the fact that his mother is the plantation's mistress. At a critical moment in his adolescence, he overhears what Jonathan Polkinghorne says about him to Ezekiel: "What I mean to say is that Andrew is my property and that his value will increase with proper training." Polkinghorne's cruel but realistic remark devastates Andrew: "What did I feel? Try as I might, I could not have told you what my body rested on, or what was under my feet" (12). Andrew finds no relief from his indeterminate position at home. In George and

Mattie's household, he is continuously required to enter into coalitions in their marital bickering. Among his fellow slaves, he is seen as an interloper. As Reb says, he "ain't folks or white" (36), since he "belonged . . . to both house and field" and felt "caught . . . in [the] crossfire" (8). Because he feels "forever poised between two worlds" (17), he has never developed enough confidence in the patterns of ethical choices to have moral character.

This situation begins to change for Andrew at Spartanburg. Johnson hints at the newly forming basis of ethical action for Andrew shortly before Andrew's wedding to Peggy. Dr. Under-cliff bestows on his daughter and future son-in-law his blessing:

> I would wish you, as they say, happiness, too, but I fear there
> *is* no happiness; it is an invention of the poets. . . . I wish you
> what the Greeks called *arete,* "doing beautifully what needs
> to be done." Not much to dance the turkey buzzard about in
> that, I daresay, but a man sleeps well at night, with *arete,*
> develops no digestive trouble, or spiritual afflictions, and
> demanding more than this *ataraxia*—another Greek notion
> —is tempting God's patience. (137)

Undercliff's benediction provides a platform for Andrew's char-acter formation in the rest of the novel. Dr. Undercliff's "virtue ethics" (as opposed to "rule ethics") derives from Aristotle's *Nicomachean Ethics. Arete* is a term from Greek philosophy signifying "virtue" or "excellence," in the sense that a person's ethical function is fulfilled and performed. For Aristotle, human beings have a function to fulfill: to express in virtuous action the harmony of rationality and feelings—what in this context could be called one's "character." The fulfillment of this function con-stitutes *arete.* Undercliff's commentary is affirmed immediately, when Andrew agrees that "the doctor was right about one thing: Virtue was doing beautifully what the moment demanded" (139). Dr. Undercliff, a man of practical wisdom who seems to combine rationality and feeling (for Aristotle, this person is a *phronemos*), is someone whom Andrew can observe and learn from.

What for Aristotle (and Johnson) are the traits of character that make a person virtuous? In *Nicomachean Ethics* Aristotle compiles a lengthy list of virtuous personality traits, then presents a systematic explanation of each virtue as a mean between extremes. A person who is self-controlled, for example, has neither Flo's sensual self-indulgence nor Ezekiel's spartan indifference to physical pleasures, but experiences a sexual enjoyment navigating between the two—which Andrew seems to enjoy in his connubial bliss with Peggy: "applying what Flo Hatfield had taught me occupied our nights for a month" (144). Constant sexual athleticism is not necessarily essential to their well being, however, since Peggy "was good on hugs" (148). For the most part, then, we can discover a virtuous trait on Aristotle's list by relating it to its corresponding (vicious) extremes.

Dr. Undercliff's benevolence represents this kind of mean. People with the trait of generosity do not give away their possessions foolishly and indiscriminately, but must perceive that their recipients need money and that they will use it properly. So Ezekiel does not behave virtuously when he gives Shem all of his wages, since he is at least partly aware of Shem's duplicity and his alcoholism. But neither is the benevolent person hardhearted or tight-fisted, as is the slave owner Polkinghorne when he refuses to free Minty and Andrew, even at Andrew's pathetic request. The mean between these two extremes seems manifest in Dr. Undercliff's wedding gift of a run-down cabin to Andrew and Peggy. The house resembles in its disrepair the shack in which Ezekiel died: "Rats and nests of squirrels I found inside, unverifiable eggs in the chimney. They left broken windows. A bad pump" (144). But while Ezekiel dies of a broken heart in his ramshackle house, Andrew and Peggy rebuild theirs. Their humble house, unlike the Cripplegate or Leviathan mansions, offers them a concentration of purpose (*telos*) in their marriage: "the house, hammering and scrubbing, kept us focused not on each other but on a spot between us and just ahead of us both" (145). A wrecked shack, the cabin has little financial worth, but as the newlyweds repair it they are infused with a "strange faith" in each other and their future together (145). Thus, their "house work" becomes an enduring value for Andrew as he begins to discover his "Way": "I discovered that my dharma, such as it was, was that of the householder" (147). Although the affluent Dr. Undercliff could have afforded a much more expensive gift, this modest wedding gift is exactly what they need to create a satisfying and enduring marriage. Undercliff's virtue is linked to his character and is expressed by his feelings, which are appropriate for the situation. Dr. Undercliff gives the gift gladly and unself-consciously, does not regret giving it, and is delighted that it brings his daughter and son-in-law happiness. His gift is virtuous not simply because it produces good results, or because it abstractly represents a mean between two extremes; rather, it is virtuous because it is performed in conformity with Dr. Undercliff's basic rationality and positive feelings toward others. Ezekiel's gift to Shem, in contrast, is self-serving, while Polkinghorne's refusal to manumit Andrew confirms his greedy character. Thus, Dr. Undercliff is an expression of *arete*.[24]

Perhaps of all the characters, Peggy is most inherently moderate in all things, and she is also an embodiment Johnson's conception of *arete*. Peggy ("Fruity" is her symbolic nickname) enacts the essential Johnson worldview whenever she appears in the novel. Her importance to Andrew's development has been noted by critics; as Timothy L. Parrish writes, Peggy represents "Johnson's relentless optimism."[25] Indeed, "Fruity" is at times insufferably cheerful. She is in some ways a comic caricature so as to avoid sentimentality—no beauty (her nose looks like a radish), she wears heavy bifocals. Peggy is "physically as plain as a pike . . . but she was, inly, energetic—an explosion of vitality, rather like a teapot set not to boil over but to bubble and steam, perhaps even beautiful in her vulnerability, candor, and openness" (124–25). But she does, as Little writes, become "the personification of the compassionate other" in her acceptance of Andrew's earlier love affair with Minty and of the fact that Andrew is black.[26] Even more important to Johnson's thematics is her joyful "singing the world"; that is, she appreciates the small, ordinary, seemingly insignificant moments of life. She seems to have an intuitive, "mindful" understanding that every moment, every choice has intrinsic moral value.

Her action expresses her character. We catch glimpses of her working on her house, making silly jokes, knitting, doing her father's accounts, putting away Andrew's books, talking with him about national and personal daily cares, even momentarily wondering whether eroticized, romantic love might be more satisfying than the daily, mundane chores of being a housewife. Peggy (like her father) embodies Johnson's thematic idea: the seriousness of "duty—the quiet, dull triumph of devoting themselves to everyday things, placing children and wife, colleagues and acquaintances in a widening circle that soon enveloped the entire community, before all else" (192). The novel's abiding symbol of morality is dramatically expressed in her responsiveness to unique people in particular situations at given moments of their lives. She inevitably does the right thing, moment by moment, seeking ways of orienting herself to act effectively in a world where things seem to fall apart constantly. As Andrew says, Peggy is an emblem of "Being, and she, bountiful without end, was so extravagantly plentiful the everyday mind closed to this explosion, this efflorescence of sense" (172). Andrew learns love for Peggy through her action, and it is his constant exposure to Peggy's and Dr. Undercliff's moral examples that begins to produce Andrew's moral transformation.

Peggy's conduct becomes a model for Andrew's moral education. If Andrew's Way becomes that of a householder, his choice must be seen in context, and not considered in abstraction from his life history or his emerging ethical character. Some readers, as Gleason understands, in discounting Andrew's character might interpret the novel as simply a ratification of the status quo.[27] Gleason writes that readers skeptical of Andrew's dharma "might claim that Johnson—even as Douglass before him—authenticates the very power structures he seeks to undermine (or, perhaps more indicting, that he never sought to undermine them at all)."[28] This possible reading, that the novel uncritically endorses middle-class living, is a gross oversimplification, since it ignores the evolution of Andrew's character and abstracts a value out of context from the novel's lived experience. The "tranquility" that Andrew constantly misspells (146) but succeeds in experiencing emerges from a continuing evolution of his character.

To refine and complicate the conception of a householder, Johnson introduces an important contrast. The unnamed householder that Andrew observes midway through the novel symbolically opposes Johnson's celebration of Andrew and Peggy's choice of life. In this scene, as Reb and Andrew are escaping Leviathan, they spy on a middle-class, white family. While Andrew gazes at them through the window, the tranquil scene of the family eating together evokes Andrew's "wretchedness and envy" (107) for their "warm, dumb domesticity" (107). But Andrew's admiration of the family's mindless immersion in a vapid domesticity is overturned immediately when their dinner is interrupted by a posse that is pursuing him and Reb. When the householder is told by the posse leader that the reward for Andrew and Reb is one hundred dollars dead or alive, he "kissed his wife, went inside the cottage, [and] came out with a .44-caliber percussion plains rifle" (108). For this householder, murder is certainly worthwhile if "they [Andrew and Reb] are worth looking for" (108). Apparently shaped by his life of ease as a white person in the South, this anonymous householder acts immorally.

Andrew realizes that simply being a householder without social conscience is immoral, a kind of solipsism: "I can't *fake* that kind of belongingness, that blithe, numbed belief that the world is an extension of my sitting room. Or myself " (109). Simple monetary success, careerism, and respectability are not sufficient ethical values as Andrew realizes, since he wants something more from life, "something greater than merely *living* from day to day" (43). The spied-on householder lacks a sense of social justice, which Andrew begins to acquire from his association with ethically good people. Even as Andrew takes pleasure in his life with Peggy and a limited satisfaction from teaching, Andrew understands that an unquestioning acceptance of middle-class values "warped the world toward Western ontology" (147). That said, however, it is important to note that Johnson does not abstractly condemn middle-class values either.

Indeed, in his essay "Black Images and Their Global Impact," he argues that adoption of some middle-class values—Johnson lists as examples "a strong work ethic, self-reliance, delayed gratification, discipline, an appreciation of the individual, a commitment to education, dedication to one's family, marital fidelity, a respect for all life, the capacity for self-sacrifice and religious piety"—could be "the cure for salvaging our ravaged, inner-city communities, for rebuilding our families and achieving economic parity with whites, Asians, Hispanics, and anyone else."[29] For Johnson, the rich context of possibilities is the most important factor in evaluating a life—not a simplistic reduction to dualistic "good" and "bad" categories of actions or modes of living.

Reb represents a Buddhist variation on *arete* in the novel. His character also directs his Way: *via negativa*—a moral life achieved through negation and renunciation. Reb is entirely free of desire for worldly goods, self-aggrandizement, and fame: "He was the man, at country market, who looked at the stands and rejoiced at what he *didn't* need; the man who, when most vigorously at work, seemed resting" (46). Reb is not a conventionally nice person; in fact, he is (like Dr. Undercliff) something of a curmudgeon, "the most disagreeable man in South Carolina" (46). In Reb, Johnson embodies his twin virtues of work and selfless commitment to art, a moral pattern that flows from his basic character. As Johnson writes in his introduction, Reb, a descendent of Johnson's mythical tribe, the Allmuseri, rejects the idea of the static self, believing that "the self is not product but process; not a noun but a verb" (xvii). In an interview, Johnson describes Reb's ethics as emerging from Asian philosophy: "Reb is the resident Taoist. His approach to creation is based on first getting himself out of the way, forgetting himself. . . . By doing

this, Reb transcends epistemological dualism, is able to act ego-
lessly, and through his art serves others."[30] His name suggesting
his resistance to a socially imposed identity of slave, Reb possesses a strong character, in the sense that his choices are consistent and directed toward an end greater than himself. He defines
his character by his diligent work as a coffin maker: "I forget all
about myself, and that's when I start looking around for a tree
that wants to be a coffin" (47). Reb's self-renunciation saves him
from Soulcatcher's derringer. "He can't be caught, he's *already*
free," says a frustrated (and now retired) Soulcatcher. Reb's
understanding that the self as always evolving—a consistent
theme in Johnson's work—literally saves his life and Andrew's.
At the end of the novel, Reb escapes to Chicago to work in service of his art, fashioning his "finest coffin, the one in which
they laid Abraham Lincoln to rest" (176). Reb's commitment
to a monastic life is entirely respectable within the Buddhist
framework of the novel, but one that Andrew does not choose
for himself.

Bannon the "Soulcatcher" balances Reb's committed monastic style of life. At first glance an unlikely character to behave
ethically, Bannon too has the potentiality to transform his life.
Like Peggy, he has an engaging though mordant sense of humor,
and an intuitive sense of human needs that he uses profession-
ally to hunt escaped slaves. He also resembles Reb in his profound commitment to work, as he tells Andrew, "Ah, too,
performs a service to Gawd, and Ah performs it well" (111).
Significantly, his very bearing resembles Reb's: "Bannon moved
like the Coffinmaker, as if Time were fiction, all that was and
would be held suspended in this single moment, which was forever" (172). As a spokesman for determinism, Bannon wants to
resist his own moral change. To Bannon, the "grim comedy" of

his life appears to him divinely ordained: "It wasn't mah *business* to change, if everythin' is Gawd's will" (112). His view of human action—God controls all—ironically permits his moral nihilism. Indifferent to what Andrew calls "the Good" (172), Bannon argues that his own self is a given, not a choice. His essential nature, he believes, determines his choice to become a murderer: "Ah knows mah nature. It ain't an *easy* thing to accept yo nature, the nature you born with. Am Ah right or wrong?" (111). He is wrong. Change he does by the novel's end, since Reb foils Bannon and makes him live up to his promise to retire from slave catching. It may be implausible to imagine at the novel's end the Soulcatcher settling down to a quiet life with the town's madam, but in Johnson's comic vision, such character transformation can indeed occur.

The starkness of Minty's death precipitates moral change in Andrew. Without a pious, didactic sermon on slavery, Johnson vividly expresses slavery's evil through Minty, who physically disintegrates at the end of the novel. Whereas at the beginning of the novel Minty represented Andrew's definition of "romantic Love" writ large, an abstraction to which he devotes himself, at the novel's end she is wrecked by pellagra, a disease brought on by her enslavement, by beatings of her vicious masters, and by her hinted sexual abuse. Once his imagined pastoral beauty, she is now "unlovely, drudgelike, sexless, the farm tool squeezed" (155)—in a word, "*Hideous*" (158). But in confronting her slow and painful death, Andrew sees beyond her appearance. She is a symbol of "Form into formlessness" (166) and of Andrew's obligation to minister generously to a messy, unattractive world. This connection, however, is ironically portrayed. He completes the quest that initiated the novel's action: he purchases Minty (with money borrowed from Dr. Undercliff) at the slave auction—buying her exactly as he had intended in the novel's beginning, but now under very different circumstances. He is now ready to perform service to a loved one, but one who is weak, sick, and who cannot repay him.

As he cares for Minty and faces Peggy's disappointment in him, Andrew has a choice between three alternatives. First, he could abandon Minty and, like Reb, leave for Canada. Second, he could simply continue to pass in Spartanburg, "milk[ing] the Self's polymorphy to elude" (159), ignoring Minty and the danger that accepting his responsibility to her would bring him. (With this option, he would resemble the sinister, white "householder" discussed above, lacking compassion for others.) Third, he could make a futile effort, at great risk to himself, to attempt to save Minty, accepting that this choice would expose his racial identity and bring Bannon's death-dealing stroke. In comforting Minty as she approaches death, Andrew chooses who he is to be and what he conceives the good life to be. In Dr. Undercliff's words, Andrew "fulfills his function," for Andrew's choice is couched in a sense of his responsibility not simply to Minty but to humanity itself. Andrew is inspired by a reasoned (not impulsive) understanding of his moral obligation to the world. He tells Peggy of the commitment he now feels toward all human beings, and that he must work to repay what he has been given:

> We are born, even slaves, into such richness, and if I cannot somehow repay them, my predecessors and that girl outside, then I am unworthy of any happiness whatsoever, here with you, or anywhere. (161)

This statement expresses the Buddhist philosophy of debt (on), connoting an obligation carried in conjunction with what one has received from another (a gift, favor, service).[31] Rationally choosing in accordance with "on," Andrew for the first time acts with courage and justice, not simply because helping Minty is courageous, benevolent, and just (it is), but because Andrew is in the process of becoming through his choices a courageous, benevolent, and just person. He is becoming the kind of person who behaves morally when the situation calls for it and whose character and feelings are in accord with his action. His life becomes an expression of *arete*.

As if on cue, the Soulcatcher reappears, seemingly ready, like Mephistopheles, to whisk Andrew away to death. The Soulcatcher's sudden appearance is Andrew's moral trial. Is his vision of the beauty and oneness of all things merely another pretense, or is his newfound perspective enduring? The only way to dramatically assess Andrew's perseverance is to subject him to the final test: Soulcatcher's derringer. The title of the final chapter is "Moksha" (169), a Hindu term meaning "deliverance" or—in Western terminology—"enlightenment." In the final chapter, Andrew confirms what he learned from taking care of Minty and living with Reb, Dr. Undercliff, and Peggy. After Minty's death and immediately before what he thinks will be his own, he rediscovers in the Soulcatcher's tattoos "the world in all its richness, ambiguity and complexity"[32] and "the delight the universe took in diversity for its own sake, the proliferation of beauty" (175). By "diversity," Johnson implies that Andrew finally experiences in gazing at Bannon's skin the full realization of the world's emptiness. In Andrew's new openness to experience, the tattoos are symbolic, presenting Andrew "in the brilliance of a silver-gray sky at dawn, an impossible flesh tapestry of a thousand individualities no longer static" (175). Before Andrew can return to the world in its fullness/emptiness, however, he must perform one more ethical action: he must reconcile with his dead father. As we have seen, Andrew has judged his father harshly from his self-centered perspective, estimating only what he believes he should have received from his idealized image of a parent, not empathizing with George's condition as a slave. Andrew's resentful sense of filial deprivation, however, is complemented in Andrew's psyche by his own nagging feeling that he himself has not been a satisfactory son, especially feeling guilty that he has betrayed George's last request, to "Be y'self" (35).

Bannon provides the opportunity for reconciliation with his father, since only Bannon, Andrew says, "knew the secrets of my history and heart" (169). Bannon shows Andrew his canvaslike, tattooed skin. In objective terms, the skin is only a screen of images, permitting the observer to project his own meanings— "a crazyquilt of other's features" (169). In Buddhist terms, the skin is an empty canvas, awaiting Andrew's own creative meditation. Thus, Bannon's skin becomes for Andrew a Buddhist object of meditation (like, for example, a candle or a colored disk), leading him to a profound insight (vipassana bhavana). As Andrew concentrates on Bannon's skin—"not tattooes at all, I saw, but forms" (175)—Andrew finally begins to understand his father in the context of cosmic mutuality, or interbeing. In a universe where the highest obligation is to love, Andrew sees his father's face and realizes his father's limited but nevertheless real love: "the profound mystery of the One and the Many gave me back my father again and again, his love, in every being from grubworms to giant sumacs" (176). Through his imaginative, empathetic acceptance of his father's difficult life, he understands that George has fulfilled the obligation to love his son to the best of his ability. He also understands that he originated dependently on his father, that his life has also been contingent on George's enslavement and the peculiar institution generally. The scene thus becomes an emblem of the continuity of generations. In his sympathy, for his father and himself, Andrew can release his father's memory into the universe: "I lost his figure in this field of energy" (176). His father, in Emerson's phrasing, becomes "part or particle of God." In his reconceptualization of his father as part of the universe, and as a part of his own inter-being, he celebrates a spiritual identity with his father—"I was my father's father, and he my child" (176). In his imaginative sympathy for his limited but loving father, Andrew can recreate his childhood from a much more compassionate and understanding perspective. Released from his own guilt as a limited but loving son, Andrew in his enlightenment is reconnected with that to which he has always belonged, and apart from which he could not exist: his father.

In Andrew, then, Johnson demonstrates that is it possible to become a virtuous person through enlightenment. Andrew synthesizes feeling, intellect, and act in compassionately uniting with his father, and through him, the world. A life of virtue rewards those who are virtuous, and in "doing beautifully what needs to be done" (137), Andrew ends the novel experiencing true happiness—what so many characters searched for but failed to find. In the beginning of *Nicomachean Ethics,* Aristotle argues that the ultimate end of human life is happiness —what Aristotle calls *eudaimonia,* denoted in Undercliff's benediction as the similar term *ataraxia* (137). Aristotle's "happiness" differs dramatically from the utilitarian's goal of pleasure or a simple feeling.[33] Andrew's happiness (like Aristotle's) is a secure tranquility, a mindful confidence in oneself and one's acts, and an openness to the world. Andrew lets go of the need for security and stability, exchanged for a sense of moral balance, coherence of character, and centeredness, which inspires him in "the business of rebuilding . . . the world" (176). Precisely what "rebuilding the world" means, however, will be contemplated in Johnson's two later novels, in which Johnson broadens his focus to national themes.

CHAPTER 4

The Sorcerer's Apprentice

> A wise man will hear, and will increase learning; and a
> man of understanding shall attain unto wise counsels: To
> understand a proverb, and the interpretation; the words of
> the wise, and their dark sayings.
>
> Proverbs 1:5–6

M. H. Abrams's classification of traditional literary critical approaches is helpful in explaining Johnson's general understanding of literature.[1] Johnson is hostile to the view that literary works are autonomous, self-sufficient entities (the critical orientation Abrams labels "objective"). As we have seen, Johnson's view of art is informed by the Buddhist doctrine of dependent origination, the fundamental relationality of all texts through history. He also has comparatively little interest in works of literature as representations of observable reality (Abrams's "mimetic" approach). In *Turning the Wheel*, Johnson writes, "For classic mimesis to work, we must first agree on what *is* before it can be imitated; since we are in strong disagreement on the Real, and have abandoned the idea that nature's meaning is pregiven, the artist is obliged, then, to reconstruct as best he can perspectives on the Real."[2]

Johnson instead emphasizes the artist's shaping design in understanding our world. Johnson's affirmation of the artist's volition in ordering and shaping the external world provides moral direction to the reader. Because Johnson takes seriously the writer's ethical position, he regards literature as a means of achieving ethical effects in a reader and also as an expression of his own ethical, social self (Abrams's "pragmatic" and "expressive" orientations). As he explains to an interviewer, "One of the things that literature ought to be about is liberation of perception and consciousness. Our voices need to be freed so that we don't fall into those traps that diminish or limit other human lives."[3] This ethical concern for the liberation of others dominates *The Sorcerer's Apprentice*.

The Sorcerer's Apprentice places the artist's antirealism in opposition to a naive realism that reduces all objects to their sheer materialistic value. In general terms, the "negative" characters of Johnson's stories are materialists, and their worldview postulates a mind-independent universe of physical objects obeying mechanistic laws of force, energy, and economics. Against these "realist" characters, Johnson deploys metaphorical artists whose job it is symbolically to restructure the world into spiritual patterns, providing a cohesive sense of connectedness. The controlling motif of the volume is a competition of alternative metaphysics, pitting the artist who unifies reality against the skeptical materialist who would segment it.

In opposing the artist to the materialist, Johnson explores alternative metaphysical positions of idealism and realism—the two fundamentally different ways people conceive of their world, think about their world, and make crucial decisions about their world and other people. In assuming the antirealist's position, Johnson merges Western idealism and Buddhist epistemology. Johnson intends to jolt emotionally the assumed realist reader into an entirely different perception of the world, making him or her forego a customary, conditioned, and ordinary version of material reality in favor of a more expansive and aesthetic sense of the world. Johnson reveals himself to be an idealist whose mission is to persuade his readers of the philosophical claims of idealism, a vocational calling that he has made his own in interviews and his book *Being and Race*. Johnson writes that the purpose of all great art is beyond conventional morality; it is to challenge our metaphysics: "Our perception—or way of seeing—has been shaken, if one is talking about great art."[4] Johnson's artist combats what he calls the "Age of Hype"—the province of the marketplace—to establish an intellectual justification for his or her art.

"The Epistemological Murphy": Johnson's Epistemology in *The Sorcerer's Apprentice*

As Johnson explains in an interview, "Moving Pictures" (1985) is "actually a story about Buddhist epistemology. No one ever gets that."[5] In the story, epistemological concerns are tied to ethical choices. The protagonist of "Moving Pictures" is a successful Hollywood writer who lives a messy life, characterized by an impending divorce, quarrels with his boss, sexual promiscuity, drug abuse, and his children whom he neglects in favor of his career. He is plagued by regrets that he has abandoned his ambitious and complex "Big Book" (a novel) for better-paying, more prestigious, but vacuous Hollywood film writing. He lives in a rat-race world that he attempts to escape one night by going to the movies.

The story dramatizes his emotional escape when he weeps for the characters on screen that he himself probably helped to create; that is, he is taken in by the patent sentimentality imaged on the screen—what he calls an "epistemological Murphy."[6] *Murphy* is a slang term for a confidence game, a criminal strategy in which a phony story created by con men hooks the victim (in the story, the film's viewer) by exploiting his or her greed. The action and characters portrayed on the screen evoke the protagonist's own self-pity and remorse over his lost opportunities and wretched circumstances, which he believes he is unable to change.[7] When he returns to his car after viewing the movie, he discovers that his car has been vandalized and he has been robbed. He loses his checkbook, his house key, and—symbolic of his rat race—"the report due tomorrow at nine sharp" (123). With despair, he learns the hard New Testament lesson: "Lay not up for yourselves treasures upon earth, where moth and rust doth corrupt, and where thieves break through and steal."[8]

As Johnson wishes his readers to see, the story is a depiction of Buddhist epistemology. The protagonist is "a seeker groping in the darkness for light"—in the double sense that he eagerly looks forward to his escapist pleasure in the theater, but also that he is very much in need of enlightenment. Johnson contrasts dramatically two different ways of knowing the external world during the protagonist's visit to his film studio's editing room. He is first shown the film frames in their singularity, with "a single frozen image, like an individual thought, complete in itself, with no connection to the others," unchanging and permanent. This vision of independent and singular frames gives way to the performance of the film itself, with the frames fusing together, "a sensuously rich world" that conveys not separateness, but a continuity of the present moment with the past and with the indefiniteness of the future. The protagonist wonders to himself how it is that these "rags of shots, conflicting ideas, and scraps of footage actually cohere" (120). His question about the film parallels Johnson's epistemological question posed in the story: how does the world hang together for a perceiver?

The protagonist's question about the perceived unity of his sensuous experience is answered in his full viewing of the feature film, first in the cutting room and then in the theater. The two film versions are Johnson's allegory of human apperception, employing both Western and Buddhist theories. First, Johnson creates a subtle dramatization of Immanuel Kant's theory of epistemology in *Critique of Pure Reason*. As viewed frame by frame in the cutting room, the protagonist's senses do not apprehend the world as a unified totality; instead, he perceives an apparently pointless procession of discrete phenomena, one unique object after another. The filmic world through the viewer appears discrete and intractable, where objects exist independently of other objects and move disparately and in randomness. When the projector is activated and the protagonist sees the film as it appears on the screen, the filmic experience is suddenly organized spatially, temporally, and causally—an actual stream of experience that does mysteriously hang together. These "scraps of footage" do finally "cohere."

This sudden apperception is no mere subjective projection of order on random flux, since all people in the theater experience this order in roughly the same manner (that is, spatially, temporally, and causally). The raw phenomena of the world are knowable only insofar as they conform to an experiential way of being organized. The protagonist's mind, like other minds in the theater perceiving the same film, achieves coherence through Kantian a priori modes and "categories" of understanding: innate and inborn structures that permit the world to be knowable. The mind is not imposing these categories onto the phenomena; the categories are constitutive of phenomena. The world's phenomena (as symbolized by the film) can be knowable only insofar as they conform to these categories; and the knowable is limited to whatever can be experienced by those categories and modes. Whatever is omnipresent, eternal, or without cause (for example, God, heaven, free will) is therefore unknowable, for we cannot perceive them with our senses. On the other hand, things next to one another in space, things before or after one another in time, and things acting in a cause-and-effect relationship as in the film are shaped into a unity through Kantian categories and subcategories.

Yet it is clear that for Johnson as a Buddhist, the perceiver's mind does much more than process reality in this Kantian sense. The protagonist also makes emotional claims on the movie, for he is not impartial, objective, or detached as he watches. Instead, he is emotionally conned by the "epistemological Murphy" that he has in part (but not totally) created for himself, and in viewing the film filtered through his personal biases and emotional requirements, he is not aware that he is producing illusions stimulated by the film's sensory data and mistaking these appearances for an emotional reality. His memories create for him a deep sense of craving and desolation that he projects onto the screen while in the theater. For example, he weeps for his own "sense of ruin" that he felt when he views the movie's cemetery scene, as he recalls his own mother's death and his "irreversible feeling of abandonment" (121). And he weeps for his lack of success with women—first in his past (high school), then with his present trophy wife who "talks now of legal separation and finding herself " (116). In other words, the protagonist's epistemology is marked by his emotional cravings (that is, his wants, wishes, felt needs, regrets, and so forth). For this unenlightened protagonist, knowing the movie, like knowing the world itself, is filtered through his own personal desire. His ignorant cognitions, and not the film, then, produce his sorrow.

The protagonist's release (that is, his true enlightenment) would be only through acceptance of the world's emptiness—its impermanence, its radical contingency, and the futility of imposing his emotional requirements on it. The theater's screen is in fact "empty" in a Buddhist sense; as a blank screen, it denies the reality that the protagonist projects onto it. Subtly, Johnson has restructured symbolically the protagonist's squalid world for the reader. Johnson shows us that the protagonist's epistemology is more incomplete than he understands, and Johnson opposes the protagonist's literalism and self-centered demand for the world to be a certain way. Ironically, the lesson should be obvious for the protagonist when he discovers his "empty," vandalized car and how "empty" he feels (123). But "emptiness" in this context is not the paradoxical, Buddhist recognition of the world's fullness and the correlative opportunity to connect with other human beings. Instead, "emptiness" registers the protagonist's refusal of enlightenment and his consequent bitterness and rage that he cannot possess everything he desires: he brings his "fists down again and again on the Fiat's roof " (124). His spirit-shattering sorrow results directly from his flawed epistemology. Of course, the protagonist may yet revise his theory of reality, since he is in charge of his life—"producer, star, director in the longest, most fabulous show of all" (124).

The story "Moving Pictures," then, supplies a lesson from Buddhist philosophy. Johnson also uses Western philosophy, especially idealist philosophy, to thematically organize his narratives. In *The Sorcerer's Apprentice,* Bishop George Berkeley's metaphysics partly guides Johnson's thematic, for in Berkeley's philosophy, Johnson discovers his ally against what he envisages as a reductionist, dualistic worldview. A commercialized version of the world is based, for Johnson, on a materialist metaphysics.

Johnson's stories depict the conflict between the artist and the marketplace in philosophical terms with Bishop Berkeley of Cloyne used metaphorically. Berkeley's philosophy assists Johnson in arguing for a view of the world appropriate to his own exalted vision of the artist as creator.

Berkeley's theory of perception, his attack on the erosive skepticism and rationalism of his own age, and his complex quarrel with materialist reality suggest a philosophical framework in which Johnson can establish art as the supreme human activity and the artist as a source of our shared world. In Buddhist terms, the artist can become a bodhisattva. With Berkeley's philosophical approach used as scaffolding, Johnson "raises the high wire of artistic performance" to make the writer the divine artificer of our culture.[9] The volume itself provides internal evidence of Johnson's philosophical debt. Johnson alludes to Berkeley the man in "Menagerie, A Child's Fable" (to his portly physical frame, "weighing more than some men" [43], and to his mental acuity: "Berkeley was, for all his woolgathering, never asleep at the switch" [43–44]); in his reference to the "playful verse attributed to Bishop Berkeley" in "Alēthia" (100); and to Berkeley the philosopher in "China" ("the body as it must be in the mind of God" [84]). Berkeley, then, is amply summoned into use throughout the volume, and these allusions hint at Berkeley's idealism as a source for Johnson's own metaphysical view.

Berkeley's influence on Johnson is seen primarily in the Bishop of Cloyne's rejection of a reality that transcends perception. Generally considered the founder of the modern school of idealism, Berkeley argues that things cannot exist on their own, separate from an imaginative agent. Berkeley's insistence on the mind's primary role in the constitution of the world mirrors

Johnson's own conception of the delicate balancing act of the artist "on the high wire," as he or she challenges our ways of knowing the world.

Berkeley's central metaphysical theory is expressed in his famous statement:

> For as to what is said of the *absolute* existence of unthinking things without any relation to their being perceived—that is to me perfectly unintelligible. Their *esse* is *percipi;* nor is it possible they should have any existence out of the minds of thinking things which perceive them.[10]

This passage from *The Principles of Human Knowledge* is the centerpiece of Berkeley's conception of "ideas" (that is, sensory objects), which exist in the mind. Berkeley insists that we do not inherit an unchanging, static reality independent of experience (John Locke's unchanging, eternal, but utterly unperceived substratum of all material things). If absolute reality were inaccessible and unknowable, if things were forever beyond the shaping powers of the creative faculties of human beings, then the artist cannot claim an independent vision of the world—let alone reconfigure the reader's morality and perception of the world. For Berkeley, there is no irreducible "something-I-know-not-what" concealed behind the sensory world, some noumenal reality that human beings can never apprehend but only intuit.

On the contrary, for Berkeley, as for Johnson, the active, creative mind continuously shapes and reshapes the world by perceiving it. The world exists directly because of the vigorous effort of the imagination that perceives it, imparts order to it, and gives it its meaning. Berkeley does not argue that human beings can conjure reality into being through imagination, however.

The world is dependent on the imagination of God, the "Author of nature" who "produces" the ideas of the consciousness: "The ideas imprinted on the senses by the Author of nature are called *real things;* and those excited in the imagination, being less regular, vivid, and constant, are more properly termed *ideas,* or *images of things* which they copy and represent."[11] In Berkeley's elevation of God's imaginative faculty, in his giving priority to the divine creative mind rather than to an unknowable noumenon, Johnson finds his own intellectual justification as a writer.

Thus, Johnson himself doubts that a writer "imitates" a world that exists independently of his consciousness; instead, the enlightened artist gives the world a reality by writing it into being, in the sense of giving the reader a new experience of the world. In an interview, Johnson deprecates the "mimetic" function of literature:

> As a writer, I don't believe that art imitates. There is a mimetic element, but I really think that what a writer does is create an experience on the pages of the book for the reader. You're not transcribing experience. If you talk about the African-American past in your work, you're obviously interpreting an experience. . . . It's all filtered through a consciousness, and the consciousness obviously of the author.[12]

Johnson's aversion to "imitation" as opposed to "creation" has a distinctly Berkeleyan ring. Berkeley writes:

> But besides all that endless variety of ideas of objects of knowledge, there is likewise *something* which knows or perceives them, and exercises divers[e] operations, as willing,

imagining, remembering, about them. This perceiving, active
being is what I call *mind, spirit, soul,* or *myself.*[13]

For Johnson, Berkeley's act of perception elevates his own artistic imagination to a position of fundamental epistemological
importance, and his philosophy provides the basis for Johnson's
own aesthetic ontology: there is no intelligibility in the world
apart from the active imagination. The centrality of this passage
in Berkeley's philosophy relates to Johnson's commitment to
his vocation as a creator, the philosophical underpinning for
his urgent need to "shake" the way we see our world. Johnson
wishes to inspire a radical revision of the materialist's understanding of the world. His artistic, Godlike perception transforms the uncreated world for the reader. In this way, Berkeley
offers Johnson a metaphor for his conception of the urgencies of
aesthetic creation in an "Age of Hype."

Berkeley's deliberations on perception allow Johnson to
create a metaphysics appropriate to his sense of artistic passion,
the crucial act of imaginative ordering of the world, of rescuing
the world from materialistic reduction—and from racism. Johnson's metaphysics is clearly tied to his vocation as an African
American writer. In his stories, racial issues form part of the
philosophical dialogue. In his essay "A Phenomenology of the
Black Body," Johnson argues that racism is the consequence
of defective (that is, materialist) metaphysics. When a African
American male body is perceived, Johnson writes, too often
racist constructions control the perception: "The mind is no way
passive; it is a participant in each act of knowing." The (white)
perceiver feels fear when perceiving an African American male
because he or she creates a meaning for the body: "I see the
[African American] student in a certain way because I fear for

my daughter while she is across town." At this point in his argument against racism, Johnson makes a Berkeleyan assertion: "to *perceive* a content is to *conceive* that content."[14] For Johnson, the writer's obligation is to undermine the reader's confidence in the social constructions of race and identity that we supposedly take for granted, to remind the reader of the metaphorical nature of reality and of his or her part in the creation of reality. The reader must know that any racist construction is a *mental* reality, formed by fear and desire. Johnson's effort to remind us that reality is mental, the intellectual significance of his debt to Berkeley, restores to the reader a transforming spiritual power. It becomes possible to recreate the world miraculously through understanding it philosophically.

In "Menagerie, A Child's Fable" (1984) Johnson introduces the Berkeleyan correlative in caricature. It is as if Johnson wishes to imagine what the world would be without Berkeley's defense of the creative mind, without the transformative powers of the imagination. As a fable, the story employs animals to set forth its admonitory moral: the disastrous consequences of the loss of artistic vision. In the pet store, things, as opposed to creative intelligence, reign supreme. Without the ordering vision of the artist, the world is analogous to a pet store gone mad, a dystopian universe of conflicting, confused, and disruptive rebellion against organic form imposed by the creative act. The "Age of Hype" Johnson inveighs against in *Being and Race* is symbolized in the story by the pet shop's collapse into a disordered, capitalistic market exchange.

As characteristic of fables, the narrative is organized by the allegorical significance assigned to the characters. Mr. Tilford, the pet store owner, allegorically represents an absent God. "A real gumboil, whose ways were mysterious" (44), Tilford has created a Noah's Ark world of diversity and conflict within the pet store that he no longer manages directly; neither does he interfere with its natural operation. Instead, like the mechanistic god postulated by the deists of the eighteenth century, Tilford expects the world to run smoothly by itself, "like an old Swiss watch that he had wound and left ticking" (53). (Bishop Berkeley himself wrote in opposition to the deistic concept of God.) He is now "sliding toward senility," gone, and perhaps dead: such is the speculation of the philosopher animals. As a creator of a marketplace economy, he debased the world by his own reduction of life to a materialistic emphasis on the profit margin: "Sometimes he treated the animals cruelly, or taunted them; he saw them not as pets but profit" (44).

In banishing the imaginative dimension of unity among animals in favor of marketplace values of profit and loss (where some animals are "worth" more than others), Tilford has guaranteed divisiveness and rancor, which become metaphors for racial conflict and multicultural wars. Without his authoritarian presence to coerce uniformity among the animals, his creation devolves into a mechanical world of bitter division and mutual antagonisms, "an entire federation of cultures . . . with a plurality of many backgrounds, needs, and viewpoints" (46). Without an artist (like Johnson) to promote mutual understanding and tolerance for different "viewpoints" among the animals, the pet store becomes a dystrophic site where individuals cannot conceive of other ways of perception because of differences they assume to be innate, genetic, or biological. Conflict becomes the norm in the shop: mammal against reptile, reptile against fish, fish against bird. In such a world, art itself is corrupted into shabby parochialism. The "reptiles" have "an elaborate theory of beauty based on the aesthetics of scales," implemented to denigrate another set of animals as "lowlifes on the evolutionary scale" (50). Each animal is "lost in [the store] with no way out, like a child in a dark forest" (54).

Berkeley, the story's "pious," doggy protagonist, functions as the parody of the Bishop of Cloyne, as the onomastic pun *Bark-ly* implies. As the watchdog with "a great deal of Tilford inside" him, Berkeley is supposed to protect the animal denizens of the pet store from the predatory world of necessity that they slip into. But he is no worthy guardian of idealism, since he is "not the smartest" (43). Johnson folds Berkeleyan idealism into the plot by making the action of his watchdog protagonist philosophically resonant. The plot hinges on Berkeley's dogged conscientiousness in never being "asleep at the switch" (44). Always awake, Berkeley seems to guard perceptually the existence of the sensory pet store world: the world continues to be, Berkeley thinks, simply because the watchdog continues to perceive it.

The plot's climax occurs when Berkeley finally takes a short nap while waiting for Tilford, exhausted from the demands of maintaining the pet store's reality. Significantly, he dreams of Tilford's Second Coming, and Tilford appears in a "burst of preternatural brilliance," blinding the animals with light. This "ancient light," however, is figured as destructive, for Tilford is dictatorial and coercive, and the animals are "somehow imprisoned in form" (56). This capitalistic pet store God is no creative artist. From this nightmarish vision of enforced uniformity and exclusion of imagination, Berkeley awakens. To his surprise, the world has gone on whether he perceived it or not; the monkey (the pet store's arch-materialist, who knows things simply because he can grasp them with his hands) gains supremacy, shoots Berkeley with Tilford's pistol, and the story ends with the world spiraling downward into chaos and destruction.

Berkeley's sleep and awakening represent Johnson's allusion to Bishop Berkeley's view in *Three Dialogues between Hylas and Philonous* of what happens to the world when all modes of perception are extinguished. Hylas asks Philonous, "Suppose you were annihilated, cannot you conceive it possible that things perceivable by sense still exist?"[15] Johnson playfully poses the same question in the story: is Berkeley's doze calamitous for the existence of his world? In the story, Berkeley the guard dog is humbled by his realization that the world continues to exist independently of his vision, his perceiving faculties. He is satirically punished for his vanity. He believed that the world depends on his own vigilant perception of it, and that his promise to protect the animals is an absolute and unconditional guarantee of their continued existence.

The dog's comeuppance is not Johnson's refutation of Berkeleyan idealism but an elaboration of it. Another mind or perceiver, Charles Johnson himself, stands behind Berkeley's consciousness of the world. In "Menagerie," through his many literary jokes and self-reflexive techniques, Johnson calls attention to himself as the creator of the pet store world that Berkeley inhabits. In this way, Johnson rewrites Philonous's answer to Hylas as to why the world remains when one ceases to perceive it (as when one is asleep or absent). Bishop Berkeley resorts to God in defending his theory of perception, claiming that whatever our perceptual condition, we are continuously perceived, "held in mind," by an "omnipresent, eternal Mind, which knows and comprehends all things, and exhibits them to our view."[16]

But Johnson's use of Berkeley avoids the metaphysical predicament that has been criticized by philosophers, for Johnson, by metaphorical substitution, replaces the Christian God of creation with himself as the artist and, thus, transposes Berkeley's

God onto an existential stage.[17] Johnson as artist performs as a substitute for Berkeley's postulation of a "universal Mind" that shapes and presents the world to the reader—unbeknownst, of course, to characters like Berkeley the watchdog. It is Johnson himself who stands behind his creation, creating and "watching," just as for Bishop Berkeley, God stood behind Creation constantly keeping it in an eternal consciousness. In Johnson's shaping imagination, all characters and events have meaning. Because the artist, like Berkeley's God, stands at the center of creation, the universe depends on him. Johnson is his own divine artificer.[18]

In "Menagerie," Berkeley reveals himself to be only a dog and not an artist after all. His hopeful, unifying vision of cooperative effort among the animals breaks down as he sleeps. Instead of his wish for justice and endurance, the animals' usurpation, invasion, and internecine feuds dominate the plot's conclusion. Though some animals are predatory by nature, their excessive violence as they destroy each other is a direct consequence of their entrapment in an economic and materialist version of experience that reduces them to the status of things: "truth was decided in the end by those who could be bloodiest in fang and claw" (55). The animals are living in a world of exchange; they are on the block, to be bought and sold according to the materialistic whims of the consumer. They are entirely devoid of the spiritually unifying vision that the artist can provide.

The pet store is a microcosm of the fragmentation of meanings that necessarily arise in the absence of the artist's controlling imagination, which Berkeley the dog cannot supply. He cannot convince the animals of their spiritual oneness because in fact he is a false idealist himself. Berkeley's naïveté consists in reducing the animals' needs within the store to their barest requirements for food and water. He believes that if only animals are fed properly and enjoy the commodities that the store offers, they should be happy to cooperate with Tilford and be commodities themselves. But this is an accommodation to a debased materialism, since "Man shall not live by bread alone, but by every word that proceedeth out of the mouth of God."[19] Johnson also avers that human beings need more than their daily bread; they need even more a transformative spiritual power, an understanding of the legitimate views of the world that other perceivers experience. Berkeley's only concern is that the animals are hungry; he never realizes that their hunger is also spiritual (in that they cannot imagine the perspectives of other animals). They need a character with expressive, artistic abilities; all Berkeley can do is howl "like a mountaintop wolf silhouetted by the moon in a Warner Brothers cartoon" (52). His simplistic version of existential needs and his inarticulateness doom his own "idealistic" project (55). In "Menagerie," Johnson employs Berkeley as an emblem of the ineffectual philosopher who is defeated by the world because he lacks confidence in his own imagination as a transforming power.

In "Menagerie," Johnson introduces the Berkeleyan correlative, not because he wishes to ridicule Berkeley but because Berkeley offers him a metaphor for his conception of aesthetic creation. Given the premise that Johnson understands Berkeley as a philosophic defender of imagination against skepticism, we can understand how Johnson uses Berkeley's posture as a metaphor for the artist's combat with the "Age of Hype." In "China" (1983), Johnson again imprisons his characters within a materialist epistemology, but he also dramatizes the means by which human beings may be released from the world of commodity. The two main characters, Rudolph and Evelyn, begin the story as a married couple enslaved by their desire for the commodities: Van de Kamp's pastry, *Self* magazine, beer, Ben-Gay, Harlequin romances, grade-B movies, color television, the Book-of-the-Month Club, Preparation H, and the countless other items found at the department stores or the local mall. It is this world, Johnson implies, that makes the two characters "*sick*" (89)—Rudolph, physically; Evelyn, spiritually. In his discovery of the martial arts, however, Rudolph liberates himself from this materialist reality as he becomes an artist, while Evelyn recognizes her own death-in-life because she can find no release from it in her own imagination.

Both "Menagerie" and "China" are constructed on concealed Berkeleyan riddles. The plot of "Menagerie" is constructed on the philosophical objection to Berkeley's idealism: does the world continue to exist when the perceiver sleeps or is otherwise absent? "China" too employs a Berkeleyan conundrum as the plot's organizing principle. In "China," Johnson revises Berkeley's concern with natural law (for example, gravity) and measurements of nature. In an immaterialist philosophy such as Berkeley's, how do we measure the natural world? If God imagines the world, is our quantitative knowledge of the world (that is, science itself) possible?

Berkeley responds to these questions by asserting that all measurements are at least to some degree dependent on the observer and that no measurement can be definitive or absolute. In this argument, Berkeley criticizes John Locke's distinction between primary qualities of objects (those characteristics existing in the objects itself, independent of the perceiver) and secondary qualities (characteristics dependent on the perceiver, and existing only in the mind). For Locke, extension, figure, and motion are primary qualities; that is, these qualities are independent of the mind and may be quantified. Color, odor, sound, and warmth are examples of secondary qualities that depend entirely on the perceiver's mind.

But Berkeley eradicates Locke's distinction. All qualities exist only in the mind; all qualities are reduced to Locke's "secondary" qualities. The world for Berkeley is therefore qualitative rather than strictly quantitative, and irreducible to exactness:

> In perusing the volume of Nature, it seems beneath the dignity of the mind to affect an exactness in reducing each particular phenomenon to general rules, or showing how it follows from them. We should propose to ourselves nobler views, such as to recreate and exalt the mind, with a prospect of the beauty, order, extent, and variety of natural things.[20]

In this passage, Berkeley regards distance and all spatial measurement as something only suggested or judged. He dismisses Newtonian ideas of absolute time and space; absolute measurements are abstractions, not realities, requiring a relative judgment of the perceiving mind. As opposed to an absolute and unequivocal conception of a quantifiable world, Berkeley elevates the creative imagination (for Johnson the Buddhist, God-in-Humanity) over empirical exactitude of physical laws. For Berkeley, the miracle, a suspension of Newtonian laws within God's will, is always a potentiality. Johnson takes much the same approach, although, as in "Menagerie," he discovers in "China" a miracle in the performance of art.

Evelyn and Rudolph wrestle with Berkeleyan questions without knowing it. They go to the movies, "pretty trashy stuff at that," and see a martial arts film, where the combatants could

> leap twenty feet through the air in perfect defiance of gravity. Rudolph's mouth hung open.

"Can people really do that?" He did not take his eyes off the screen, but talked at her from the right side of his mouth. "Leap that high?"

"It's a *movie*," sighed Evelyn. "A *bad* movie."

He nodded, then asked again, "But can they?" (65)

Can human beings leap twenty feet? Can they defy Newtonian laws of gravity? Like the protagonist of "Moving Pictures," Rudolph reads his own desire into the theater's screen. But unlike the miserable scriptwriter, Rudolph does not merely deposit his desire onto an empty object. Despite Evelyn's derision; Rudolph commits himself to achieving this goal by studying the martial arts, and at the story's climax, he leaps "twenty feet off the ground in a perfect flying kick" (95). The story explores the meaning of Rudolph's victory over gravity within a Berkeleyan framework.

In "China," marital arts provide Rudolph with the means of overcoming his psychological limitations. Karate represents for Johnson a form of art through which, in creating an alternative world, the artist does not work but "plays" at the creation of his or her body. Rudolph says, "I've never been able to give *every*thing to *any*thing. The world never let me. It won't let me put all of myself into play" (76). The martial arts are transformative, as is literature. In *Being and Race,* Johnson defends his analogy of writing to karate, just as Hemingway compared writing to boxing: "It's fair to compare the severe discipline of the Asian martial arts to writing."[21] As a ludic artist himself, Johnson allows Rudolph true liberation: he creates in Rudolph's self-created body "the body as it must be in the mind of God" (84), an explicit allusion to Berkeley's philosophy. Rudolph believes that he can miraculously suspend

Newtonian laws by submitting to the "severe discipline" of his art, and the narrative voice asserts that he succeeds—succeeds in refashioning not only his body but his mind, and therefore the world he inhabits.

In describing Rudolph's new vision of the world, acquired through practice of his art, Johnson employs specifically Berkeleyan language: "himself, Rudolph Lee Jackson, at the center of the universe; for if the universe was infinite, any point where he stood would be at its center—it would shift and move with him" (87). As artist, Rudolph's perception transforms the uncreated world. Rudolph's consciousness becomes the measure of all space; all matter radiates from him. His art engages the world: matter is the void awaiting his imaginative fiat. Everything ("things" in a Berkeleyan sense) becomes a matter of reading and perceiving. Space becomes contingent on the creative mind.

Rudolph's liberating artistic vision is in stark contrast to Evelyn's pessimistic Christian pietism. For her, no miracles are possible, and nature is an arid space of economic, religious, and physical laws. She dismisses Rudolph as a "faker" (87), not understanding her own pun (fakir). But her vision of the world (associated in Johnson's philosophical subtext with Berkeley's antagonists: Locke, Hobbes, and Newton) demeans humankind: "man was evil—she'd told him that a thousand times—or, if not evil, hopelessly flawed. Everything failed; it was some sort of law" (78). If the world is controlled by "some sort of law" —be it gravity or the imperfection of humanity—no miracle could be possible, even for the artist. Evelyn's problem is her reduction of all experience to lifeless matter, a world without spirit or energy. Her unenlightened perspective in confirmed by the escapist literature she reads, works that dismiss the world before our eyes in favor of foolish fantasy. The image of lovers "clinging to one another" in the Harlequin romances parodies her relationship with Rudolph (78), since she clings to him, trying to control all aspects of his life. Rudolph, unlike Evelyn, has recognized that the marketplace is not "fulfillment of his potential" (79). Her reaction to the new Rudolph is summarized in this sentence: "Rudolph, I want you back the way you were: *sick*" (89).

The story's title, the story's epigraph from *The Dhamma-pada,* and Rudolph's martial arts are set against Evelyn's puritanism and her Westernized commodification of her life. Although at the plot's beginning both characters are identifiably American and middle-class, Johnson's dichotomy of East/West implies Johnson's privileging of idealism in the story as a means of racial transcendence. The story's controlling pattern is the revelation of idealism and its effects in the practical world: Evelyn's revelation of her comparatively wasted life that has been devoted to a materialized vision of existence; and Rudolph's revelation of the potentiality of miracle implicit in an imaginative reordering of space and physical law. Rudolph's massive and miraculous reordering is available to him only through the commitment that art demands.

Even more significant than his defiance of gravity at the story's end, however, is Rudolph's feeling of oneness with other people (human beings different from him in race, geography, religion, age, and culture), and his appreciation for the Asian worldview that he had not taken seriously before. Evelyn derogates his art by pointing out that he "didn't grow up in China" and that he "can't be Chinese" (90, 91). Ignoring her specious racial divisiveness, Rudolph becomes engrossed in a different way of seeing reality. In Johnson's words in a different context, Rudolph gets "beneath those sedimented meanings, all the calcified, rigid perceptions of the object."[22] Perhaps for Johnson, this transformation of vision, attainable through art, is the *real* miracle.

Rudolph's miracle occurs because he abandons a life prescribed for him by American culture. Rather than continue to assume that the world exists independently, filled with threatening Others, he realizes that the world's existence depends on him and his own ordering vision. He relinquishes his former metaphysics (materialism) in favor of Idealism. In doing so, he accomplishes what Johnson himself argues is the purpose of art. Johnson defends art that would allow individuals to understand the Other. His mission as artist is evoking "the intuition of other lives":

> Using imagination and the techniques of variation, we try to occupy the real place of the other and view from this standpoint the world as it is present in all its texture, limitations, and possibilities. . . . We must quit the familiarity of our own lives momentarily to experience this.[23]

These three stories in particular give his mission a philosophical substructure. His use of Berkeleyan and Buddhist doctrines keeps him balanced on the high wire.

"Exchange Value" (1982), like the three preceding stories, is organized around epistemological concerns that lead to moral issues. On the surface, as Jonathan Little and William Nash explain, the story is a depiction of the social causes of ghetto corruption, for Johnson improvises on Richard Wright's theme of the terrible effects of the dominant racist power structure on African Americans.[24] Two brothers, Loftis and Cooter, dramatize the depressing struggle of African Americans attempting to escape the tight social space to which they have been relegated. Loftis, an honors graduate of DuSable High School, buys *Esquire,* reads *Black Scholar* and borrowed library books, and has a full-time job (ironically, as a night watchman). Nevertheless, he has resigned himself to a life of crime, looking for the "Big Score." Cooter, the narrator, has fully absorbed the worst racist stereotypes and, unemployed, spends his time watching television and reading comics, "'bout as useful on a hustle—or when it comes to getting ahead—as a headcold" (29). As his name implies, Loftis originally was the enterprising individual, while Cooter (whose name denotes his foolishness, "crazy as a coot") cannot combat the depression apparently suffered by his parents.

The brothers' lives hint that these two seemingly opposite paths of life are in fact subtly intertwined, since white, deterministic assumptions about race have been accepted by both characters. Petty thieves, they seem to be stereotypes of inner-city thugs, and the story revolves around their burglary of Miss Bailey, an elderly African American woman who is their own neighbor in the projects. Ironically, they come to ruin because they are exceptionally successful. Instead of an "old shoebox full of money" they set out to steal (27), they steal the old woman's hidden cache, which she inherited years earlier from her industrialist-magnate employer, now worth $879,543. They conceal this princely sum in their own apartment. But the story ends with the vanity of their success, as they duplicate her life of reclusiveness, her eccentric parsimony, and her demented paranoia. Like her, they deliberately imprison themselves in the apartment at the story's end, apparently to wait for their own deaths. The story, however, is not limited to its social commentary.

Johnson dramatizes in the brothers an unenlightened understanding of the world, which leads them into moral confusion. Marxism offers one approach to the story, and Linda Furgerson Selzer cogently and perceptively demonstrates how the story employs Marxist theoretics. As she explains, Johnson's allusive field is the Marxist distinction between "use-value" and "exchange-value," as signified by his title.[25] Marx distinguishes "use-value" from "exchange-value" by observing that prior to capitalism, items were made solely for their intrinsic usefulness: a loaf of bread to be eaten, a pair of shoes to be worn, a table to be set. Capitalism, however, transforms the thing that is valuable because it can be used for comfort, pleasure, and function (bread, shoes, a table) into an abstraction that is valuable because it can be exchanged for something else, usually money to be used to yield still more money or to purchase some object or service. Marx writes, "Exchange value presents itself at a quantitative relations, as the proportion in which values in use of one sort are exchanged for those of another sort, a relation constantly changing with time and place."[26] As Selzer writes, "Johnson in fact offers a fictional investigation of Marx's account of commodity fetishism to uncover the hidden logic—or sorcery—performed by both capitalism and racism."[27]

Both brothers understand Marx's distinction of "use" and "exchange" value on an intuitive level. Cooter is eager to "use" his stolen wealth, "like wizards" to "transform her stuff into anything else at will" (35), while Loftis wishes to hoard the treasure, telling Cooter, "Don't you touch *any*thing! . . . Not until we inventory this stuff!" (31). These two brothers could become "sorcerer-like" in that they can magically convert their cash into wish: "we had $879,543 worth of wishes, if you can deal with that" (34). However, Cooter discovers the disappointment in his self-centered "use" of his ill-gotten wealth. He initially intends to splurge in a "high-hat restaurant," but then struggles with his diffidence and his guilt, feeling like "just another jig putting on airs." He later buys some expensive clothing, but when he returns to the apartment, "a funny, Pandora-like feeling hit me. I took off the jacket, boxed it—it looked trifling in the hallway's weak light" (35). Cooter's craving for his own sense gratification is the actual source of his disappointment, not the material things that he purchases or attempts to purchase. It is his emotion that renders both coat and restaurant inadequate, not the coat or meal as objects. His anguish arises from an epistemological mistake, misunderstanding the transitory and unsubstantial nature of the things themselves, imprinted as they are by his own fluctuating desire.

Rather than engaging in a meditative self-scrutiny that could lead to changing the way they view the world, the two brothers blame the wealth itself for their suffering. Cooter experiences the wealth as a curse: "something ain't *right* about this stash. There could be a curse on it" (31). In fact, their wealth forces them to confront Johnson's paradox of freedom. They have enough money to buy whatever they desire (what they would have earlier described as "freedom"), but as Loftis explains to his younger brother, "As soon as you buy something you *lose* the power to buy something" (36). Given their intensely individualistic but conventional, rapacious, and sometimes contradictory desires, their loot leads them into an entanglement with their own emotions. The wealth, if used on behalf of a wider community, would not be "cursed"; viewed rationally, the money is a morally neutral object, simply a screen (as in "Moving Pictures") that absorbs the myriad human desires projected onto it. Incapable of transcending their own desire in order to understand the loot's emptiness, its radical lack of intrinsic meaning, the two brothers slip into the worst kind of bondage: to their own desire. Cooter's egotism brings him to a conclusion similar to Thoreau's in *Walden:* "*every* purchase has to be a poor buy: a loss of life" (38). The story's ending sentence emphasizes the brothers' failure of imagination. Cooter discovers a lost penny, then conceals the penny in a jar, "with the rest of our things" (40). The story's final word reveals how because of their failure of understanding, the brothers have exchanged a world of possibilities for entrapment in a world of "things."

The alternative to the brothers' bondage to their own desire is a Buddhist knowledge of the world as it truly is. This epistemological lesson is given graphically in one of the most ghastly descriptions of a decaying human body in contemporary literature. It is no wonder that Cooter does "a Hollywood faint" when he sees poor Miss Bailey, his burglary victim (32). Miss Bailey's bloated, putrescent corpse—in the process of being consumed by rats, roaches, and maggots—should be an inducement to the brothers to seek wisdom rather than riches. Wisdom, in the story's context, means acquiring new convictions about values, a choice to perform actions that do not degrade the self or others, a preference for a more compassionate, related form of living over self-gratification. For the Buddhist as well as Judeo-Christian tradition, meditation on the various stages of the body's decomposition is intended to foster a detachment from worldly things, a waking from the dream of a subhuman existence to a sense of greater, ultimately social ends. Wisdom becomes inseparable from compassion, from a nonself-centered openness to the needs of other human beings. In this sense, philosophy is not simply a mode of knowledge but a way of life, pointing the way toward discriminating judgments and a worthwhile future for oneself and the world.

Cooter and Loftis are "free" in a larger sense than they realize. They can with their wealth dedicate themselves to fostering a community in their neighborhood instead of being its fearsome, nighttime predators. This would mean, of course, accepting with equanimity the constraints that the creation of such a community would entail. They have the freedom, to express this differently, to create a "sangha" (that is, a Buddhist community or monastery that fosters togetherness). The two brothers, however, are not ready for this meditative transformation and this more nuanced idea of freedom. Indeed, there is a chance the brothers will change their ways, since Cooter asserts "we could change" (40). But as the story ends, they build "for now" (40) a demonic sangha for themselves in their apartment. They construct a cloacal-like prison, a "booby-trapped tunnel of cardboard and razor blades" (35) in front of their door to protect their treasure.

Their pathetic burglary victim, Miss Bailey, represents another distinctly unenlightened way of life and shares with Cooter and Loftis an individualistic bias. She has devoted her life to working for "chump change—a pitiful li'l bowl of porridge" (29–30), as Cooter and Loftis's parents did. When she inherited her fortune, she became a Howard Hughes–like recluse who carefully hoarded her inheritance, begged for food, avoided cleaning her own apartment (though she had worked as a maid), and exhibited a bizarre peculiarity: she saved her own excrement in coffee cans (perhaps because, as Cooter tells us, she began to eat her coins). Miss Bailey's grim fate—apparently starving herself to death, despite the presence of food nearby —underscores the tragedy of misunderstanding the nature of material things and human freedom. She imagines a world of scarcity and loss, not one that is empty/full:

> she'd been poor as Job's turkey for thirty years, suffering that special Negro fear of using up what little we get in this life— Loftis, he call that entropy—believing in her belly, and for all her faith, jim, that there just ain't no more coming tomorrow from grace, or the Lord, or from her own labor . . . she be spellbound, possessed by the promise of life, panicky about depletion, and locked now in the past 'cause *every* purchase, you know, has to be a poor buy: a loss of life. (37–38)

As Little points out, the wealth "identifies all the things that Loftis, Cooter, Miss Bailey and their parents and their parents' parents and so on have been denied because of the color of their skin."[28] They were "locked in the past" by a racist system that led them to think of the world only in contraries: things either gained or lost, things either saved or spent. She, like the brothers and their ancestors, originated dependent on a racist system that may nevertheless be susceptible to efforts of reform.

"The Secret of Doing Good": Ethics and "Revisable Theories of Reality" in *The Sorcerer's Apprentice*

To reform a social system, however, one must begin by a pragmatic testing of one's epistemology. In Cornel West's excellent discussion of American pragmatic philosophy, West explains that our understanding of reality, to have validity, must be put into practice. We can then determine, according to West, "the best available, yet revisable theories of reality."[29] What actions we decide to perform will be based on our beliefs about our world, our understanding of reality, but this understanding is necessarily provisional. We consider and reconsider the truth, testing and retesting, the truth being contingent on what is known at the time. As we entertain "revisable theories of reality," we discover through our experience what Johnson calls "the secret of doing good" (151). The second part of this discussion deals with Johnson's dramatization of revisable—or potentially revisable—versions of reality that lead to positive ethical action. As Johnson makes clear, such a condition must be constantly open to growth.

The volume's first story, "The Education of Mingo" (1977), introduces the theme of the artist's ethical responsibility to awaken his or her reader in order to induce change. Little writes, "Johnson portrays Moses as the didactic and polemic artist," and from Little's perspective, Moses is the satiric target because he tries "to colonialize, civilize, and christianize Mingo."[30] Although Johnson deplores didacticism, as the story's form he chooses a traditionally didactic mode, "a rigid New Testament parable" (3–4). Johnson has commented on the insistent but elusive moral dimension of the story in *Being and Race*:

> Underpinning [the parable's] world are esoteric and moral laws often unknown to the protagonist, who must act nevertheless and, in ignorance of the way things work beneath the level of mere appearances, finds his actions turn out wrong or prove themselves too ambiguous for reason, so limited, to fully grasp, as in my story "The Education of Mingo."[31]

In this story, Johnson wrestles with the moral consequences of his antirealist philosophical position. How is it possible for him to be a moral writer, even as he denies the existence of absolute moral truths (for example, as found in conventional religion)? In "The Education of Mingo," Johnson dramatically demonstrates that we inhabit a world of human situations, and moral judgment in these situations involves not an abstract moral model (be it Christian, Kantian, utilitarian, or another system), but the emotional life of others.

Moses Green, whose first name mocks his identity as slave master and his second as thinker, is Johnson's satiric surrogate for the author, "an artist fingering something fine and noble from a rude chump of foreign clay."[32] But in a way Moses does not realize, his own "education . . . was as serious as a heart attack" (5). Moses reduces his world to material objects that have an existence apart from his perceiving mind, and it is this epistemologically flawed vision that he tries to impart to his servant, Mingo. Moses was "a man for whom nothing was more absolute than an ax handle, or the weight of a plow." Moses has purchased Mingo, his African slave, with "Mexican coin," and now he teaches Mingo only his brand of American technique, such as how to hold a fork, or how to identify lightning. What Moses does not realize is the world-shifting change from intuition to technique that Mingo's education requires; Mingo's education "involved the evaporation of one coherent, consistent, complete universe and the embracing of another one alien, contradictory, strange" (6). In giving up an African culture emphasizing intuition, trust, and imagination, Mingo must learn mere technique, seemingly without any purpose or moral end. In attempting to make Mingo into "his own spitting image" (7), Moses confidently tells Mingo, "Teach you everything I know, son, which ain't so joe-fired much—just common sense" (4), always guided in his teaching strategies by (Johnson repeats) "common sense" (6).

Beneath Moses's simple prescription of common sense lies Johnson's elaborate philosophical joke: he covertly alludes to Aristotle's *sensus communis.* Aristotle's "common sense" is a cognitive faculty residing in the person's soul that recognizes "common sensibles," properties of a thing (such as movement or shape) directly perceived by more than one sense. Mingo moves, has shape, makes sounds, and otherwise behaves as a thing to be perceived by more than one sense; on the other hand, he is also from Moses's perspective similar to a gun, a mirror, a plow, or any of Moses's other tools. Moses's wish to educate Mingo is thus somewhat contradictory; he perceives Mingo as only a thing to be reduced to other things on his farm, though initially he purchases Mingo because he "felt the need for a field hand and helpmate—a friend, to speak the truth plainly" (3).

Moses's fiancée, Harriet Bridgewater, sustains the allusive Aristotelian joke. Because she is desperate to win Moses as a husband, she uses Aristotle's writings only to belittle Mingo and intimidate Moses. Harriet disguises her anxiety over Moses's friendship with Mingo by quoting Aristotle's commentary on slavery in his *Politics:* "Slaves are tools with life in them, Moses, and tools are lifeless slaves" (10). In alluding to Aristotle, Harriet represents Johnson's opposite: she uses philosophy not as a moral guide used to awaken people, but only as respectable credentials to conceal her own racism and justify her efforts to control Moses's affections. Though she possesses a "well stocked mind" (7), Harriet, a former schoolteacher, is the worst kind of teacher, one who denies the possible validity of her students' differing perspectives. Harriet reduces both Moses (her actual student and hoped-for husband) and the slave Mingo (Moses's student and Johnson's sign for the reader) as mere things, extensions of her desire, both sexual and economic.

Although Harriet has not written anything, Moses suspects that much of her conversation is "spun from thin air" (7), implying her writerly aspirations. But Johnson shows how this use of the imagination is degraded, since it is only employed to enforce a sense of difference. She positions herself against and above all others, insisting unequivocally on separation between gender, race, and class. "I know I'm right," she tells Moses (11). Moses's secret appraisal of her—"haughty, worldly, so clear at times" (8)—mirrors the reader's own. As Moses's superior, she is incapable of imagining herself in another's place, and her "endless chatter" (9) is only a weapon to make Moses feel inferior. Significantly, her most important "instruction" to Moses regards private property and its identity with the owner: "You kick a man's mule, for example, and isn't it just like ramming a boot heel in that man's belly?" (8). For her, "being and having were sorta the same thing" (8). Her disrespect of Mingo's own capacity for change—"he'll never completely adjust" (9)— expresses her negative attitude toward anyone outside of her own tightly guarded consciousness.

Moses is not persuaded by Harriet's denunciation of Mingo. Since Moses does not entirely think of Mingo as a person, but as one more object he possesses, Moses believes that he can make a moral purchase on his world by educating Mingo to become "his own spitting image" (7). Through Mingo, Moses wishes to recreate his moral dualism and enforce it with a terrible violence: "It was like aiming a shotgun at the whole world through the African, blasting away all that Moses, according to his lights, tagged evil, and cultivating the good" (5). By "good," Moses means that he wants only a universe that is "more familiar" (6). He does not want the challenge of "revisable theories of reality," since he confidently believes that he can witness evil without sharing it or being compromised by it. From a Buddhist perspective, Moses commits a basic error. He understands the world as if taking place separately from his own self-determined position, not realizing that he originates dependent on the actions, thoughts, and desires of other human beings.

Unlike Harriet, Moses revises his theory of reality. Initially dwelling on only the surface reality, Moses congratulates himself that "that African . . . inside a year, was exactly the product of his own way of seeing, as much one of his products and judgments as his choice of tobacco" (7). But Mingo's murder of Isaiah Jenson is a rebuke to Moses's self-congratulatory position. When Moses first discovers Isaiah's blood-soaked corpse, he does not hold himself responsible for Isaiah's death, but blames his student's obtuseness. When Mingo kills Isaiah, Moses thinks (commonsensically) that Mingo has simply reversed his direct, rational, to-the-point instruction. Instead of being kind to Isaiah and killing chicken hawks, as Moses had told him, Mingo killed Isaiah and was kind to chicken hawks. In this way, Moses places the entire moral burden of Isaiah's murder on Mingo.

But when Mingo kills Harriet, Moses discovers his own complicity in Mingo's crimes. Mingo takes seriously Moses's injunctions—not simply his instructions but his inner thoughts and desires. One of the "esoteric and moral laws often unknown to the protagonist" that Johnson alludes to in his commentary on the story is Mingo's intuitive understanding of Moses's inner moral life. Mingo sensed that beneath Moses's neighborly and decorous behavior, Moses actually disliked Isaiah and wished him harm. Similarly, Moses did not love Harriet, and he yearned to escape her matrimonial clutches. As Moses's "instrument," Mingo acts on his master's negative subjective states rather than his surface, socially oriented behaviors.

Mingo's imagination was capable of understanding Moses's affection for him, that "he felt closer to the black African than to Harriet" (11), and he acted on that sensibility in murdering Harriet.

Mingo enacts the "New Testament" parable's meaning, which also arises from the central Buddhist precept of "Right Thoughts." For utilitarian ethics, it is acceptable ethically if a person feels aggression toward others, so long as he or she does not act on that aggression and harm others. In contrast, from Buddhist and Christian perspectives, the truly ethical person cannot be separated from his or her action. In this more holistic sense, it is not enough for Moses merely to perform good actions and refrain from bad actions. As we have seen in *Oxherding Tale,* virtue more importantly entails the person's character—feelings, compassion, positive desires, and goodwill to others emerging from a person's inner life. Though Moses attempts to live respectably on life's surface, his inner life is marked by turmoil: anger, anxieties, envy, insecurities, resentment, and competition. Moses is therefore always "policing his gestures" (5), attempting to prevent his hidden aggressions from bursting through into his social world, a sense captured in Johnson's image of Moses imagining himself firing a shotgun at the world. Mingo responds instead to Moses's hidden intentions (for a Buddhist, his "Wrong Thoughts"), which Mingo intuits as a member of the magical Allmuseri tribe. In a sense, Mingo makes plain that which Moses wants concealed.

With his commonsensical world collapsing around him, Moses can only flee with Mingo to the territory "somewheres in the west" (23). But once again with Moses, appearances belie reality, for Moses is not merely evading responsibility. Immediately after Harriet's murder, Moses decides to execute Mingo with his shotgun, just as he earlier wished to aim a shotgun at the world to rid it of its perceived excesses, evils, and injustices. But he does not kill Mingo in full recognition of his own implication in Mingo's murders: "I'm guilty. It was me set the gears in motion. Me" (22). In this beginning of a self-critique, in this revelatory moment of empathetic understanding of another person, Moses acknowledges his complicity in the world's grief and guilt. He learns to understand the world from Mingo's perspective. He understands for the first time the doctrine of dependent origination: that Mingo's murderous acts have a context that includes him and the institution of slavery. For the first time Moses understands that he is immersed in the world that earlier he wanted self-righteously to condemn. As a white person (and perhaps as a representative of the white reader), he accepts his complicity: to what extent are all people complicit in any one individual's crime? As Selzer writes in an excellent article on the story, "Ironically, Johnson's narrative closes as Moses—who initially purchases a slave in hopes of making his world look 'more familiar'—rides with Mingo into unfamiliar territory."[33]

The reader is superior to Moses in his simple, inchoate understanding of his radical relationality. The reader also begins to understand the relationship between writer and reader. Johnson's reader realizes that in accepting an artist's tutelage, imaginatively inhabiting his or her inner self, the reader may discover dimensions of that self unknown even to the teacher/writer. Like the artist, the reader discovers that his own reading of a text must necessarily be provisional, and may not in fact be the final and conclusive one. Mingo represents Johnson's satire of the student/reader. As an Allmuseri, Johnson's mythically magic tribe, Mingo is also forced to accept a revised theory of reality. He must experience "the evaporation of one coherent, consistent, complete universe and the embracing of another one alien, contradictory, strange." This is, of course, precisely what the ideal reader experiences in processing Johnson's text, especially those thematic depths beneath the surface, so that the reader and writer "magically [dissolve] into each other like two crossing shafts of light" (19). Mingo, however, "reads" Moses with perspicuity but with too much literalness. He does not exercise his own moral judgment within the context of Moses's real, concealed meanings. That is, he reads critically, but with a moral sightlessness; with an exceptional interpretive competence, but with an ethical obtuseness. It is as if Johnson's introductory story admonishes the reader to read symbolically, but also with moral clarity.

Like "The Education of Mingo," "Alēthia" (1979) centers on moral writing. The title itself calls attention to the act of reading closely, implying the necessity of uncovering occluded meanings. As the narrator explains, "Alēthia," taken from Max Scheler's commentary on Edmund Husserl's phenomenology, means "'to call forth from concealedness'" (104). "Alēthia's" narrator is an African American professor of philosophy who, near his career's end, wonders if his life of devotion to knowledge was in fact a concealed flight from his human condition—racial, sexual, political. He thinks of himself as a "two-reel comedy" (101), though he does not recognize the significance of his own pun ("too real"). Like Moses Green, the philosopher is a failed "artist"; unlike Moses, he attempts writing, for his room is filled with "half-finished books" (101). His inability to complete his manuscripts reveals his troubled inner self; he distrusts his discipline even as he secretly despises his own identity. In his solitary act of writing, he attempts to construct his own isolated identity, but he fails because he divorces his work from his world. Although he assures his reader that "I know my faults" (99), he has in fact hidden from his faults. Certainly, it is the professor's faults that the reader must "call forth from concealedness." A self-professed skeptic (99), the professor is not skeptical enough about his own self-analysis.

Again like Moses, the professor does not take seriously enough the moral responsibility that comes with his teaching position, instead holding everyone else responsible for his shortcomings. Lecturing on Kant, "thumbs hooked in my vest" (100), the narrator smugly separates himself from the social conditions of his existence in favor of what he thinks is the "medieval fortress" of Northwestern University (101). His commitment to knowledge is a strategy that disavows any possibility of social commitment. His repudiation of the world takes its toll physically, implied by his many psychosomatic symptoms: an ulcer, bad digestion, migraines, stomach cramps, insomnia, and possible impotence.

The professor has also concealed from himself his perception of his own race. This dimension is expressed ironically in his "feeling his twoness," an allusion to W. E. B. Du Bois's famous definition of "double-consciousness" in *The Souls of Black Folk* (1903): "an American, a Negro; two souls, two thoughts, two warring ideals in one dark body" (102). Because of the protagonist's self-absorption, he interprets Du Bois in an entirely self-centered way, assuming that Du Bois refers only to an African American's wish to be black and American simultaneously. This fusion the protagonist believes he has accomplished, since he congratulates himself on escaping from the racist societal expectations for a black male: prison, the post office, fundamentalist Christianity, or the cemetery. But Du Boisian "double-consciousness" does not actually refer to a conflict between two entirely different, warring identities (American versus Negro), but instead to an evolution and merging of identities that goes on in both whites and blacks as they interact. As Du Bois goes on to write,

> It is a peculiar sensation, this double-consciousness, this sense of always looking at one's self through the eyes of others, of measuring one's soul by the tape of a world that looks on in amused contempt and pity.[34]

The Du Boisian "double-consciousness," the central concept of his book, is that a person's self-conception is a function of how other people perceive one, of "looking at one's self through the eyes of others." For Du Bois as for Buddhism, one's identity is not biological, innate, or static; instead, it is social and relational. Ironically, the professor has absorbed precisely those stereotypes that he has avoided personally.

The challenge to the narrator's assumption that he has transcended stereotypes and to his sense of resolute self-determination comes in the form of black Wendy Barnes, a student whom he considers "vulgar" (105), but only because that is how she is perceived by white society. *Vulgar,* of course, is derived from Latin *vulgaris,* meaning "of the common people." It is she in her "vulgarity" who will force him to revise his theories of reality. An African American woman in her mid-twenties, Wendy has been reduced by the professor to a racist stereotype of the ill-prepared, black, Equal Opportunity Program woman. But in her office visit she presents a quite different identity—that of a young, intellectual student whom he should be trying to reach. Although the visit begins unpropitiously—she tells him that unless she receives an A in his course, she will accuse him of sexual harassment—she soon reveals herself to be an adept student of philosophy. Because stereotypes have blinded the narrator to Wendy's potentiality, he has not taken her seriously. In part because of the oppression she has suffered as an African American woman, Wendy is (paradoxically) a lyrical nihilist. She tells him her philosophy:

> Civil rights is high comedy. The old values are dead. Our money is plastic. Our art is murder. Our philosophy is a cackle, obscene and touching, from the tower. The universe explodes silently nowhere. (108)

Wendy's ideas are precisely what this narrator should be attempting to combat as an ethical writer, since this philosophy denies the whole meaning of his life of scholarship. Wendy represents an opportunity for the professor to truly teach. Saving her means salvation for him, a way to enrich both his life and hers and to rescue both from despair and meaninglessness. But he is at first incapable of overcoming age, gender, and class barriers to sympathize with her.

For the narrator and Johnson's reader, then, multiple dimensions of experience—personal, political, racial, philosophical—are called forth from "concealedness" in his encounter with Wendy. In this book, reality is not readily understood, either by an illiterate Illinois farmer or by the Chicago professor of philosophy, since reality is reduced by them to a simplistic plane. As in "The Education of Mingo," the professor's buried identity begins to emerge, obscured by decades of self-delusion. As the narrator states, "meaning [is] in masquerade" (109); but to successfully negotiate the extraordinary experiences dramatized in the story, both the narrator and the reader are required to uncover significance "masquerading" in ordinary events, since merely looking at a spectacle in itself is not enough. The educator himself becomes educated, while his student becomes his source of understanding.

But this change only occurs after his internal conflict is resolved, a resolution that occurs in his discovered bond to others. The issue of sympathy is foregrounded in this text through a philosophical allusion to Max Scheler, a disciple of Edmund Husserl. As it relates to the story, Scheler's philosophy extensively analyzes sympathy in a general approach to the human construction of values; he diverges from Kant (also alluded to in the story) by arguing that the Kantian imperative is artificial and disingenuous because it leads to coerced ethical acts, while "true" ethics (the Good) is spontaneous and honest. Sympathy is important because in sympathy, as Scheler defines it, we "recognize, meet, and respect unequivocally the subjectivity of another human existence in a genuine encounter."[35] Love, the highest expression of sympathy, occurs with a sense of a complete "adumbration of human possibilities . . . it is the basis for the religious ideal of infinite compassion and unqualified acceptance."[36]

The narrator begins his epiphanic journey toward "infinite compassion and unqualified acceptance" by traveling with Wendy into Southside Chicago. While this trip seems unpromising to him—he describes the black neighborhood as a "sewer" (107)—it is his site of spiritual renewal. As he takes drugs and drinks alcohol, "a new prehension" takes hold of him; his acute self-consciousness is annihilated as he sees the true beauty of the people surrounding him:

> If I existed at all, it was in this kaleidoscopic party, this pinwheel of color, the I just a function, a flickerflash creation of

this black chaos, the chaos no more, or less than the *I*. There was an awful beauty in this. (110–11)

The professor's psychedelic experience brings him close to the concept he claims to believe early in the story, "seeing beauty in every tissue and every vein of a world lacking discipline and obedience to law" (104). For the first time, looking has become an ethical moment for the narrator. He, like Moses, sees himself within the context of dependent origination—this is the site of his "origination," literally as his birthplace and figuratively as his rebirth with Wendy. He makes love to Wendy, then "lets [his] mind sleep" (112). As he awakens (always a symbolic moment for Johnson), the narrator for once senses himself as a part of a whole, united in spirit with his former neighborhood. When he returns to the classroom, he presumably will offer worthy instruction to students like Wendy, finish his manuscripts, and take himself both less and more seriously.

Like "Alēthia" and "Moving Pictures," "Popper's Disease" (1982) elaborates the theme of the potential artist who has exchanged a vocation in writing for the status, wealth, and public recognition of another career, in this case, medicine. Dr. Henry Popper, whose story is his own autobiography, reveals his "dis-ease" in writing a science fiction tale about confronting the Monster: a double of himself. Like the Monster, he also feels "the same primordial feeling of *thrownness* that every Negro experiences when hurled into a society that simultaneously supports and . . . annihilates him" (134). Popper invites the reader's suspicion of his status as narrator when he assures us, "I am the most reliable of men" (128), and his self-description bears out this suspicion.

On the surface, Dr. Popper is a genuinely good human being, performing that rarest of medical operations: house calls. Yet his self-commentary betrays the real motives behind his laudable service. Like the professor in "Alēthia," Dr. Popper is burdened with a sense of double-consciousness as an African American professional. The only black student in his class at Harvard medical school, Harry married his wife, Mildred, not out of love, but out of self-doubt: "I so doubted myself it seemed miraculous that a woman as beautiful as Mildred, with her light voice and brilliant eyes, would have me" (134). Now, many years later, he is tired of his trophy wife, though he assures us she "still has her looks" (128). She, we discover in the story, is busy having affairs while Dr. Popper is out on his house calls. He is equally disenchanted with his position in the upper-middle class, where his white neighbors "cautiously avoid the topic of race" (128). He attends compulsory neighborly "get-togethers," but complains, "I'm not sure I understand them, and sometimes I'm convinced they don't understand me" (129). Indeed, he infers that his neighbors see him (as Du Bois would say), as "a problem," determined by social forces, not by his own hard work and perseverance: "to ask, 'Who am I?' is to ask, 'By what social forces have I been shaped?'" (128).

His altruistic house calls to his patients, then, are revealed to be his way of avoiding his wife, his neighbors, and his possible self-discovery. He is doing the right thing by visiting his patients, but from a Buddhist perspective he does not present the "Right Thoughts." That is, he is not motivated by compassion for others, but by a desire to escape a world he dislikes. Perhaps most important of all, Dr. Popper has entirely adopted the same Westernized, materialist "cultural assumptions" as his neighbors: "that history, for example, is linear, not circular, reason is preferable to emotion, and that one event 'causes' another" (129). Understandably, he is deeply unhappy, though his life has been marked by an unrelenting quest for materialist happiness.

Redemption is possible for Dr. Popper if he revises his theory of reality. He understands that there may be an alternative to the constricting social role he has adopted and the worldview he has accepted. The solution lies partly in his African heritage. Like Mingo, he senses because of the culture of his ancestors that there are other ways of imagining human identity and community besides the model of Western individualism:

> My ancestors—or so I've read—had a hundred concepts for the African community, but none for the "individual," who, as we define him today—the lonely Leibnizean monad—is an invention of the Industrial Age, as romantic love is the product of medieval poets. My ancestors, I've also heard, were pre-Industrial and, therefore, are no test of reality. (134)

Although he commits himself to saving only the body, he also senses that there is an "invisible realm of values and belief" that transcends the illnesses of the physical world but may play a part in producing physical illness. He begins the story as an uneasy materialist, then, but he is ready for the challenge to revise his theory of reality.

This challenge comes in the form of the Monster. When Henry meets the Monster, he truly confronts an alien, whose speech puns on contemporary existential discourse: the sick alien suffers dread and nausea (he threatens to vomit), refers to the "Plague" (an allusion to Albert Camus's novel), and has instruments that measure the world in "*angst*roms" (emphasis added). Indeed, this confrontation may not be an experience at all, but a Buddhist dream in which the narrator confronts his own worst demon. He mentions twice in the story that he is sleepy, and that he is concerned that he will doze off while driving.

Whether an actual experience or a nightmare, the encounter with the Monster forces Popper to confront his own evasions. The Monster tells Henry the truth about Henry's own existential illness: "It seems we are both strangers here" (141). The Monster is from a planet whose culture resembles Popper's ancestral African one, for in the Monster's culture, "Dualism was death" (144). In a unique reversal, the Monster plays the role of existential rebel on its planet, for it is dying because it has resisted its planet's healthy repudiation of Dualism. It suffers from a terminal case of the "Plague," a disease that is more an epistemological disorder than a physical one. The Plague resembles Henry's Westernized worldview; the Plague has led the Monster to insist on its unique self, its separation from "everything in [its] perceptual field," and a repudiation of literal, concrete meanings. These things outside the self, it tells Popper, "threaten to absorb me, engulf me, annihilate me completely, because I am, in a word, deeply and inexorably *different* from them" (138). As the Monster is dying, it reveals its own ontological solipsism, for Johnson the consequence of its own reluctance to revise its theory of reality. Its last words are, "the idea has just occurred to me that all phenomena are products of my ego" (142), including Popper himself.

The Monster's body disintegrates in death ("Thermogenesis"), and (as so often in Johnson's fiction) this event gives Popper the opportunity to meditate on his own end. Henry may yet break down the self-enclosed, self-determining idea of the self that he and the Monster share. However, Henry is not yet enlightened himself, so he cannot help the Monster recover from its terminal disease. Instead, Henry lacks compassion for the Monster, and he sees this opportunity to help the Monster only as a means of self-exaltation: "The Nobel Prize would be a *gift* to whoever diagnosed, then cured this uncanny disease. It was front-page stuff. Medical history, I hoped, might even rename it after me" (139). At the end of the story he is locked within the spaceship and sealed off (just as the Monster was sealed off) in his world, confronting his own demons, his own buried but exalted sense of self. Popper gazes into the Telecipher, which tells him that the nature of the Monster's (and his own) disease: "*It's the Self* and *There is no cure*" (146). Ironically, Dr. Popper's cure may be in front of him, in the Telecipher, the Monster's television machine that resembles the movie-theater screen in "Moving Pictures." The Telecipher is Johnson's symbol for the Buddhist concept of emptiness:

> Continuous in time, everywhere in space, the field was the idea of polymorphy made fact, its particles mere concretions of energy, as if Being delighted in playing hide-and-seek with itself, dressing up, so to speak, as Everything, then sloughed off particularities when bored with the game. (144–45)

As Dr. Popper stares at the Telecipher, he prepares to understand who he is and what he really wants for himself.[37] The doctor may eventually be able to cure himself. Johnson dramatizes a possible "cure" for Popper's disease in the final, title story of the volume, "The Sorcerer's Apprentice" (1983). Johnson directly confronts the issue that underlies the volume, the author's ethical connection to art, of critical importance because art is a "means to transform the world" (159). The story's protagonist is Allan Jackson, who embarks on a career of sorcery,

Johnson's metaphor for art. Allan is the apprentice of Rubin, the village sorcerer. In the past, Rubin had worked a miracle by supposedly healing Richard's (Allan's father's) hand. Allan leads us to understand that Richard venerates Rubin and wants his son to be just like him. The story's plot centers on Allan's overcoming his self-absorption in order to discover a "mindful" freedom from his father, from Rubin, and from his own desires. To create art with "mindfulness"—complete commitment to one's project without regard to self-exultation or the rewards offered by another—is Allan's ethical goal. Until he abandons his notion of individual achievement as the only significant value, he cannot be a keeper of Rubin's symbolic art.

Although Allan begins his apprenticeship by reducing art to a mastery of technique, he soon learns that artistry is much more than "a question of know-how" (152). Like misguided apprentices from Goethe's *Der Zauberlehrling* to Walt Disney's *Fantasia*, Allan naively sees the artist's powers as an alternative to the drudgery of ordinary, unremarkable experience, since immersion in daily toil reduces his sense of self-importance. As Rubin's mere apprentice, he feels "unessential, anonymous, like a tool" (156). Tired of such menial chores as cleaning, bringing water, and cooking, Allan wishes to practice what he believes is a more important, more expansive art. But by dismissing ordinary experience, Allan cannot envisage this as his source of morality. For the Buddhist, chopping wood and carrying water, the most ordinary of tasks, were to be seen as the extraordinary "Way" itself.[38]

Not realizing that the central challenge of Rubin's role is both epistemological *and* practical, Allan is nevertheless a good and worthy character. His potentiality is evidenced by the respect accorded him by Rubin and his village, his indifference to money (he will not take fees from his patients), and his willingness to work hard and sacrifice his life for his craft: "So many sacrifices. So many hours spent hunched over yellow, wormholed scrolls. . . . He must have knowledge, an armory of techniques, a thousand strategies, if he is to unfailingly do good" (157). Central to his worldview is his affirmative understanding of ethics that Johnson's fiction has consistently endorsed: "that the secret of doing good is a good heart" (151). It is Allan's practical goal as a sorcerer to use his art to make sick people in a sick world healthy, to restore ethical harmony to a world out of joint.

Because Allan so deeply wishes to succeed in this apparently selfless labor, he does not understand Rubin's enigmatic advice: "You are the best of students. And you wish to do good, but you can't be too faithful, or too eager, or the good becomes evil" (150). Rubin senses in Allan, despite Allan's manifest generosity and unstinting commitment, a degree of self-congratulation in his craft. Allan cannot manage to get himself "out of the way" in his work.[39] The hidden obstacle to Allan's fulfillment as an artist is his profound love for his father, Richard. Allan is initially motivated to become a sorcerer because of his father, for Allan wishes to win the same recognition from Richard that Richard gives Rubin. Allan's private, hidden purpose is egotistical yet understandable, but he must learn the difficult lesson that "love could disfigure the thing loved" (167).

Allan tries so hard because Richard, a former slave, is a difficult man to please. Allan implies that Richard, "the sort of man who held his feelings in" (152), is partly responsible for the suicide of Allan's mother, Beatrice, who loses the family's life savings because of her naive trust in a criminal (who plays a "Murphy game" with her). Instead of being compassionate toward Beatrice's foolish mistake, Richard stood "smoking cigars and watching only Lord knew what in the darkness." She later commits suicide, presumably in grief caused partly by Richard's unrelenting reserve. Allan experiences this same emotional coldness from his father, though Allan feels no bitterness against him. Allan sympathetically understands that Richard's stunted emotional life is a direct result of his experience as a slave: "it was risky to feel if you had grown up . . . in a world of nightriders. There was too much to lose. Any attachment ended in separation, grief. If once you let yourself care, the crying might never stop" (153). He realizes that the blight of slavery has harmed Richard emotionally, even though "people took this [emotional repression] for strength" (152).

Allan's drive to win his father's acceptance, then, is one obstacle to mindful creation. His slavish reliance on Rubin's technique, rather than his own self-expression, is the second obstacle. As an apprentice, Allan dedicates himself to imitating his master rather than perfecting his techniques as expressions of his individuality. As Nash writes, "Despite everything he hears from his teacher, Allan remains unwilling to explore what his own creative voice might have to offer."[40] Allan is much like any slave to a master, though Rubin is an unwilling "Master." Allan lacks his own authentic style because he desperately wants Rubin's success. Thus, Allan does not worry about self-expression. Instead, he worries about a merely inconsistent success, since he believes sorcery was "a gift, given to a few, like poetry" (158).

Rubin tries to disabuse him of this view by emphasizing that sorcery is a merging of conventions and ancestral traditions that have been passed down throughout the centuries, much like literature itself:

the spells had been in circulation for centuries. They were a web of history and culture, like the king-sized quilts you saw as curiosities at country fairs, sewn by every woman in Abbeville, each having finished only a section, a single flower perhaps, so no man, strictly speaking, could own a mystic spell. (154)

Rubin's vision of art is a continuum, as in *Oxherding Tale,* where no one person can claim "originality" in the Romantic sense, though every artist of whatever talent contributes, even if it be "a single flower." Art for Rubin is an ongoing process, as it originates dependent (as in Rubin's analogy of the quilt) on generation after generation of artists, working in a myriad of diverse traditions. At the same time, Rubin's art itself was individualized, modified by his unique identity. Rubin modified his own instructor's magical gestures, using his left hand because Rubin was arthritic in his right hand. Allan, misunderstanding Rubin's practice, uses his left hand too, thinking that mastery of technique is the essence of sorcery/art. If Allan would only, Rubin implies, immerse himself in his art and forget his over-reliance on technique, he would inevitably experience more success than failure. Immersion, however, carries the risk of utter failure. In a test of Allan's ability, a sick child, Pearl, is brought to him for a cure; Allan valiantly attempts to help Pearl with the techniques he has learned, imitating Rubin "so perfectly it seemed that Rubin, not Allan, worked magic in the room" (163). When Allan's incantations fail and Pearl dies, Allan must face not only his failure but also the attack of his internalized demon, Bazazath.

Set against Rubin and his generous view of art, Bazazath, the Demon of the West, is the spirit of personal inadequacy.

Bazazath tells Allan that he failed and will always fail because he is imperfect; his art will be only the product of his (the author's) temperamental flaws, stylistic obsessions, prejudices, and similar limitations inherent in individuality:

> to labor on and will the work when you are obviously *beneath* this service is to parody them [the good, the beautiful], twist them beyond recognition, to lay hold of what was once beautiful and make it a monstrosity. It becomes *black* magic. Sorcery is relative, student—dialectical, if you like expensive speech. (167)

Bazazath's argument is that art that is located in the particular, literature that is an honest expression of an individual creator, leads inevitably to the writer's egotism and self-promotion. And no human being—Allan especially, given his troubled relationship with his father—can escape from the defects and limitations inherent in individuality. Bazazath argues that Allan cannot condense in his art the purely universal because he is "beneath" the practice of art. Central to Bazazath's view is the conventional (and illusory) binary of "black" magic, which inevitably qualifies as inferior because of its blackness, and "white" magic, the socially approved art—metaphors for African American literature set against white, "mainstream" American literature. From Bazazath's demonic perspective, "black" art is necessarily inferior and defective. But the reader must remember that Bazazath is a devil, the demon of drunkenness, "the father of lies," and nothing he says should be taken as truth.[41] He is the Demon of the "West," and like Dr. Popper's neighbors, subscribes to a Western dualistic philosophy. Worst of all, Bazazath inveighs against parody, Johnson's favorite art form.

Bazazath's argument must be disregarded, leading as it must to artistic inaction, even the artist's suicide. Allan momentarily accepts Bazazath's decree as truth, and seeing a future of failure, decides to commit suicide. Enlightenment occurs when he affirms his connection with his father, Richard, and by extension with his ancestral, racial lineage. This reconciliation occurs, ironically, immediately after Allan's most humiliating failure. Allan fails to save Pearl, he thinks, because he persisted in using his left hand: "the fingers of his left hand spread over the bony ledge of her brow" (155). But to ascribe his failing to a mere mistake in technique misses the story's point; in this world, disappointment and failure will happen eventually, despite our best intentions and efforts. A mature, rational person is willing to accept this risk as a cost of helping others. Allan learns to accept his failure in front of the person he assumes is his worst critic, his father. His father as harsh critic, however, is not what Richard actually is, but what Allan imagines him to be: "Don't want me, thought Allan. Don't love me as I am" (168). Allan courageously revises his theory of reality and chooses the more difficult thing (over suicide): to live with his own imperfection and failures for his father's sake. That is, Allan sacrifices his vain quest for perfection out of compassion for Richard. Knowing that if he commits suicide he "would drag his father's last treasure, dirtied as it was" into hell and hurt Richard one more time, Allan miraculously "scrubs away part of the chalk circle"—which, as the impersonal narrator has claimed, "no man or devil could break" (167).

Yet Allan has broken it, and in doing so, reaches out to his father and embraces him as he falls. It is then Allan makes his momentous discovery: Rubin the Sorcerer (earlier imagined by Allan as perfect) has also failed. In squeezing "the old man's thick, ruined fingers," Allan discovers that Richard has not been healed by Rubin after all. Allan learns that art can never be entirely successful, and that Richard (and all human beings with him) needs his son's art of emotional healing. Allan is a Buddhist artist because he finally "gets himself out of the way." He learns to accept his own imperfections through selfless love for his father. Allan recognizes that it is his obligation to write out of his existential situation, though his execution may be imperfect; to produce a "black" magic that incorporates "white"; to write in affirmation of his race. This revision of reality, Johnson implies, will truly lead to greater and more satisfying levels of enlightenment.

The Sorcerer's Apprentice explores ways an individual may revise a theory of reality in order to transform the self. In Johnson's succeeding books, he boldly extends his analysis of necessary transformations from the individual to the world.

CHAPTER 5

Middle Passage

> Every major character for me is a character of evolution
> and change. They are not the same at the end of the book
> as when we first saw them. The ideal novel would be one
> in which there are no minor characters, where there are no
> flat characters. Everybody is in this situation of process
> and change. Everybody is forced and pressured, as the main
> characters are, to move forward with their lives, to have
> their perceptions changed, to react differently in different
> situations. That would be the ideal novel.
>
> Charles Johnson, *I Call Myself an Artist*

The 1990 National Book Award winner *Middle Passage* focuses
on a historical moment that many Americans do not understand
or might want to forget: the Middle Passage. As Johnson tells an
interviewer, educating America about African American history
is his responsibility as a writer: "Most of [African American]
history is not known, and that's where we get assumptions, prejudices, and misinformation, which causes a lot of suffering. Literature can address some of that."[1] In addressing this subject,
Johnson forthrightly confronts the nation's shame. Johnson's
assumption is that understanding the past will explain the present and ease "a lot of suffering," liberating people by confronting
the past's trauma. By knowing the past, people will be better prepared to change the present.

The book's setting is on board the ship *Republic* during
the shipment of slaves from their capture in Africa to their

enslavement in the United States. The Middle Passage refers to the "middle" part of the voyage across the Atlantic in the triangular trading route between Africa, the West Indies, and the slaveholding states. While the suffering of captured Africans was intense during every aspect of their enslavement, the Middle Passage was especially horrific. The Africans suffered starvation, diseases, psychological and physical trauma from the inhumanly tight quarters, and abuse from the slaver's crews. Many Africans died or were murdered by the crew during the voyage. Johnson's intention is educative for a wide readership, since he clarifies the ghastly nature of this often concealed or forgotten part of American history. Johnson's talent for describing the human body in decay, a characteristic in all his works, comes to the fore in this text, and the reader will never forget the vivid description of the varieties of intense physical pain, brutality, and the physical putrescence and corruption on board the slaver. Indeed, America's history of slavery is akin to the ship's sewage, located out of sight below the deck, but its stench and toxicity a constant presence to all on board.

Despite Johnson's subject matter, the novel is a comedy. Johnson reconciles the novel's subject with its tone by making the novel an investigation of history, both personal and national. As is typical for Johnson, identity from a Buddhist perspective is the primary theme: the misplaced confidence in the idea of a substantialist, psychic core, and the liberating effects of discovering its emptiness. In his previous fiction, Johnson has limited himself to an individual's enlightenment. But in this novel, Johnson links his theme of personal identity to the question of America's national identity: how it is imagined with the corporate cooperation of its citizens, then constantly revised communally through time. In *Oxherding Tale*, Andrew tells Peggy, "There are no 'nations.' We tear down one shop sign, *America;* we put another, *Atlantis.* And we blunder along as usual."[2] In *Oxherding Tale,* however, this illusory nature of an American static identity is only asserted; in *Middle Passage,* it is dramatized.

The parallel between American history and a personal biography is inspired by the psychoanalytic concept of repression: that those important experiences (national and personal) that are buried cause "a lot of suffering." Johnson's purpose is to relieve that suffering by exposing what is hidden, what is "beneath the deck" both nationally and personally, and finally telling the truth. Johnson's view of history in this sense is fundamentally pragmatic. Knowledge of the past is important primarily as a means toward a greater end: improving the health of the present. Johnson stresses the freedom and power of the present to use the past, recognizing that the past is always, like the nation itself, a continuous and evolving creation in the present moment. In this way, history is a "useful fiction" as we Americans commit "to the business of rebuilding . . . the world."[3]

"Useful fiction" is the novel's organizing principle.[4] Toward the novel's conclusion, when the *Republic* is about to go down, Johnson adopts the term when Rutherford tells the fearful, crying child Baleka that all will be well. Though he has compulsively lied throughout the novel—"I always lied" (90)—this time his (presumed) falsehood has a "useful" significance, since it calms the child. Although he is certain that the *Republic* will sink, Rutherford lies to Baleka. He explains that "the 'useful fiction' of this lie got the injured through the night and gave the children reason not to hurl themselves overboard" (162). As he reassures the child, Rutherford begins to believe the statement "all will be well" himself: "soon enough I came to desperately believe in it myself, for them I believed we would reach home, and even I was more peaceful" (163).

In this context, a "useful fiction" is a construction of the world that may not have an absolutely objective referential basis, but which nevertheless provides social guidance and understanding and promotes compassionate conduct. In the novel, a narrative about the world (a "useful fiction") is evaluated in terms of how well it satisfies the need for faith in humanity and hope for the future, both individual and collective, and to what degree it contributes to the community's survival. The term *useful fiction* should not be interpreted as the notion that all accounts of our experience are mere falsehoods. Not all "fictions" are of equal fictionality, and some are superior to others in promoting humane actions. Similarly, a "useful fiction" for Johnson does not denote a simple relativism that denies that any account of experience can be said to be better than any other. Instead, the term "fiction" denies that there exists some ultimate accounting of our world that would be literally true, some final story of our experiences that would conclusively and definitively explain our lives. "Useful fiction," instead, correlates with Johnson's antirealist philosophical orientation. At least for Baleka and Rutherford, all *is* well at the novel's end. Rutherford's "lie" turns out to be true.

"Each Man Outpictured His World from Deep within His Own Heart": "Useful Fiction" as American History

Johnson's novel is not dominated by a tragic consciousness of an irredeemable American past. Instead, Johnson expresses a faith that the past's mistakes produce effects that are susceptible to efforts of reform in the present and future. People and nations can change. To ameliorate conditions in the present, however, it is essential to have a "useful fiction" of what happened in the past—a story that offers meaning and guidance and provides hope for correction. In the sense that history is always written in the future (just as Rutherford writes the *Republic*'s log when he is safely on the *Juno*), history is intended for the people of the present. The needs of this readership, however, are diverse. White readers, for example, may respond to African American history somewhat differently than African American readers; ideally, white readers should work to correct the lingering effects of slavery, while African Americans may take justifiable pride in their ancestors who, as Rutherford writes, "did not commit suicide" (187), even under incredible, inhuman conditions. Ideally, American history should be a "useful fiction" that inspires and fortifies all its citizens.

Johnson shows America in a constant state of assembly and deconstruction, created by its citizens' ever-renewed faith. The symbol for the nation is, in Melvillean tradition, a "physically unstable" ship aptly named the *Republic*. As with Herman Melville's sea novels, the ship has macrocosmic meaning:

> She was perpetually flying apart and re-forming during the voyage, falling to pieces beneath us, the great sails ripping to rags in high winds, the rot, cracks, and parasites in old wood so cancerously swift, springing up where least expected, that Captain Falcon's crew spent most of their time literally rebuilding the *Republic* as we crawled along the waves. In a word, she was, from stem to stern, a process. She would not be, Cringle warned me, the same vessel that left New Orleans. . . . And a seaman's first duty was to keep her afloat at any cost. (36)

The ship's symbolism operates on two fundamental levels, expressing both Johnson's national theme and his Buddhist antirealism. First, the ship symbolizes American identity itself, as narrated through history. Symbolically, the ship of state is in constant dissolution and rebuilding. There is no solidity on the ship, just as there is no terminal, definitive, or authoritative version of the nation. In fact, there is "no ship" from moment to moment, in the sense of the ship having a definitive, substantialist identity; it is "empty" in the Buddhist sense. Johnson instead imagines a cooperative community that constantly makes and remakes the world that cradles it, adjusting the world as constantly changing circumstances demand. Through the efforts of human beings the ship persists and "crawls along" above the void, escaping the abyss because of cooperative work of its crew. As an ongoing product of human labor, the ship (in spite of its use) is "strikingly beautiful" (20). In this way, the nation's identity evolves in a "process" toward a greater sense of coherence, never entirely to be achieved but only imagined as a goal by those who have faith in its future. At no point is America ever finished, and it is a citizen's duty "at any cost" to preserve this fragile thing—disorderly, "flying apart," but coming together again with its citizens' concerted efforts. American history is not simply made but is remade again and again.

Ironically, the making of American history is most vividly fought out by two Africans, Diamelo and Ngonyama. Each is engaged in making a history, as each African attempts to impose a particular and personal interpretation of his experiences. Although they are rivals, they equally suffer the evils on board during the Middle Passage. Each character is richly entitled to his outrage for what is happening to him, and they both plot the African uprising that concludes the novel. Both could present

precisely the same history of the Middle Passage—abuse, humiliations, injustice, deprivation, kidnapping, torture, betrayal.
The way they conceptualize their experience, however, is very
different; yet neither is "wrong" in the sense that they deliberately distort events or deceive others or themselves about what
they have suffered. As Rutherford says about the Allmuseri,
"each man had his atrocity to tell" (134). All Africans suffer the
evil of slavery, and from Johnson's perspective, the real test of
their accounting is not their referentiality to past events (very
much the same kinds of atrocities), but in its consequences for
the present moment. Understanding that each action produces
unknown effects in the future, Rutherford supplies the reader
with an understanding of the Buddhist doctrine of karma. He
says their stories are "seeds . . . that would flower into other
deeds—good and evil—in no time at all" (140). The real question of their stories, then, is the "usefulness" of their "fictions"
—the karmic possibilities of the faith and commitment their
narratives may provide for others.

It is certainly accurate to understand Diamelo within a contemporary context, as critics suggest. Little writes that Diamelo
represents "the late sixties' Black Power movement and contemporary beliefs in Afrocentrism."[5] William Nash agrees: Diamelo
represents "an extreme version of the fundamental principles
of black cultural nationalism."[6] Both Jonathan Little and Nash
understand that Johnson opposes Diamelo's extremism. Yet
Diamelo's story cannot be dismissed. Diamelo's accusations
against the *Republic*'s crew correlate with what the reader
knows occurred during the Middle Passage, and the "American
crimes perpetrated" on Africans on the *Republic* are verifiable
historically (134). Diamelo has earned "the purity of his racial
outrage" (153) with his own suffering. But in articulating the

pain he has experienced, Diamelo cuts himself off from pragmatic action in the present. As Rutherford ruefully points out, "a champion must keep his dragon alive" (154). So it is that Diamelo, in his rage against those who hurt him, creates impractical rules for the survivors on the drifting ship. He insists that only Allmuseri may be spoken and that only African maps and Allmuseri medicine may be used. Most impractical of all, the starving survivors were "to dine only on dishes familiar to the Allmuseri" (155). His history of the *Republic*'s voyage is not a "useful fiction" in that it fails to empower others to take constructive and cooperative action. His history leads to no pragmatic benefit on the *Republic*. In fact, Diamelo is responsible for the *Republic*'s sinking, when he misfires a cannon that bursts on deck and sets the ship afire. The symbolic point is clear: if the past is something to be used pragmatically to promote faith and encourage self-correction, Diamelo's history, dwelling on hatred and revenge, can lead only to the destruction of America.

Diamelo's spiritual error, from a Buddhist perspective, is that he is unable to overcome evil. He has certainly experienced evil, but he has hypostatized evil; that is, he has converted the wrongs done to him into an object, clinging to a fixed, never-changing entity to be conceptualized as an eternal grievance. He lacks faith that the evil effects of slavery can be meliorated by human effort. He understands the distinction between right and wrong, but he cannot understand that the wrong done to him is not indicative of an essence eternally perpetuated. Diamelo fails to make a critical distinction. On a human dimension, slavery must be condemned as an evil that we must never commit. But from a religious point of view, it is not an absolute; its effects can be transformed in the future with goodwill, understanding, concerted effort, and commitment.

A wiser perspective seems to be offered by Ngonyama, who separates himself from Diamelo after the revolt. He, to use a Zen phrase, goes "beyond good and evil." Rather than insist on absolute and exact justice, Ngonyama pleads for Cringle's life. This generosity is Johnson's interpretive comment on the Allmuseri suffering on the *Republic,* and by extension the history of slavery itself. One scene in particular presents Johnson's pragmatic view of American history, and as so often for Johnson's thematic moments, wisdom is delivered in the face of death, waste, and the putrescence of a human body. This moment occurs when Rutherford is ordered to assist in throwing overboard an Allmuseri corpse. In a ghastly description of the disintegrating body, Rutherford notes that "the last stages of rigor mortis froze the body hunched forward in a grotesque hunker, like Lot's wife" (121). Rutherford immediately identifies with the dead African youth, saying "he was close to my own age" (122), and senses in the comparison his own spiritual rot: "The young rot quickest, you know" (122). Because he intuitively understands his connection to the dead youth, Rutherford's revulsion toward the corpse is matched by his fascination: "I cannot say how sickened I felt. The sight and smell of him was a wild thing turned loose in my mind" (122). As he gazes into the dead youth's eyes, he attempts to learn the lesson the corpse reveals: "I found myself poised vertiginously on their edge, falling through these dead holes deeper into the empty hulk he had become, as if his spirit had flown and mine was being sucked there in its place" (123).

Momentarily, Rutherford is caught in a double bind. If he throws the body into the ocean, he is tied forever to the evils of the slave trade; but if he desists, he betrays himself to the crew, already suspicious of him because of his race. With either action, he defines himself irrevocably, in such a way that he cannot control the immediate effects of his choice. So he resolves his crisis "without thinking" (123)—another characteristic of Johnson's unenlightened protagonists—and throws the body into the sea.

This unthinking response, however, comes at a price. A portion of the rotting leg comes off the African's body and marks Rutherford's hand. Rutherford gazes down at his hand, covered with the corrupted, stinking flesh of the African boy. The stain, of course, is symbolic, for he is now marked physically; he, as the dead African boy was, is a slave, if not literally then spiritually. Rutherford suddenly understands his entrapment in the system of slavery, and his own participation that stains him (unwillingly)—both by his act and by his race. Rutherford writes, "My stained hand tingled. . . . it would never be clean again, no matter how often I scrubbed it or with what stinging chemicals" (123). He raises his knife to cut off his stained hand—clearly a scriptural allusion, "And if thy right hand offend thee, cut it off, and cast it from thee."[7] But Ngonyama stops Rutherford from his self-mutilation. A wronged man himself, Ngonyama nevertheless forgives Rutherford for his involvement in the slave trade, and by stopping his self-mutilation encourages Rutherford's own self-forgiveness. He silently leads Rutherford to the rail, "where I gasped for wind, wanting to retch but unable to" (123). Ngonyama says nothing as Rutherford stands by the rail (just as Johnson himself refrains from a didactic commentary on racism). Instead, Ngonyama allows Rutherford to "decipher" his own interpretation of the event (124).

Unlike Diamelo, Rutherford supposes, Ngonyama understands the radical contingency of human experience. Expressing in his "empty" eyes (124) a compassionate understanding of

Rutherford's context for his act, Ngonyama rescues Rutherford from his self-mutilation because he, unlike Rutherford, understands each action as entirely contingent. Ngonyama knows that Rutherford acts only within the context of his limited understanding of slavery and race, his callowness, and his lack of appreciation for the Allmuseri. Because Ngonyama is enlightened, he does not demand perfect retribution, but sees Rutherford's behavior is not self-determined. Rutherford's involvement in slavery originates dependent on the universe of factors in his life—Rutherford's past, his youth, his race, his American citizenship. Thus, "like Lot's wife" (121), Rutherford must not look back and dwell constantly on his sin; to do so would transform him into an object, as if he were a pillar of salt. Nor, the reader is led to understand, can America—even in knowing the truth—dwell forever on its evil, but must, using knowledge of it and its effects, change the present and work toward a better future. Rutherford realizes that he can do nothing to change the past. Nor can he or anyone individually control the future. As he says, "the mills of the gods were still grinding, killing and remaking us all, and nothing I or anyone else did might stop the terrible forces and transformations our voyage had set free" (125). Changing the future requires communal effort and enlightenment. Instead, he can change only himself. He begins to repent of his aimlessness and irresponsibility: "I cried for all the sewage I carried in my spirit, my failures and crimes, foolish hopes and vanities, the very faults and structural flaws in the blueprint of my brain" (127). History, if it has any meaning for the present, must lead to changing America's "structural flaws," slavery's baleful effects—among them, racism and discrimination. Individual change may not immediately transform America, just as Rutherford's self-transformation does not save

Ngonyama, who goes down with the ship. But Ngonyama dies at the helm, faithfully trying to guide the ship of state.

"I Was No One—or Nothing—in My Own Right": Rutherford's Futile Quest for a Permanent Identity

The ship's second symbolic meaning has to do with a deluded conception of a personal, fixed, substantialist self. While we may aspire to a sense of fixity in our identity, the inescapably temporal nature of our world renders this aspiration vain. The novel's example of the formed and reformed self is Rutherford —the protagonist, a premier confidence man. As we have seen in Johnson's fiction, the con game (the "epistemological Murphy") has serious philosophical consequences. Rutherford Calhoun is literally the American self-made man, who creates, then revises, himself as he goes along (much as the crew rebuilds the *Republic*). He is nothing but what he passes himself off as being. For Rutherford, identity itself is only a performance, not an enduring truth but another person's momentary belief that affirms the reality to which it refers. His identities are indeed "useful fictions," since his survival depends on the willingness of others to grant him their belief in his fictions (his con games).

Rutherford Calhoun is the text's historian and autobiographer, and he is also the embodiment of the "middle" in the Middle Passage. As S. X. Goudie explains, he occupies a liminal position throughout the novel as he shifts from allegiance to allegiance.[8] As "middle," he straddles a boundary between the sea and the land, between Captain Falcon and the crew, and between the crew and the Allmuseri. He is asked by each party to commit himself wholly to their cause and their cause only. He is asked to commit himself to Isadora in marriage; to Falcon, who needs "someone to keep his eyes open and tell me of any signs of trouble" (57); to Cringle, who asks, "are you with me?" (63); to Ngonyama, "that crafty bastard" who plots rebellion (83); and to McGaffin, whom Rutherford asks, "How can I help?" (87). Rutherford's ontological position is unsettled and unclear, even to him.

Rutherford, like his nation, is constantly engaged in self-making. He is always on the move, like any good con man, because he does not want to be caught in the fixity of a simple definition. He is situated between the extremes with which he is asked throughout his life to identify, and his talent is to easily assume the identities that with the assistance of others he creates. When he is coerced to accept a stable but manufactured identity, that of Isadora's husband, he immediately flees. His flight from marriage sets in motion the novel's plot, which is organized around a series of confrontations between Rutherford and opposing entities that seek to nail him down. Rutherford's travels finally lead him to see his self not as independent and absolute, but as an aggregate of various selves. He is a cluster of incorporated elements, like a quilt, "where everybody in the quarters adds a stitch or knits a flower, so the finished thing is greater'n any of them" (117).

Rutherford thinks of himself as the con man, yet he unconsciously repudiates that designation and desires the permanence that a fixed identity would bring him. Although Rutherford seems a feckless character, he is in reality suffering because he lacks a stable sense of self. From a Buddhist perspective, Rutherford is entrapped in samsara, endlessly attempting to satisfy his voracious appetite for sensual experience but inevitably becoming disappointed with the transient world. He pretends to be a carefree young man whose only preoccupation in life is finding a diversion, the more outrageous the better. For him, women, wine, and song are life's only worthwhile goals. No "Middle Way" for him!

But even he has an uneasy sense that his compulsion to seek thrills is somewhat strange, even pathological. He senses his own addiction to thrill seeking: "I have always been drawn by nature to extremes. . . . in the face of freedom, I have never been able to do things halfway, and I hungered—literally *hungered*—for life in all its shades and hues: I was hooked on sensation" (3). Rutherford's seeming insouciance, then, is belied by his troubled psyche. He feels anguish about his lack of identity, his existential "drifting" (2), and his awareness that he is a liar, a philanderer, a cheat, a "social parasite," and a "petty thief " (3). His own history is complicated by his inability to accept who he actually is: "I was no one—or nothing—in my own right" (47). Rutherford's narrative task, paradoxically, is to accept this emptiness as an understanding of his true being, though on a deeper and more reflective level than he is capable of when the novel begins. In a literal and figurative way, Rutherford will end where he begins.

Rutherford's conflicted feelings about paternity partly account for his emotional distress. The novel is partly a history of Rutherford's father quest. A pattern in the novel is his relationship with his real father (Riley Calhoun) and the series of surrogate fathers whom he encounters. A manumitted slave, Rutherford was abandoned by his biological, black father, who escaped the plantation where he was enslaved. Rutherford's account of his father is based not only on the perceptions of others, but also on his own desires and attachments. Although it might be possible for Rutherford to create a history/fiction of Riley as a heroic slave, resisting slavery against all odds by escaping into the night, he instead writes a narrative picturing Riley as an irresponsible coward whose indifference to his children fills Rutherford with contempt and anger. For Rutherford, his father is emphatically *not* the heroic slave, but a wastrel who left his two young sons in a selfish search for pleasure. Rutherford continues to feel his abandonment in childhood, even though he is now twenty-three. Rutherford says that for fifteen years

> I have searched the faces of black men on Illinois farms and streets, . . . hoping to identify this man named Riley Calhoun, primarily to give him a piece of my mind, followed by the drubbing he so richly deserved for selfishly enjoying his individual liberty. (112)

Rutherford keeps his own dragon alive, to use his own metaphor (154). Since Rutherford was too young to know Riley when he disappeared, what Rutherford presents as history is in fact his most elaborate fiction.

How "useful" is this fiction for Rutherford? First, creating this history—as opposed to one more generous or compassionate—allows Rutherford a certain degree of license for his own misbehavior. Rutherford dimly understands that this fiction has in some manner contributed to his present misconduct, since he imitates his father's rebellious search for pleasure. Also, his unconscious identification with Riley is made clear in his description of his life as a slave on the plantation: he attempted "outright sedition. . . . Setting Peleg's barn on fire once, breaking things, petty theft, lies, swearing, keeping bad company, . . . fighting, . . . small acts of revolt" (114). In contrast to Riley's flight to freedom, however, Rutherford's are merely "small acts of revolt." Rutherford's flight on the *Republic* is not heroic, since (as a manumitted slave) he does not need to escape, and when he does flee New Orleans he escapes not the brutality of slavery, but only Isadora, a pious and somewhat dull school-teacher. In fact, then, Rutherford's fiction is "useful" for only self-serving purposes; yet he has not improved his own life nor has he compassionately contributed to the well-being of others. Pragmatically speaking, this "useful fiction" has failed him, and to lead a worthwhile life he must work at revising it.

Riley is replaced as Rutherford's father by his master, Reverend Peleg Chandler. In Chandler's case too Rutherford creates for himself a serviceable history, and Chandler's description suits Rutherford's emotional needs because of its ambiguity. Despite his status as Chandler's slave, Rutherford describes him as "a fair, sympathetic, and well-meaning man, as whites go" (111) who was "generous with his slaves for their years of devoted service" (109). On the one hand, then, Rutherford makes Chandler appear as the benevolent slave master, similar to a reformed and enlightened Moses Green in "The Education of Mingo." By elevating Chandler, his "adoptive" father in this way, Rutherford may by comparison vilify Riley.

On the other hand, his description of Chandler is rife with contradictions that undermine his report of Chandler's goodness. Chandler, as a slave owner, is a self-deluded man who wishes he were better; Rutherford assures us that he was a "reluctant slave owner" who "hated the Peculiar Institution" (111). Yet he is reluctant to free his slaves, though he eventually frees them all except Rutherford and Jackson, whom he finally manumits on his deathbed. Chandler's words and acts seldom go together in Rutherford's account. For example, Chandler piously tells Rutherford, "Wealth, you know, isn't what a man has, but what he *is*" (118), even though he allows his slaves to starve because of his selfishness; they also suffer from cold and a lack of clothing on his farm. There is even a hint that Chandler resorts to murder, since we discover later that Riley is killed close to Chandler's farm shortly after he escapes.

It cannot be argued that Reverend Chandler is the ideal surrogate parent for Rutherford. Chandler's paternalism and racial condescension render him ignorant of what Rutherford as a young child requires emotionally, since Chandler instills a sense of worthlessness in Rutherford at an early age. When as a child Rutherford, understandably jealous of the attention given Jackson, asks Chandler what he can do for others, Chandler's reply is a rebuke: "'Yes, that *is* the question, Rutherford. What *can* you do?' That helped my morale not at all," explains Rutherford, "It made me feel as if everything of value lay outside me. Beyond. It fueled my urge to steal things" (162). Rutherford's misery results at least partially from this rejection. Chandler may be religious, but he cannot act on his religious understanding until he dies. At that moment, he enunciates one of the novel's primary themes: "love is infallible; it has no errors, for all errors are the want of love" (111). Ironically, however, he has withheld his love from Rutherford.

Reverend Chandler hopes that Rutherford will fashion himself in Chandler's own image and become "a Negro preacher, perhaps even a black saint" (3). But Chandler's self-centered hope has seemingly not affected Rutherford, for he is in full oedipal revolt against both his master and Riley. It is as if Rutherford has attempted to become precisely the opposite of what Chandler hoped for him, explaining to us that his favorite activity is burglary: "Theft, if the truth be told, was the closest thing I knew to transcendence" (46). Rutherford, then, can have it both ways with his constructed history: he can choose to narrate, as it fits his emotional need, either Chandler the vile master or Chandler the good man. The usefulness of this dualistic history is that Rutherford can minimize the seriousness of his thrill-seeking addiction: he is "hooked on sensation . . . a lecher for perception and the nerve-knocking thrill" (3). His choice of sensual New Orleans seems to him the satisfaction of addiction, the antithesis of puritanical southern Illinois: *"Here, Rutherford is home"* (2). "Home" is not, however, a physical site for Rutherford but a self-deluded description of a metaphysical condition; he fervently wishes for the permanence that "home" metaphorically points to. As a twice-over orphan, "a fatherless child" (126), feeling abandoned by his slave father and rejecting his master, Rutherford longs for stability and permanence.

The excessiveness of his inclinations may also be accounted for by examining his relationship with his brother, Jackson, who is "so gentle, so self-emptied" (112). Rutherford understands Jackson's influence on his behavior, since he is Jackson's antithesis. Rutherford subscribes to a dualism structured by his own past. For Rutherford, Jackson is "a negative of myself . . . the possible-me that lived my life's alternate options, the me I fled. Me. Yet not me. Me if I let go. Me if I gave in" (112). Rutherford, as if he wishes to identify with his image of his departed father, wants to play the "bad" brother to what he perceives as Jackson's Uncle Tomism, his "obsequious" (113) and "subservien[t]" (9) "role of manservant" to Chandler. He wants to play Cain to Jackson's Abel. He sees himself as Jackson's "shadow-self, the social parasite, the black picklock and worldling" (113). Jackson, in contrast, seems to him "shackled to subservience" (9), helping his fellow slaves and attempting modest acts of "plodding reform" (114).

Jackson's description, like Riley's and Chandler's, is a "useful fiction" that rationalizes Rutherford's own irresponsibility and self-evasion. Whereas Rutherford seeks fights with other slaves, Jackson generously acts as peacemaker and servant of his people; his "plodding reforms" are reforms nevertheless. Significantly, Rutherford intends to repeat Chandler's worst actions by becoming a slave owner himself (by inheriting Chandler's estate), while Jackson insists that the estate be "divided equally among . . . servants and hired hands, presently and formerly employed, for their labor helped create it" (117). Rather than seeing Jackson's "self-emptying" (comparable to Jesus's kenosis) as a spiritual concern for the slaves' welfare, Rutherford interprets his behavior as "spineless" (3).

In reaction against his three models (Riley, Chandler, and Jackson), Rutherford chooses to live as the metaphoric son of "Papa" Zeringue. Papa Zeringue is "the very Ur-type of Gangster" (13), a lord of misrule who presides over the world of sheer appetite and self-indulgence, precisely the domain that Rutherford thinks he wants. Papa is "a black lord in ruins, a fallen angel who, like Lucifer, controlled the lower depths of the city . . . but held his dark kingdom, and all within it, in the greatest contempt. He was wicked. Wicked and self-serving" (13). The allusion to Lucifer alerts the reader to an important recognition: like Lucifer, Papa knows the truth but deliberately perverts it. This insight is conveyed in Papa's conversation with Rutherford, in explaining to him how "worldly things work": "The Social Wheel, as I unnerstand it after forty years in business for myself," Papa tells Rutherford, "is oiled by debts, each man owing the other somethin' in a kinda web of endless obligations" (15). Taken out of context, Papa's "wicked" speech expresses an insight about the communal life imaged in the

Buddhist wheel of life: that all human beings are interconnected in a weblike system of obligation, an understanding that is akin to Nhat Hanh's concept of interbeing. But Papa perverts this spiritual truth into an issue of financial accounting of debtors and creditors. Ironically, Rutherford's challenge to mature coincides with Papa's command that he marry Isadora, and given Rutherford's past life as a slave, he comically dreads the thought that his future identity will coalesce in the "shackles" (10) of a husband and home keeper, "to settle down and start a family so [he] can give to others in even greater measure" (8).

The final father surrogate is the *Republic*'s insane, dwarf captain, an Ahab-like Ebenezer Falcon, whose name implies Charles Dickens's parsimonious hero and is suggestive of America's national bird. Falcon is the worst surrogate father in the novel, since he denies Rutherford's inner reality: "I suppose [other people have] never been real to me. Only I'm real to me. Even you're not real to me, Mr. Calhoun" (95). Falcon deprives himself of any contact with the world, discounting any human need but his own. His rejection of Rutherford's reality mirrors his attitude toward other countries and their citizens: "he was a patriot whose burning passion was the manifest destiny of the United States to Americanize the entire planet" (30). Falcon represents a false sense of American history, that of a nation resolutely formed independently of all others—a perspective opposite of Johnson's Buddhist vision of interconnectedness and dependent origination. Falcon is a grim warning of what Rutherford can become. Rutherford also needs to feel human contact, for part of his motivation for stealing is to come into contact with another person: "a familiar, sensual tingle that came whenever I broke into someone's home, as if I were slipping inside another's soul" (46). Falcon's self-determined philosophy is mirrored by his locked, cavelike cabin, with its carefully crafted booby traps symbolic of his repudiation of companionship.

Like Rutherford, Falcon is also fleeing a domestic world of wife and household, and in Falcon, Rutherford discovers his double: "I saw something—or thought I did—of myself in him" (33). Also like Rutherford, Falcon sets himself as an antagonist against the world:

> Conflict *is* what it means to be conscious. Dualism is a bloody structure of the mind. Subject and object, perceiver and perceived, self and other—these ancient twins are built into the mind like the stem-piece of a merchantman. We cannot *think* without them, sir. . . . Slavery, if you think this through, forcing yourself not to flinch, is the social correlate of a deeper, ontic wound. (97–98)

For Falcon, conflict is similar to a Kantian category of understanding: to perceive others is to perceive the Other in conflict, a competition leading to mastery. Slavery is thus inevitable given Falcon's dualism. For Johnson, this metaphysic is the basis of the Western worldview that subjugates people perceived as "different." Falcon's speech momentarily defeats Rutherford, for it confirms his sense of worthlessness as an African American: "I sat for a moment in misery and methought myself outdone. I stank. I could smell myself, and stood, wanting a defense against Falcon's dark counsel and arguments. . . . To my everlasting shame, I knew of none" (98). Falcon's vision of life as perpetual competition, of a Hobbesian struggle between monadic individuals, makes the "stink" of existence almost unendurable to Rutherford, though he cannot refute Falcon's self-entrapped

vision. The novel's trajectory is Rutherford's emotional separation from Falcon, toward a Buddhist understanding of emptiness and dependent origination. Only this philosophy can rescue
Rutherford from Falcon's fatalistic dualism.

The crew, like Rutherford, is also ensnared in a life of
desire. The *Republic*'s microcosmic crew is a group of outcasts,
though a solidarity of sorts, composed of "social failure[s]"
(35), all of whom "failed at bourgeois life in one way or
another" (39). These men "seemed to hunger for 'experience' as
the bourgeois Creoles desired possessions" (38). Among this
ship of fools, two crewmembers especially serve symbolic functions, both parodic transformations of Melville's characters in
Moby-Dick: Peter Cringle, the first mate and quartermaster who
is Johnson's parody of Melville's Starbuck; and Josiah Squibb,
the *Republic*'s cook, Johnson's parody of Melville's cook Stubb.
Johnson utilizes each character to comment on contemporary
Americans.

Cringle represents a modern-day liberal. Marked by his
"New England gentility," his primary physical characteristic is
that his "skin was as white as wax" (23). However, it is Cringle,
not Rutherford, who is obsessed with his own whiteness, and
his self-conscious focus on his race and class is the most conspic-
uous of all the characters. Although Cringle attempts to help
his crew and defend them from Falcon's unreasonableness—
he often rages at Falcon for driving the crew too hard—he is
ineffectual in his attempts to protect them. His concern for
Tommy's welfare, for example, is genuine, but he does nothing
but expose himself to his own humiliation when confronted
with Tommy's continual rape by Falcon: "the mate wouldn't
look me in the eye; he chewed the inside of his cheek" (26).
Unsurprisingly, it is he and not Falcon who is usually the target

of the crew's derision. His discourse is interpreted as "pomposity" by the crew (41), and they see him as "weak" and "enfeebled" (42), effeminate in a "ship of *men*" (41). Seemingly Falcon's emotional antithesis, he too feels detached from his social world, though unlike Falcon, he regrets the emotional distance between himself and others. He is obsessed with his separation, a distance created by his sense of guilt caused by class difference: "he hated not to be 'regular,' yet who, it was clear, carried a core of aloneness within him that nothing on shore could touch" (25). His guilt feeds on his own shame, self-pity, and resentment of his father, since he can blame his father for his choices. "It wasn't my decision" (158): Cringle's answer for all his own quandaries conveniently releases him of moral responsibility.

In Cringle, Johnson explores the implications of present-day, white, liberal guilt, a characteristic usually associated with people who are at least minimally middle class. He is "someone who'd grown up with a great deal of wealth, privileges, or personal gifts, and felt guilty about them in the presence of those who hadn't" (25). Coming from a wealthy family, Cringle understands that because of his race and class, he has immensely benefited from the American system, and that his privileged status has contributed to keeping African Americans oppressed. He senses that he originates dependent on a network of class distinctions, but he is unable to bring this intuition to full consciousness and act on it. Because he responds to Rutherford as one of the deprived, he is especially friendly to him, but his friendliness comes from his sense of guilt and not from a genuine feeling of Rutherford's fellow humanity. For example, he defends Rutherford from crewmembers, though he does not understand that Rutherford will betray him too if Rutherford must for his own survival. He simply cannot understand Rutherford as a human being on Rutherford's own terms.

Cringle's guilt, though treated sympathetically by Rutherford, is symptomatic of liberal ineffectuality in leadership. Because his guilt is so self-absorbed, he fails to provide firm moral leadership on the *Republic,* and he provides the crew with no pragmatic benefit. Guilt, of course, can be rational or irrational. It can be based on a rational, regretful evaluation of one's immoral actions that leads to self-change; or it can be an irrational response to an irrevocable situation or irreversible event, an excessive self-flagellation that leads nowhere. Rutherford too feels this irrational guilt. After Rutherford is rescued, he feels "guilty simply for being alive" (188), an excessive survivor guilt so intense that he momentarily considers hanging himself. Cringle's primary guilt is also irrational, since his birth in an America riddled by class distinction and slavery is an event he did not cause.

Yet in pragmatic terms, Cringle has ample reason to feel guilty for his actual choices. By acting as first mate on the *Republic,* he knowingly and willingly participates in the slave trade, and he is therefore complicit in the evil of slavery, despite his professions of regret over the peculiar institution and his pity for the captured Allmuseri. His unconscious moral confusion leads to contradictions in his behavior on the *Republic.* When he witnesses the maltreatment of the Allmuseri on board, he feels pity for "the poor bastards" (62), but (as with Rutherford) his pity lacks any kind of human identification with them— his version of compassion is mere sentimentality. Furthermore, when his own life is on the line, he does not hesitate to use deadly force; he shoots and kills an Allmuseri when he is attacked. He, much like Falcon, despises the Allmuseri as the unalterable "Other"—"devil-worshiping, spell-casting wizards" (43). Thus, he tells Rutherford that the Allmuseri are "not like us at all. No, not like you either, though you are black" (43). Johnson demonstrates Cringle's vague and confused sense of morality ironically when Cringle uses his Bible only to clean his pipe: "He banged his large calabash pipe on the Bible he carried, bound in pressed pigskin, to shake loose the dottle" (62). Cringle's troubled conscience is a source of his own disharmony, of a divided personality in which one part (his rebellion against and acquiescence to his father) legislates and commands the other. He has interiorized the master-slave relationship; he is, like Rutherford, a slave to his own desire both to attach to and release himself from his father.

Cringle's liberal guilt, producing nothing but his own alien-ation and self-distrust, exposes a concealed dimension of liber-alism. Beneath his genial surface, Cringle resembles the fascist Falcon more than he realizes. Like Falcon, he has no faith. Cringle senses that the era of white domination may be coming to an end; that a new, fearsome era—as yet to be actualized—may emerge with white power diminished. Cringle's anxiety about what the future will bring America is symbolized in his vacant gaze at the sea, which he imagines as completely hostile. A sea gazer, like Rutherford, Cringle sees the world as a chaos needing Euro-American, "civilized" control: "I dislike it, Cal-houn, being hemmed in by Nothing, this bottomless chaos breeding all manner of monstrosities and creatures that defy civ-ilized law" (42)—"civilized law" being his expression in part of a white hegemony that rationalizes slavery. Later in the novel, Falcon as he dies will express the same anxiety as Cringle does, that "the civilized values and visions of high culture, have all gone to hell in fine old hamlets filled high with garbage" (145).

The "monstrosities and creatures" that defy both Cringle and Falcon can be none other than the Allmuseri, the racial Other. Cringle's statement resembles Falcon's own vision of universal and irresistible conflict. As Falcon says, "For a self to act, it must have somethin' to act *on*. A nonself—some call this Nature—that resists, thwarts the will, and *vetoes* the actor" (97). Cringle feels this "veto" constantly. Like Falcon, he envisages culture as a contest between powers, with the elevation of one power (or race) leading to a necessary diminution of the other. He fears that the world's mutability must necessarily efface or destroy Euro-American achievements. Cringle laments, "all our reasoning and works are so provisional, so damned fragile, and someday we pass away like the stain of breath on a mirror and sink back into *that* from whence we've come" (42). His fear of personal death is also an expression of his lack of faith in the future, his conviction that cultural change inevitably brings disruption and dissension, rather than wider benefit and more pervasive order.

Cringle is also Johnson's ironic symbol of the contemporary, existential man, filled with despair over an absence of absolute values. Cringle's staring into the sea—like Rutherford's—is a direct allusion to the "Look," Jean-Paul Sartre's most famous metaphor in *Being and Nothingness* (1943). Cringle represents Johnson's satire of the Sartrean "lost man," alienated from family, friends, and—exceptionally important for this text—the "Other." The sea is identified by Cringle with "the Void" (36), while Cringle typifies the absurd Sartrean individual peering into the abyss and contemplating the death that will release him from his anguish. Sartre writes, "I approach the precipice, and my scrutiny is searching for myself in my very depths. In terms of this moment, I play with my possibilities. My eyes, running over the abyss from top to bottom, imitate the possible fall and realize it symbolically."⁹ Cringle's despair of connection and ambivalence about his death revolve specifically around his sense of separateness from the Allmuseri. He even more than Falcon articulates the debased sense of pragmatism when he complains about his duties on the *Republic:* "Truth is what *works,* pragmatically, in the sphere of commerce. . . . [Cringle's father] judges everything in terms of profit" (160). As a minor character, Cringle undergoes drastic change in drastic circumstances. His enlightenment occurs when he begins to understand people (and pragmatism) in an entirely different way.

Squibb the cook, Rutherford's immediate superior, represents a broader plane of American experience, the average person's lack of awareness of a moral quandary in America's racialized history. In fact, Squibb's life is characterized by his uninterest in all philosophical issues. He is perhaps the most prominent example of enslavement to desire in the novel, in his addiction to alcohol and in his pathological attachment to his memory of "Stinky," his affectionate nickname for his ex-wife. For Squibb as for Rutherford, "*life* was a commodity, a *thing* we could cram into ourselves" (38). Squibb feels no sense of guilt or responsibility for being employed as a cook on a slaver; in fact, because of his alcoholism he is usually oblivious to the events aboard the ship. Squibb most clearly embodies what Cringle says about the crew in general: "They skim along the surface, the others" (42).

Steering toward America: America's Confrontation with the Allmuseri

The Allmuseri rebellion mutually transforms the whites and the Africans on the *Republic.* In the slave revolt, both parties originate dependent on each other, just as African Americans and Euro-Americans interweave. Partly, Johnson uses their rebellion as consistent with his novel's educative purpose. The resistance of the captured Africans shows that, historically, slaves-to-be were not mere passive victims on slavers but often fought back when the opportunity arose against an almost always insuperable power. As Nash points out, the Allmuseri uprising is based on the rebellion aboard the slaver *Amistad* in 1839, nine years after the novel's setting.[10] The *Amistad* rebellion, of course, was successful in that most of the captured Africans were returned to Africa, whereas the *Republic* is sent to the ocean's bottom—but not before demonstrating Johnson's theme of interbeing.

A variety of theories have been advanced regarding the ethnography of the name Allmuseri, but in an interview, Johnson implies that the tribe's name has only a casual significance.[11] The tribe has engrossed him since 1977, while writing "The Education of Mingo": "I needed a tribe . . . there was this little place in this African village called an Allmuseri. It was a hut, and magic went on in there. . . . I needed another tribe in another story so I just said, Allmuseri."[12] The philosophical significance of the Allmuseri, however, looms large in this novel, as they embody several of Johnson's themes developed throughout his career. The tribe appreciates a Buddhist sense of eternal unity: "The failure to experience the unity of Being everywhere was the Allmuseri vision of Hell" (65). Resisting abstractions that categorize reality, they "are a people so incapable of abstraction no two instances of 'hot' or 'cold' were the same for them, this hot porridge today being so specific, unique, and bound to the present that it had only a nominal resemblance to the hot porridge of yesterday." The Allmuseri also accept the

Buddhist doctrine of the no-self, for as the mysterious "Ur-tribe of humanity" (61), they symbolically lack fingerprints. They celebrate rather than resist elemental change: "they were process and Heraclitean change, like any men, not fixed but evolving" (124). As a consequence, the Allmuseri embrace the Buddhist concept of emptiness; ironically, Europeans were once members of the tribe but had fallen away into "the madness of multiplicity" (65). But in their adopting violence to thwart their enslavers, they have transformed themselves, Rutherford understands, forever.

Among the Americans, Cringle and Squibb initially seem resistant to spiritual transformation: Cringle because of his fear of the Allmuseri, "creatures that defy civilized law" (42); and Squibb because of his alcoholism and laziness. When the rebellion occurs, both characters are galvanized, but their responses diverge. At first, Cringle expresses defiance against the victorious Allmuseri: "They'll see hell quicker'n they'll see help from me" (134). His life is saved when Rutherford intercedes on his behalf, asking Ngonyama, "I ask you to make him *your* slave" (136). By actually living the life of a captured African, Cringle begins to understand through his own experience the suffering that the slaves had to endure, and though he attempts to steer the ship toward American ports, he fails because his cosmos is symbolically altered by his servitude: "The heavens are all wrong. That's what baffles me. They've not been in the right place" (158). Accordingly, he begins to revise his own theories of reality. His physical disorientation leads to a clearer spiritual direction of what he must do to help the ship's community, and he loses confidence in his "civilized laws" (42) as his sole moral guide. As the ship drifts, his illness becomes worse, but he is capable of overcoming his concern for his own health. Instead, he accepts the necessity of cannibalism, presumably one of the "uncivilized" practices he formerly associated only with Africa, a "bottomless chaos" (42), but now the only pragmatic action to be taken for the benefit of others. He asks that both Americans and Africans eat him so that they can continue to live, in the hopes that they eventually are rescued by another ship. In his self-sacrifice, he "won his wings," says Squibb (174).

Cringle's self-sacrificing transformation may represent a symbolic continuation of his civilized perspective, literally "in" Rutherford and the rest of the survivors.[13] Also, his selfless gesture implies in its imagery the Eucharist. However, the impact of Cringle's death is not primarily symbolic but emotional, for Johnson does not shield us from the horror of his death. His murder at Squibb's hands is described in macabre detail. In Squibb's recounting of the event, which takes place while Rutherford is unconscious, Cringle instructs Squibb on knifing his vulnerable areas so as to kill him efficiently: the heart, the jugular vein, and "the soft flesh behind his ear, pokin' straight through the brain" (174). When the Allmuseri butcher Cringle's body, Squibb says, "it hit me, that I'd killed a man" (174). Fully confronting the horror of Cringle's death, the reader can only agree.

The text's intellectual challenge revolves around awful ethical issues for contemporary America: assisted suicide and euthanasia. Onboard the *Republic,* lofty, disembodied "civilized law" gives way to performative knowledge discovered in lived experience. In Cringle's death, the characters' profound moral commitments are a matter of personal experience shaped by circumstance rather than abstract principles. Cringle knows he is dying, and medical assistance is unavailable on the drifting ship; furthermore, Cringle's telling others to consume his flesh expresses his hope that the starving Africans and Americans will survive the ordeal, and may inspire hope in them too. More important, he has accepted the Other he had formerly disdained, so he dies, Squibb tells us, without suffering, despite his excruciating pain. Cringle's assisted suicide, in other words, is a moral achievement, for it originates dependent on the welfare and good will of others.

Johnson's meditation on morality is also played out in Squibb's change. At first Squibb is an example of those people who only "skim the surface" of life (42), but after the Allmuseri revolt he too undergoes a transformation. A drunk, before the revolt he was useless, but now his labor is desperately needed for those onboard to survive. He begins to resemble the Allmuseri; in Squibb, Rutherford feels "perfectly balanced crosscurrents of culture" that help him "solve whatever problem was at hand" (176). When he understands that people really need his help, "whatever was needful he did" (176). To use a familiar Buddhist metaphor, he mindfully fetches wood and carries water, and he intuits others' needs, shown when he can "anticipate [Rutherford's] pain before [he] felt it" (176). But Johnson also places Squibb on a high level of understanding in the terrible extremity of circumstances. Slaughtering your good friend is much different from swabbing the deck, mindfully or not. Squibb's change of character permits him to thrust the knife blade. Understanding Cringle's "need" to die for others, this simple man himself becomes profoundly philosophical, asking, "what was the limit of bein' human?" (174). Murdering Cringle, he finds out.

Dramatically, we are to contrast Cringle's and Squibb's transformations with Falcon's adamant re-entrenchment in self. Consistent with the rest of his work, in *Middle Passage* Johnson asks readers to concern themselves not simply with individual, isolated actions (suicide or cannibalism) but with the evaluation of character traits that make an individual's act good or bad. While Cringle and Squibb act to save other people, Falcon annuls his link to humanity. He does not change. Earlier, he explains that he too is a cannibal, and he terrifies Rutherford with his story of eating a cabin boy when shipwrecked. But consistent with his character, he enjoys his cannibalism, since it feeds his "desire to be [a] fascinating object in the eyes of others" (33). Like Cringle, Falcon commits suicide, but does so out of a hate-filled rejection of the world that he cannot control. Moreover, his suicide is quick and his death (compared to Cringle's) relatively painless, since he shoots himself in the head. Cringle's and Falcon's intentions (to commit suicide) are identical, but their motivations are completely different.

The most significant change in the novel, of course, is Rutherford's. Pragmatically, this change is expressed in his adoption of Jackson's persistent "burning for things to work out well" (126). Rutherford attempts to "forget my personal cares, my pains, and my hopes . . . I prayed, like my brother, that all would be well" (161). Rutherford's encounter with the Allmuseri's "shape-shifting god" marks a critical stage in his discovery of the world's unity in spirit. The scene recalls Rutherford, overcome by nausea but unable to vomit, throwing the youth's body into the ocean. The god appears to him as the psychologically repressed element Rutherford must confront, "with whom I had bloody, unfinished business" (167)—Riley Calhoun, Rutherford's father. Suddenly, Rutherford "stares" at the text's sign for the world's interbeing, "the antecedent universe to which my father, as a single thread, belonged" (169). Riley is no longer the villain who abandoned his family; instead, his life's narrative is part of the world's fabric of stories—"A thousand soft undervoices" (171) that compose human life. In empathizing with who his father really was—a terrified slave who tried to escape but was murdered only a few miles from Chandler's farm—Rutherford gives up his anger and resentment and adopts the Allmuseri manner of forgiveness and acceptance. Just as Ngonyama's generous forgiveness of him led Rutherford to self-acceptance, Rutherford forgives his father by imaginatively understanding Riley's way of seeing the world. He realizes Riley's interbeing, the context of his actions as a slave. Rutherford can now understand Riley as a person on his own terms: not a weak, hateful coward but a person who, like the Allmuseri, survived the Middle Passage and suffered on Chandler's farm. He realizes that his father was entrapped in an evil system, and that his escape was not a betrayal of him but occurred within the context of the brutality he had suffered. His father momentarily disappears within the god, then reappears in an expansive vision of the connectedness of "We." Instead of Riley the individual person, Rutherford envisages a mystic unity with his father and all people, "as waves vanish into water" (171).

This vision has racial implications, for Rutherford knows that "I could only feel that identity was imagined; I had to listen harder to isolate him from the We that swelled each particle and pore of him, as if the (black) self was the greatest of all fictions" (171). His recognition of his personhood with his father's—"Suddenly I knew the god's name: Rutherford" (171)—literally makes the world sing: "the effect of all this was that from bowsprit to stern she seemed to *sing* like the fabled *Argo*" (171). He is at last released from his need for thrills and excitement, and from his need for vengeance and cosmic justice. His "faint" or "death" (171) is a sign that he has relinquished personal identity, with all its desires, resentments, and petty grievances.

Rutherford's new sense of the world is registered in images of rebirth. He lies "as in a chrysalis" (181), Johnson puns, "at the foot of the berth [birth]" (178); and Rutherford says, "Try as I might, I could not remember my full name" (179). His "ontic" restoration is accompanied by a fully realized concern for his companions on board: "I did not care for myself anymore, only that my mates should survive" (181). His acquisition of a new identity is symbolized later, when, as the *Republic* sinks, he is baptized by being thrown into the Atlantic Ocean; at this point in the narrative, however, the ocean is not an image of the "Void," but instead is a symbol for Buddhist emptiness/ fullness, with its "dancing, lemon-colored lights" (184). His acceptance of the world also releases him from his con game; no longer does he wish to control the minds of the crew and the will of the Allmuseri. He "felt no need to possess or dominate, only appreciate in the ever extended present" (187). He does not renounce his experience or attempt to reshape it in a more self-flattering way as he writes in the log; rather, he acknowledges that he is "a wreck of the *Republic*" (190). Rutherford mindfully turns to writing to make his now "useful fiction" accessible to a wide population. He "transfigure[s] all we had experienced, and . . . make[s] . . . peace with the recent past by turning it into Word" (190). He thus makes his writing a form of meditation.

Johnson ends his philosophical novel in a satiric romp with the conventions of romantic comedy—certainly a needed comic relief after the grimmest aspects of the *Republic*'s destruction. Rutherford is reintegrated into society by means of his marriage to Isadora, and with his adopted children and Isadora's pets, together they form a ready-made family. After being tossed into the Atlantic, Rutherford, Squibb, and three Allmuseri children are rescued by the *Juno,* named after the goddess of marriage. Coincidentally, Isadora is also on the *Juno;* a nineteenth-century Penelope, she has been weaving and then unweaving clothes for her pets to stave off an unlikely marriage partner—none other than Papa Zeringue, whom Rutherford successfully blackmails in order to win Isadora's hand. Isadora, who now has decided to transform herself into a sexual vamp for Rutherford's sake, is momentarily taken aback by Rutherford's appearance and lack of sexual desire. Whereas earlier he had only the most sexist assumptions about women, now—balding, arthritic, and at least temporarily uninterested in passionate sex—Rutherford comically thinks "desire was too much of a wound, a rip of insufficiency and incompleteness" (208). Instead, he wishes for an enduring relationship with his wife-to-be: "I wanted our futures blended, not our limbs, our histories perfectly twined for all time, not our flesh" (208). Rutherford adopts the orphaned Allmuseri children, marries Isadora, and returns to Illinois to farm, becoming a householder with Jackson. Society is renewed with their marriage, and Papa Zeringue (revealed as the *Republic*'s primary financial sponsor) is punished (both physically by Santos and emotionally with the loss of his wealth). All ends well.

Beneath the amusing implausibility of comic conventions, however, Johnson stresses the serious transformation that has occurred. Rutherford has changed from reprobate to reformed man, from insouciant player to committed householder, exchanging a "misspent manhood" (170) for a life of domesticity and adoptive fatherhood. Accepting his father's failures and understanding the reasons behind them, he can now fulfill the role of the father he did not have. Rutherford accepts that the most important life moments are not the thrilling, romantic ones that earlier he thought he needed (was "hooked on") but the small and prosaic ones, the most ordinary and everyday events that we do not appreciate simply because they are so commonplace. Rutherford resolves to live moment by moment, his goodness now entirely undramatic. His ethical orientation is the moment-to-moment conscientiousness of being a good father, husband, and citizen. For his presumptive future, moral decisions are matters of responsiveness to unique people in particular situations. In *Oxherding Tale* and *Middle Passage*, Johnson shows how enlightenment can transform a person. In *Dreamer*, he shows how it can possibly transform a nation.

CHAPTER 6

Dreamer

And the light shineth in darkness; and the darkness compre-
hended it not.

John 1:5

In *Dreamer,* Charles Johnson most fully realizes his vision of the
enacted social responsibilities of the spiritually enlightened in
his portrayal of Dr. Martin Luther King Jr. In an excellent article, John Whalen-Bridge explains that Johnson dramatizes what
a social movement that synthesizes Judeo-Christian and Buddhist principles looks like.[1] According to Whalen-Bridge, King
himself is the exemplar of the syncretistic self, and his movement actualizes its ideals: "King was fond of saying, Jesus provided the message, Gandhi the method for their social mission"
(114). Historically, King visited India, and he recommended
the Vietnamese Buddhist Thich Nhat Hanh as a candidate for
the Nobel Peace Prize, as Johnson notes (18). Johnson's King
seems highly motivated by Buddhist ideals, such as "ahimsa,"
the refusal to harm other living things, when he does not kill
roaches in his apartment (47). He also recommends to his con-
gregation "digging a little grave for the ego" (139), an allusion
to the Buddhist idea of "no-self." Nevertheless, King is a committed Christian: "*the words of Christ were the horn of his salvation*" (218).

Johnson's typical artistic organization of employing foils is
made explicit in the novel's two doubles, King and Chaym (or

Cain). Johnson's technique in this novel is complicated by a third character, Matthew, whose novelistic point of view alternates with an authorial perspective on King's consciousness. The novel's central symbol, the dream, is for Johnson double-edged. It signifies both the Judeo-Christian dream of a more harmonious society, created by human imagination and labor; and a Buddhist understanding of the world itself as an illusory dream, which teaches that the world of our daily lives is constructed only from the sensory projections formulated from our own self-centered desires. For the first, the dream must be intensified and consciously enacted; for the second, awakening from the dream is essential for personal growth. King works selflessly toward his own dream: his "city upon a hill," his "beloved community" (208).

The main characters are all dreamers. Each of Johnson's three characters—Matthew, Chaym, and Martin Luther King Jr.—evolves toward a spiritual awakening on three different but interwoven levels: the personal concerns of the individual (summarized by Matthew's felt inferiority); the social dimension of injustice and criminality (represented by Chaym's behavior and his cynical view of King's moral position); and the responsibility of national engagement (dramatized by King's Gethsemane-like conflict). At the novel's beginning, none of them feels "at home—*really* at home—anywhere" (100), but each seeks a different kind of awakening from their world of sin and sorrow. Each seeks an alternative to a bitterly nihilistic (non-Buddhist) vision of the world as "empty" core: "there's nothing underneath. . . . Just emptiness" (86).

Feeling entrapped, all three characters attempt to escape their existential condition, and escape—freedom—is possible but not unequivocal. Central to the novel is Johnson's faith in the spiritual transformation of the individual, though change may never be complete or permanent. Perhaps because the reader knows very well what history holds in store for King as he prepares for Memphis, Johnson's tone verges toward the tragic in this novel. As William Nash writes, "this is admittedly the grimmest scenario [Johnson] constructs."[2] This darker understanding is especially made clear in Johnson's character development. Each character evolves slowly toward a stable position, then unexpectedly moves away from stability. King wrestles with accepting the personal cost of his social burden in the civil rights movement, but as soon as he achieves his personal resignation, he seemingly begins to question the philosophical basis of civil disobedience and nonviolence. Chaym attempts to move philosophically away from his bitter, materialist worldview to embrace King's idealism, but as soon as this change seems effected, he surrenders to the pressure of the FBI, disappearing into "everywhere," as Matthew tells Amy (236). Finally, Matthew becomes committed to creating a more harmonious and cooperative society, but first must accept that "in each of us there was a wound, an emptiness that would not be filled in our lifetime" (236). Thus, character development is never definitive or absolute, but always open to further change.

Johnson illustrates the theme of evolving selves and the artist's responsibility to depict the need for moral evolution in a scene where Matthew examines Chaym's drawings. He finds several portraits of himself by Chaym, varying from a naive, realistic portraiture to a postmodernist impressionism, where "I barely recognized myself. Me as he envisioned I might be in a decade. . . . I stared and stared at these portraits" (209). Matthew's meditation on his own portraits as he might appear in a future mirror conveys Johnson's theme that one's identity evolves as surely as one's physical features. One's identity is a process that "reveal[s] the world's mystery and wonder" (209), and the artist, like Chaym, can "reinvent [the world] from scratch" in art and action. The artist limns out the "constantly mutating soul" (59) of human beings, thereby guiding them toward what they can be "in a decade" and beyond. Thus, the artist's moral burden is immense. Because the nature of human change is unpredictable, the novel finally reminds us that the struggle for a civil society is not an automatic growth but is an effect of conscious human resolve, inspired by exemplary people like King, but also in part by the artist's work.

"Creative Tension": Martin Luther King Jr. as Johnson's Prophetic Pragmatist

The historical King was not a "pragmatist" in the colloquial sense of the word. Indeed, Johnson in *Turning the Wheel* writes that the historical King in one of his speeches denounced "'pragmatism' applied to questions of right and wrong."[3] Yet as Whalen-Bridge has convincingly argued, Johnson's literary purpose is not simply to depict the historical King but to give us a contemporary moral guide. Nor, would I add, is Johnson concerned with pragmatism in its vernacular connotation: the relativistic idea that whatever works is right. As we have seen in *Middle Passage,* Johnson evokes a more complex, highly nuanced view of pragmatism, consistent with Cornel West's concept of "prophetic pragmatism." West uses "prophetic" in the Old Testament sense, as in the prophet Elijah confronting a decayed society, seeking radical transformation by forthrightly exposing its moral failures. West, like Johnson throughout the novel, blends political engagement, philosophy, and religion, and although Johnson has not commented on West's work, they share a common interest in eclectic borrowing, so that any philosophical or religious tradition can help any other. In the novel, King is Johnson's own incarnation of prophetic pragmatism.

In West's description of American pragmatism, a pragmatist always begins with profound faith, not doubt or skepticism. This faith is held firmly despite the world's radical lack of certainty. Because the world is constantly evolving, there is no absolute principle to be adhered to rigidly, nor is there some underlying, presocial rule in which an ethical person can take refuge. In a world of constant change, there cannot be a recourse to an absolute source of moral truth; instead, ethical action must reflect, according to West, an "experiential" method. An experiential method, as West notes, is "self-correcting," always open to revisions; and it is "communal," for the view of reality it operates on is centered in a community of opinions, a consensus contingent on whatever is known or capable of being known. Our ethical action—as individuals, as a community, and as a nation—is a result of our experiential knowledge, which is necessarily "revisable"[4] as we continually learn that our picture of the world is only partial. Thus, even the most hallowed religious or moral principles are only assumptions of truth, to be validated by testing and by experience. Johnson in *Turning the Wheel* argues that this pragmatic turn is embraced by the American political structure itself: "America was founded on principles, ideals, and documents . . . that forced it to be forever self-correcting."[5] West writes, "ultimately, convergence and agreement among scientists will disclose reality. Of course, such ultimate agreement never comes; it is simply a regulative ideal and a hope."[6] "Centrality of contingency," West argues, is at the center of American pragmatism. Abstract moral principles like religious or secular laws may offer a guide, but these may be forsaken in specific circumstances. As we saw in *Middle Passage,* suicide, murder, euthanasia, and cannibalism all have precedence over adherence to abstract "civilized" principles, given a scrupulous decision that principle in certain circumstances must be overruled. For both Cringle and Squibb, boundaries of personal conscience dissolve in desperate decisions about what must be saved and what lost. These terrible decisions provide the answer to Squibb's hard question, "What was the limit of bein' human?"[7]

In this way for West, prophetic pragmatism is always based on human values, and the "prophetic pragmatist" courageously founds all action on those human values. Human initiative can transform the world, but such action, issuing from the character of the actor, should have consequences that are equitable, compassionate, and altruistic for the world. But because all knowledge of an action's results are ex post facto, the pragmatist must carefully examine all possibilities before any action can be taken, and even then the pattern of action can only be performed in faith and belief. Choosing the moral pattern (dharma) is always a risk and a struggle; in fact, our only certainty is that we will never be entirely successful in our undertaking, and we may be entirely wrong. Johnson's King makes choices in the context of his faith, but for him, choosing is a terrifying risk, and there are no guarantees that his choice is the correct one. Johnson's aesthetic task in *Dreamer* is to give a sense of King's existential dilemma on a national stage during the 1960s, which may not be immediately clear to a reader in 1998 (*Dreamer*'s publication date). Given King's "curse of canonization" (Johnson's description of how King has been transformed over three decades), it may be difficult for a reader to recover imaginatively King's formidable obstacles, since King has been sanitized and made devoid of any radical perspectives on American society.[8] He has been turned into the archetypal nice man. In the novel, however, Johnson portrays a King who is willing to coerce society to undergo the pain of revising itself. In terms of the novel's organizing scriptural allusion, King is a "paradoxical fusion of Cain and Abel" (125).

King is as much the Cain figure as he is the Abel. He is, of course, "Abel," the accepted, middle-class avatar of virtue that, in Whalen-Bridge's words, "is very much a bodhisattva dedicated to the idea of healing-through-integration."[9] Certainly his ongoing goodness to all people around him confirms King as the bodhisattva. But as a Cain figure, King is also like an Old Testament prophet, for he knows that a spiritual revolution is needed to reverse discrimination, end injustice, and promote a life worth living for all people. To bring his nation to the bitter recognition of moral failure, King must, like Christ, "come to send fire on the earth."[10] King must inflict emotional suffering on his fellow (white) citizens with "creative tension," allowing the "long-buried hatreds to surface, where they were exposed for the world to see." As Matthew explains, "King's philosophy not withstanding, 'creative tension' was an act of violence, the murder of a repressive past so that a new order—God's order—could be born" (125).

Johnson's phrase "creative tension" is derived from King's famous "Letter from Birmingham Jail," written on April 16, 1963, while King was incarcerated for civil disobedience in Birmingham, Alabama. In the essay, he admonishes those whites who agreed with the aims of the civil rights movement but who opposed King's breaking laws. He criticizes those "who constantly [say], 'I agree with you in the goal you seek, but I cannot agree with your methods.'"[11] As West's "prophetic pragmatist" would understand (and as King argues in "Letter from Birmingham Jail"), the "methods" are essential. Those who criticize him are the people, King implies, for whom property rights, laws, and social order (all abstract principles) are more important than the lived-through, prolonged suffering of African Americans. These white and black conservatives are the people whom King must confront—not necessarily evil people, but people who value abstract principles over the welfare of others. King makes his indictment clear with a graphic image of a pierced boil:

> We who engage in nonviolent direct action are not the creators of tension. We merely bring to the surface the hidden tension that is already alive. We bring it out into the open where it can be seen and dealt with. Like a boil that can never be cured so long as it is covered up but must be opened with all its pus-flowing ugliness to the natural medicines of air and light, injustice must be exposed, with all the tension its exposure creates, to the light of human conscience and the air of national opinion before it can be cured.[12]

The purpose of King's civil disobedience was to reveal the partly concealed disorder and injustice to whites so that it might be corrected. He rejected opposing violence with violence, since the karmic fruit of such action would be rotten: it would only continue the cycle of suffering and retribution. He understood that social change could only occur when the light shone on darkness and people became ashamed of living in darkness—fear, guilt, bigotry, and the refusal to allow a whole population of Americans to receive their due rights.

Shining the light on evil, Johnson understands, is painful. Johnson's King is willing, nevertheless, to commit "the murder of a repressive past" (125). For his goal, justice for all, he looks beyond the abstract principles held by those who criticized him, and he brings terrific emotional pain to those who would retain the status quo. In King's aggressive civil disobedience, Johnson fuses the offerings of Cain and Abel because his political activism draws attention to the hateful consequences of static laws, even as the movement promotes progressive ideals. Yet for Johnson, King's "creative tension" is an optimistic social practice, for its faith is that America, despite its past of slavery and racial oppression, is worth fighting for.

In this fight, it is the revolutionary potential of King's faith that inspires and supports him. Johnson shows that it was certainly not obvious in King's time that provoking the reactions of bigots, lancing the boil of national lies—"creative tension" —was the best way ultimately to achieve justice. As Whalen-Bridge writes, King "comes to symbolize painful division" even among those closest to him, since even his advisors debate the wisdom of his strategy.[13] On the face of it, his strategy *does* seem unwise. King insists that white people might have to work against their own immediate interests for a greater, social good; that they would have to experience temporary pain to achieve less suffering in the future. But King's faith leads him to believe that people of all races live both deeply and shallowly, with multiple allegiances rather than a single allegiance to themselves, and with unconscious commitments to a future life as well as rudimentary concerns for the present. In Johnson's novel, King's faith is that people can change and that his advisors are wrong. He believes that after his shining the light, people could forgive themselves and one another, make a new start, and join the "beloved community."

Johnson dramatizes the alternative to King's "prophetic pragmatism" in the radical Yahya Zubena's complete absence of faith. Matthew and Amy return to Chicago to attend a lecture given by Zubena at the Black People's Liberation Library. As Nash points out, Zubena is probably based on Eldridge Cleaver, and Nash is surely correct when he writes that Johnson "makes that mouthpiece morally repugnant and intellectually limited."[14] Zubena's is indeed a debased "pragmatism." In his lecture, Zubena points to a map of Chicago and, demarcating the areas where African Americans live, he claims that segregation is actually a plot to "contain" the race in case of race war: "Being concentrated like that means when y'all start rebelling against your miserable conditions . . . all Charlie's got to do is move his tanks and trucks and National Guard troops right down the freeways and Illinois Central tracks to your front door" (172). Zubena requires retaliation. Matthew, ever the optimist, dismisses Zubena's polemic of hate as "*kitsch*. Revolutionary *kitsch*" (174).

Yet in the mid-1960s, Zubena's diatribe could not have been so glibly dismissed, and Johnson encourages readers to exercise their historical imagination and evoke the 1960s. This was a period, after all, when African American children were blown up in churches and civil rights leaders like Medgar Evers were shot in the back late at night as they walked to their front door. In this terrifying time, it certainly was not so obvious that Zubena's call for violent, armed resistance is "kitsch"; in fact, it could have been a provisional "truth." Johnson makes this interpretation of Zubena possible by showing that it was shared in its time; he grounds the scene in African American literature of the 1960s, implying that Zubena's political accusations were plausible on some level. As Matthew enters the outer room to hear Zubena's lecture, he notices "a row of works by Chester Himes" (170), an allusion to Himes's novels published during the 1960s about race wars (for example, *Blind Man with a Pistol* and the posthumously published *Plan B*). And Zubena's seemingly paranoiac conviction of African Americans held in concentration camps is an allusion to the genocidal "King Alfred Plan" in John A. Williams's hugely successful novel *The Man Who Cried I Am* (1967). Zubena, then, makes a case that may seem outrageous for a 1998 reader, but that during the 1960s was not entirely unbelievable.

Johnson encourages the reader to ask, what is the fruit of Zubena's violent philosophy as opposed to King's nonviolent demonstrations? Thankfully, through the efforts of King and people like him, the bloodshed and suffering of a race war were averted; Johnson's novel emphasizes King's struggle against not only racist whites, but also violently militant blacks. Nevertheless, in essays Johnson reminds us of the legacy of Zubena's absence of faith. In "The King We Left Behind," Johnson argues that radicals of the 1960s represented by Zubena (such as Cleaver, Huey Newton, and Malcolm X) "are the true spiritual fathers of today's Crips and Bloods."[15] And in *Turning the Wheel,* Johnson (employing specifically the terminology of pragmatism) asserts the immorality of a lack of vision: "*the social payoff* of this grim perception [of victimization], particularly when it smothers all others in a fiction (or life), is . . . immoral. We are responsible for the way the world appears before us, for its depth and richness (if we are open to others) or its poverty (if we are not), and for the impact our vision has on others" (emphasis mine).[16] Zubena lacks faith and a vision of a life worth living. In contrast, Johnson's King (and the historical King too) lives in faith. Sensing his life might soon end, King chooses Christ, who walked before him, suffering for the sake of righteousness, justice, and love. Johnson's novel vividly presents King's example to us, and the force of his writing makes obligatory our love for others. Johnson lets us understand that it is our shame that during these three decades, we have let King down. But Johnson reminds us that each moment we have an opportunity to garner the "social payoff" of spiritual change; that justice and equality are superior to any immediate profit; that love is stronger than death.

Chaym and the "Drum Major Instinct": The Desire to Be First in *Dreamer*

In *Dreamer,* Johnson shows that employing a syncretistic combination of Buddhism and Judeo-Christian principles can create King's "beloved community" (235). As Whalen-Bridges writes, "Neither a strictly Christian nor a strictly Buddhist interpretation of the novel will work."[17] But King's goal of mutuality is continually frustrated by a vision of life as competition, what King calls the "drum major instinct—a desire to be out front, a desire to lead the parade, a desire to be first" (234). Chaym most clearly embodies this instinct, though it is not entirely absent in any of the characters. Chaym is designed as King's mirror, his doppelgänger, and on a narrative level, Johnson balances the two characters. Even though he bears a twinlike resemblance to King, he is, in Matthew's words, "the kind of Negro the Movement had for years kept away from the world's cameras: sullen, ill-kept, the very embodiment of the blues" (33). Most obviously, Chaym violates the Buddhist doctrine of ahimsa, "noninjury to everything that exists" (108), while King cannot bring himself to kill even the roaches that infest his Chicago apartment. Chaym is a thief, an arsonist, and possibly a murderer, while King consistently acts benevolently. Chaym's impoverished background opposes King's relatively comfortable, middle-class upbringing. Chaym's understanding of Eastern philosophy and background in Zen Buddhism balances King's immersion in Western philosophy and his Christian faith. Both characters are to a differing extent game players. Chaym, however, is lost within his own game playing.

It is ironic that Chaym's game is played out in the very arena he pretends to reject: American society. Chaym more than anything wishes to have what he believes King enjoys: "*Immortality*" (43). By "immortality," Chaym does not mean heaven, nor even the nirvana he studied in Zen. By stipulating *King's* "immortality," he means his national and international fame; Chaym wants to be the greatest celebrity in America's celebrity culture, as he perceives King to be. Chaym's burning desire "to be first" discloses the depth of his spiritual illness, his entrapment in a cycle of corporately created illusions. His orbit around a substantialized self expresses itself brutally in his imagined zero-sum game with King, a game that he can win if King will lose: "I can do anything *he* does. Just watch me—and I'll fucking do it better" (112). The illusion that one individual can be "immortal," even be more important than another, depends on the belief that fame itself is a reality. When we see King's life from his own perspective, in the novel's italicized chapters, we understand the very real problems that King confronted: weariness, physical discomfort, fear, guilt, disappointment, homesickness, sleeplessness, pain, disillusionment, exhaustion. Being a celebrity is not enviable in this book, and King's own personal troubles, which Chaym cannot imagine, are vividly conveyed to the reader.

But Chaym has uncritically adopted the generally accepted view of King as a transcendent person, impervious to human frailties. Chaym's delusion regarding King is strengthened through his interactions with those who should know better—those close to King, like Amy and Matthew. They too fail to understand King's inner turbulence, and that he is subject to human, negative emotions. No one seems to realize that King is a "rebel messiah" (125), and the novel presents his Gethsemane experience, his "midnight in the soul" (23). Instead of feeling compassion for King, Chaym perceives him only as an opponent. Thus, Chaym's own set of illusions are constantly reinforced by his few glimpses of King and the limited awareness of others, but also by the assumptions of an American culture that elevates famous people like King. Johnson's allusion to *The Great Gatsby* emphasizes that Chaym thinks he can change himself with values from the very culture he wants to escape. For Chaym, real life is always in the future—"a day of redemption that forever receded like the horizon" (63).

The corollary of King's personal fame, within the context of Chaym's rigid dualism, is all other people's degradation and subjugation. For Chaym, any African American besides him can fill that designation, since Chaym himself feels a great sense of pride. He adopts a Hobbesian worldview that in his own mind justifies his criminality: "There's two kinds of people in this world. Predators and prey. Lions and *lunch*. You see it any other way, buddy, and people will chump you off" (55). Concealed in this bleak assessment is Chaym's own self-exultation. He really believes that he is the roaring lion, "king" of beasts, and his sense of innate superiority accompanies his denigration of other African Americans. It is in the context of Chaym's own pride that his derogation of African Americans must be understood:

"You got to remember that nobody on earth likes Negroes. Not even Negroes. We're outcasts. And outcasts can't never create a community. . . . You ever thought we might be second-class citizens because generally we *are* second-rate? . . . We don't count for shit" (65–66).

Chaym's dualistic vision of lions and lunch, winners and losers, insiders and outcasts underscores his inability to envisage his world in a lucid, rational manner and accept King's own social role without evaluating it next to his own. From Chaym's dualistic perspective, King's public triumphs mean only his own (unnoticed) personal defeat. This is made specifically poignant when Chaym thinks that he is to speak as King's double at a church function. But King speaks, and Chaym's humiliation occurs when he watches King embraced by his parishioners:

Smith watched with perfect, everyman impotence and awe the love and admiration showered on his famous twin, seeing the Good but powerless to be it, lost in his littleness, and to me it seemed King's double was undergoing a kind of living death in the great man's presence, despite his intense training and desire to be remembered by God. Obviously, His children did not see Chaym in the shadows. Nor, I thought, would they ever. (142)

As Whalen-Bridge writes, "Smith's vanity is pierced by King's brilliantly unself-conscious self-presentation."[18] For Johnson, being "in the shadows" is not the worst condition, since if viewed objectively, good work is often accomplished "in the shadows." But Chaym above all wants to be seen, and because "His children" did not see him, Chaym undergoes "a kind of living death" because he is not "first."

Because he cannot liberate himself from "the drum major instinct," even his virtuous actions are tinged with self-regard. As is typical for a Johnson character, Chaym's attempt to reform comes after a brush with death. After he is wounded by a deranged assassin who mistakes him for King, he recovers physically by studying King's sermons. Like Andrew in *Oxherding Tale*, Chaym begins his self-reformation with the help of an ethical model, King as presented in his sermons. This new meditation allows Chaym's renewal of interest in "everyday things that had no scribe" (154)—always a sign of emerging spiritual health in Johnson. When Chaym seeks diversion at the Bethel A.M.E. Church, he is assigned to tend a cemetery garden, where "names and dates for the dead . . . were all but obliterated" (160). However, the memento mori theme implied by the setting is not entirely grasped by Smith, though he works at enlightenment.[19] Although Smith asks for no wages, his labor is deceptive because it is not performed in the proper frame of mind. From a Buddhist perspective, he lacks mindfulness; that is, he cannot get his ego out of the way. Matthew notes that "*he* was doing this to work out his own demons" (160). Because Chaym is not liberated from his own craving and self-regard, he cannot achieve mindfulness at the moment he performs his work. It comes as no surprise, then, when Chaym agrees, under the threat of imprisonment, to cooperate with the FBI in their conspiracy against King. Chaym exchanges true, spiritual liberation for a comfortable apartment, a new suit of clothes, a "fat wallet" (212), and the false sense of freedom outside of prison. "I don't have much choice," he tells Matthew (213).

Chaym *does* have a choice, and his belief that his choice is determined is a result of misunderstanding both the Judeo-Christian and Buddhist notions of freedom. His ignorance is exposed in his remark to Bishop, when threatened with imprisonment for his past crimes: "It's just a li'l karma catching up with me, I guess. Check your Deuteronomy 32:35" (206). Chaym misinterprets both the concept of karma and the scriptural verse. Chaym conceives of karma as a mechanistic system of cause and effect, an almost materialistic accounting of human action where he is certain to suffer rigid retribution for his past. This is a misunderstanding of karma, in that Chaym dualistically opposes freedom to obedient submission. Karma is not an implacable determinism. As Dale S. Wright writes, karma "makes freedom both possible and available" by pointing to an obedience to a greater good, "the communal context . . . socially ordained ideals and projects."[20] Only within the restraint offered by "the communal context," Wright shows, is freedom possible. Chaym has the opportunity to submit himself to "socially ordained ideals and projects"—King's movement. But he chooses not to. As a human being, Chaym has the opportunity to interrupt karmic direction and alter his life situation. In a similar manner, Chaym misreads the passage from Deuteronomy 32:35. The Bible verse reads, "To me belongeth vengeance, and recompence; their foot shall slide in due time: for the day of their calamity is at hand, and the things that shall come upon them make haste." In the verse, a favorite of Jonathan Edwards, Jehovah claims the right of vengeance for Himself, but the FBI agents are usurping this divine prerogative in Chaym's case. In his misunderstanding, Chaym preoccupies himself with his own past, and he thereby denies himself the freedom to choose in the present moment. And so Chaym disappears into "everywhere," as Matthew tells Amy (236). Yet he had the opportunity to change his life, and in the novel, he very nearly did; in Chaym, Johnson reminds the reader that anyone, even a recidivistic criminal, may reform. Thus, human beings can never give up hope for each other.

"God's Athlete": Martin Luther King Jr. as the American Bodhisattva

For Martin Luther King Jr. the present moment is filled with opportunities to do good, from sparing the cockroaches in his dingy hotel room, to accommodating the stewardess who asks him to autograph forty copies of his book. These good acts flow from his character naturally, for we sense that he has made virtue a part of his ordinary life. He does not seek escape, autonomy, or triumphant self-creation, as his double, Chaym, does. His triumph is not really a triumph of principle, but of clear perception, unclouded by craving and preconceived, self-important assumptions. King lives in his day-to-day existence what Chaym cannot achieve: the freedom to deal mindfully with the simple activities of life. He, unlike Chaym, grows to see the world clearly, apart from what he wishes it were. This attainment, however, is expressed in a paradox: King's arduous quest brings nothing that he did not previously have before his quest began. What he experiences from his enlightenment is something from which he was never separated—his family, friends, work, his national purpose.

King's movement toward enlightenment is not easy, however. The novel's primary aesthetic problem is to avoid sentimentalizing King, to avoid "the curse of canonization."[21] To make King's persona heroic would detract from the novel's theme of the fundamental equality of all people. Also, King has become a manipulated political commodity. Throughout the 1990s, the complexity of his social legacy and his prophetic ministry has been oversimplified and in some cases deliberately distorted by those opposed to racial progress.[22] Johnson's narrative dilemma is to preserve King's radical, courageously proclaimed critique of America's social order, while simultaneous dramatizing King's struggles as a human being. Sentimentality is avoided as Johnson recreates King's inner life. In the interwoven italicized chapters, the reader sees not history's hero, but an anxious, doubtful, soul-weary human being. He grimly thinks of his life as *"suicide on the installment plan"* (187) as he wrestles with the terrible price he must pay for his activism. Unknown to the other characters in the novel, Johnson's private King recapitulates in his thoughts their same sense of an injured soul, their common sorrow.

Like these characters, King is a player. With King, Johnson varies the motif of competition, since King wishes "to be first in love . . . first in moral excellence" (234). Accordingly, his "game" has high stakes. As he reflects on his trip to Chicago, King thinks, *"If they could triumph here . . . then they could conquer any citadel of inequality in the world"* (16). When he enters Chicago he discovers that his competition has many fronts, and he nearly experiences an emotional implosion. Suddenly, everyone seems to be against him, and King realizes that *"no one thought he could win"* (16). Not only does he face the political sophistication of Chicago's Mayor Richard Daley, but he must also contend with the vanities of other ministers in his own SCLC; the potential betrayal of the radical Black Panthers, CORE, and SNCC; and the resentment and skepticism of Chicago's African Americans, long used to racism's urban rituals and the betrayals of their nation. In the North, he begins to wonder if the game is worth the playing. Suddenly, he is tired of being *"God's athlete"* (14). He wishes he could escape to the comfort and safety of his family, "*his beautiful wife and four children*" (20)—in Johnson's past novels, the family being the idealized refuge and primary source of value. But such a refuge is not available to King. He thinks of himself trapped in American history, "*a nightmare in the mind of some devil who could not roll himself awake*" (82). King's sense of his lost freedom parallels Chaym's own: "*He felt caged. Chained. In bondage and no longer belonging to himself*" (81). As with Jesus in Gethsemane, it is no wonder that King wishes this cup to be passed from him.

Paradoxically for such a public figure, the resolution of King's narrative occurs entirely within King's consciousness. Only the reader recognizes the change King undergoes, presented in a series of interpolated, italicized chapters reflecting King's inner turmoil. King's thoughts resemble both Judeo-Christian and Buddhist contemplation, wherein through prayer or meditation the person arrives at a resolution or spiritual breakthrough. King achieves five distinct resolutions. Though they are interwoven, each resolution depends dramatically on the preceding one. In this way, Johnson distinguishes King from the other characters. Though they may struggle with the same existential conflicts, his engagement occurs at a much deeper, more philosophical level.

The resolutions are arranged in an ascending scale of complexity. First, after acknowledging the vast inequality in America, King explicitly endorses a Lockean view of the social contract: "*The least advantaged had every right to break the social contract that had so miserably failed to meet their needs. They would rebel, riot as they were doing now in Chicago*" (50). In this way, King expresses his compassion for those unlike him, who are inarticulate, poor, desolate, and forgotten.

They find no other way, King realizes, but to "rebel, riot" to protest injustice. Unlike either Chaym or Matthew, King does not stand in judgment of rioters in the street; nor does he hate or fear them. Instead, he empathizes with them.

King's second resolution is an elaboration of his first. He resolves that because "*Race was an illusion, all children were literally—genetically—their own,*" segregation laws must be "*torn down*" (84). The argument that race is illusory is a familiar theme in Johnson's work, but in this instance he elaborates his idea within a political activist discourse. To obey segregationist laws founded on the unreality of race simply because these laws were in place would make of law an immutable fixture, elevated above human welfare. What, King asks himself, is the purpose of law? What human ends do laws pragmatically serve? Paradoxically, King concludes, laws are instituted only to extend and preserve human freedom; good laws create freedom. Bad laws, on the contrary, make people "mental and spiritual slave[s]" (67). In this manner, King reveals that he understands freedom in a much deeper and more impersonal way than either Chaym or Matthew, who want to restrict freedom's meaning to doing and having what they would like. King's more nuanced conception of freedom brings with it a terrific sense of responsibility to the wider community and to the nation itself. If he is free to break a bad law, this disobedience must occur within a context of total mindfulness; otherwise, the self would get in the way. So it is that King's third resolution places civil disobedience within a purely religious, ecumenical context, as a spiritual consequence of the first two resolutions. He thinks, "*The challenge of the spiritual was simply this: to be good, truly moral, and in control of oneself for this moment only*" (196)—to live, in Buddhist terms, mindfully in the "Now." In this fourth meditation,

Johnson's King narratively translates religious faith into political principles.

Perhaps King's final inner resolution is the most complex of all. In this resolution, he renounces life as game. Accompanying King's resolution, however, is an emotional state that others find difficult to understand. Just as, from Johnson's perspective, the end of the historical King's life may have been misunderstood by King's biographers, Johnson's King is misinterpreted by the novel's characters.[23] This distortion is reflected by Matthew, who wants to preserve his idealization of King. When Daley meets King in Chicago's Palmer House, Daley makes the concession that "his city had not done enough." Matthew assumes that because "the mayor blinked" (151), King has "won" his competition with Mayor Daley. This optimistic assessment is certainly debatable, both in the novel and historically, and Matthew's sanguine view is challenged by other characters, including King himself. Because the conclusion of King's Chicago campaign is dubious, other characters can offer a negative view of King. This analysis comes from his worst enemies, however. The FBI agents, Groat and Withersby, tell Chaym and Matthew that because of his travail in Chicago, King has simply lost his faith. King, they explain, has undergone a personality transformation; he suffers "despair, fits of depression" (198) because "damn near every hand is turned against this man" (200). "He's over the edge" (200) is their succinct diagnosis of King.

On the surface this interpretation seems corroborated. King tells Ralph Abernathy:

Nonviolence as a way of life may be asking too much of people. Maybe it goes against the grain of something tribal in our genes. Or against the ego. Or the carnal mind, which can only perceive in terms of polarities. . . . But the apes, black, and white, are out there. And their goal is to make the world a jungle. I say, let them kill each other and tear it all down, then God-hungry men and women can make a fresh start. (223)

What the FBI agents (and King's biographers) term "depression," however, is for Johnson the final stage of Buddhist enlightenment. For Johnson, the diagnosis of King's psychopathology in his final days is an epistemological misunderstanding, since it assumes the dualism of winners and losers repudiated by the novel and by King himself. Throughout the novel, King has struggled as "God's athlete," attempting to win a game of social justice that cannot be won definitively, permanently, or conclusively. King accepts this hard lesson that Johnson conveys in the essay "A Sangha by Another Name." In the essay, Johnson warns against the utopian hope that the struggle for justice can ever be complete; he admonishes citizens not to project themselves magically into a wonderful "tomorrow that never comes." Instead, Johnson recommends in the article an alertness to the creative potentiality of every moment, "no matter how humble the activity."[24]

King is Johnson's consummate symbol of Buddhist mindfulness as he accepts the world's bitter divisions. The limitations of his action lie not in him, King comes to realize, but in the nature of the world. Like Rutherford on the *Republic*, King accepts that he cannot transform the world by himself. If King feels "*trapped . . . stuck in a hole*" (223), it is now not because of his inadequacies, but because the world itself is "*a cradle-to-crypt dream, in which all men were caught and only the blessed allowed to awaken*" (224). And awaken King does. The "depression" perceived by others is in actuality his final renunciation of self, his willingness to forego the competition and—in Johnson's deeply moving phrasing—accept "*a fuller, deeper, and more perfectly realized broken heart*" (225) by knowing that despite his best, most dedicated efforts, injustice will continue.[25] King accepts that he will never usher in the City of God, but this does not mean for him that his career has been a failure. King continues with his routine, his daily life—checking out of his hotel, calling his wife, meeting the press, boarding a plane—and in this attention to the mundane and ordinary, he spiritually renews his commitment to social justice.

He now understands that any one particular choice (and all are important) is a result of a holistic process in which he and the entire nation choose second by second. He accepts the world's emptiness: the idea that all things are converging in an instant of time and will inevitably change. He alone cannot change the direction of history, but he has unconditional faith in the process itself. He has renounced the game that declares winners and losers in an unequivocal manner. Johnson's King has ended his "clinging" to a world inherently and inevitably disappointing: he recovers from his suffering, described by the word he remembers from India, "dukkha" (224). This release is the most "*comfortable position*" (224) that he could possibly take, and in this Gethsemane experience, King goes to his eventual crucifixion with a profoundly Buddhist enlightenment.

Being a "Good Prop": Matthew, Standing in the Shadows

King's enlightenment is replayed in a minor chord by Matthew's own awakening. Although Matthew does not engage in King's profound philosophical struggle, Matthew also confronts his own problems of belief. Closely related to Matthew's plot is his loss of belief in Christianity. Despite bearing an apostle's name, Matthew has abandoned his Christian faith, just as Chaym is alienated from Buddhism. Matthew's apostasy occurs with the death of his mother. Before her death, he was a faithful Christian, but his faith evaporates with his tears when she dies. As she lies on her deathbed, he prays for her life:

> I'd prayed. Bent over her . . . I begged the god she'd given me
> when I was a child to return to me whole the only person in
> this world who'd cared if I lived or died, but He did not
> accept the offering of my tears, and she was taken from me,
> I was orphaned, and whatever flame of faith she'd nurtured
> in me flimmered out forever (149).

Once again in Johnson's work, the extinguished flame as an image of nirvana is used ironically. Because he wishes he could regain his faith, Matthew clings to conventional Christianity as if it were magic. Carrying the Bible "as a kind of talisman for times of trouble" (54), he nevertheless has little faith that this "talisman" will provide any kind of safeguard or guidance. He is (like Faith, Andrew, and Rutherford) spiritually adrift.

Chaym reveals Matthew's character when he tells Matthew, "You want to be among the anointed, the blessed—to *belong*" (65). Significantly studying Nietzsche when he meets King, Matthew represents the secular, postmodernist person, suffering from a life (he thinks) not worth living.[26] Symbolically and literally an orphan, Matthew's burden is his overwhelming sense of shame. Matthew has no father, and he (unlike King) has made little of his life, since he has dropped out of college. He tries to relieve this shame by adopting a surrogate father, King, but even

King cannot relieve Matthew of his pervasive sense of worthlessness. Though he acts as the movement's historian, he has little satisfaction from this role; it simply, he feels, makes him a "good prop" (165). Like Chaym, Matthew cannot tolerate standing in the shadows: "I blended easily into the background, as bland and undistinguished as a piece of furniture, so anonymous most people forgot I was there" (25). Viewed objectively, Matthew's position as chronicler of one of the century's most important social movements should endow his life with purpose and meaning. But because he wants more recognition and praise than his own position could bring him, he is only diminished in his mind.

Matthew desperately wishes for an important identity. This he suddenly receives with King's instructions regarding Chaym: "I want you to work with him. Get him back on his feet. Help him understand what the Movement's about—and have him sign the Commitment Blank" (42). But Matthew reshapes King's words to make them conform to his desire for importance. After King's meeting with Chaym, Matthew eagerly takes charge of Chaym, assuring him that King "thinks you might be able to help" (43), though King had said only that he would like to help Chaym, not that he expects Chaym to help him. Indeed, it is clear that King is encouraging Matthew to "be first in generosity" (234). Matthew, not King, decides King needs a body double, and since Chaym looks very much like King, Matthew is naively confident that Chaym can be King's substitute: "I began to feel that, for all his exasperating qualities, perhaps he could stand in for King" (86). Although King apparently does request later that Chaym stand in for him at a church function (a request that King apparently rescinds), Matthew misinterprets King's words to create a hubristic challenge: to remake another human being.

Matthew's self-deception in manipulating Chaym (and King too) is not for his own material benefit. He expects neither monetary payment nor fame (as does Chaym) in "working with" Chaym, and he hopes his efforts will redound for King's and the movement's benefit. Nevertheless, he cannot honestly examine his own self-serving motives for this project. Like Chaym, Matthew follows the "drum major instinct" and wants to be an important "player" in the civil rights game. Matthew embarks on his goal with considerable dedication and redoubled discipline. If he succeeds in reforming Chaym to fulfill this mission—"a task so impossible that the thought of it kept my Protestant stomach perpetually cramped, knotted, and queasy" (64)—he would in his own imagination be heroic, as King (Matthew believes) is heroic. A measure of Matthew's pride reveals itself when he criticizes King because King does not avail himself of Chaym's and Matthew's services: "I felt his decision to keep us on the sidelines was a tactical error" (116).

Matthew's self-created mission is hopeless, for his project stunts rather than enlarges his life. Matthew becomes even more the victim of anxiety than he was previously, with his knotted and cramped stomach, particularly since he now makes himself responsible for Chaym's safe passage through life; he must control not only Chaym but the world also. It is now Matthew's self-assumed responsibility to ensure nothing happens to Chaym, though Matthew quickly learns he cannot command circumstances. The attempted murder of Chaym foils his plans. Ironically playing King's role while *not* in the public eye (when Chaym supposes it is not necessary), Chaym offers a seemingly harmless old man a ride. The old man is in fact mentally deranged, and mistaking Chaym for King, blames him for all his troubles. He fires his gun wildly at Chaym, wounding him. The attempted murder is presented by Johnson as a random, chaotic absurdity. Chaym, pretending benevolence toward another person but feeling none, is almost killed by Chaym's own double —an alienated, bitter, chronically enraged outcast, who (like Chaym) lives in a depressed urban wasteland, with "the stain of industrial smoke and soot spread across broken windows, broken doors, and broken walls scrawled with the graffiti of street gangs" (146).

Matthew's narrative does not linger on the old man's desolate social condition, even though reflection on this old man's desperate poverty and degraded living conditions might help Matthew understand more clearly the movement's humanistic goals. Instead, his thoughts shift immediately to himself. Though he attempted to dissuade Chaym from offering the old man a ride, Matthew nevertheless feels overwhelming guilt for somehow causing the incident: "If he died, it was my doing" (149). His harsh and unreasonable self-criticism—"I'd frozen, paralyzed by my own fear"—almost makes him, not the old man, responsible for the attack. Ironically, Matthew has a model for how to react in this kind of crisis: Martin Luther King Jr. Johnson makes the comparison explicit when Matthew remembers Izola Ware Curry, who stabbed King in 1958. Although King was almost killed in Curry's attack, he responded to Curry with generosity, empathy, and compassion. He said, "Don't do anything to her; don't prosecute her; get her healed."[27] King, in contrast to Chaym and Matthew, can see beyond his own situation and feel compassion for suffering human beings.

When Matthew is not feeling guilty for not accomplishing his project, he feels anger toward Chaym for not progressing as expeditiously as Matthew wishes. Describing Chaym as "wicked" satisfies Matthew's dualistic moral calculus. However,

Matthew's observation of Chaym's fallen nature is complicated by a growing sense of psychological identification with Chaym, a process that begins when Matthew first meets him: "Smith looked straight at me, flashing that ironical, almost erotic smirk again, as if somehow we were co-conspirators, or maybe he knew something scandalous about me" (35). This ironic fellowship is confirmed later, when Chaym tells Matthew that "you like most of the rest of us. Brothers, I mean" (65).

Part of the test of Matthew's character is to discover that he is not in fact unique, but that he does bear a brotherly relationship with Chaym, whom he initially scorns. Chaym, Matthew wants to believe, is his opposite: while Matthew is thoughtful and quiet, Chaym is brutal and swaggering. But Matthew discovers his own capacity for violence that dissolves this insistence on his uniqueness. This moment occurs when Matthew suffers a racial insult from a waitress at a cheap diner. When Matthew pays his bill, the racist, ignorant waitress, Arlene, refuses to touch his skin, instead placing his change on the counter. Just as Chaym would do, he responds with unthinking violence:

> Something inside me (I don't know what) snapped (I don't know how), flooding me with a hatred so hot, like a drug, I was nearly blinded by it as I threw the food in her face, hurled from the counter sugar canisters and ketchup bottles smashing against the wall behind the grill, screaming so loud and long my glasses streamed. (73)

Matthew's reaction to his outburst, an atypical exhilaration and joy, inspires him to look more closely at himself and his act. He remembers his "sad but stoic" mother (72), who in a similar circumstance accepts a waitress's humiliating treatment so that she can feed him, her small son; Matthew's mother withheld her anger to achieve a greater purpose. His mother, long before King's movement, had intuited exactly what King exhorts his followers to do in the ugly face of injustice. As Nash writes, his mother's "unwillingness to submit, either to oppression or to bitterness, embodies the resilience that all of the chosen in the novel share."[28] In his attack on the waitress, Matthew senses that he has failed "the minister, my mother, myself " (74).

This scene also has a literary context, for in it Johnson pays homage to James Baldwin's powerful restaurant scene in *Notes of a Native Son*. This episode, the reader infers, was one of many that finally led to Baldwin's expatriation to France, and it is politically significant that Baldwin narrates it against the backdrop of the racial riots in Harlem that occurred shortly after the incident. Baldwin tells of how he, furious at the treatment of racists, enters a diner in New York, knowing that Jim Crow restrictions will lead to denying him service. When the waitress predictably tells him to leave, he feels rage, "a kind of blind fever, a pounding in the skull and fire in the bowels." Like Matthew, Baldwin is overcome by his rage "to strike from a distance," and he throws a water glass at her, which misses her and smashes against a mirror; then he quickly leaves the restaurant, pursued by the other (white) patrons. In this incident, Baldwin sees his action as wholly determined by circumstance, since an African American "has the choice, merely, of living with [rage] consciously or surrendering to it."[29]

Writing almost fifty years after Baldwin's essay, Johnson understands (as any reader must) Baldwin's emotional situation, but he revisits Baldwin's stark choice between total acceptance of or total surrender to rage. Is there another, unimagined alternative? In answering the question, Johnson explores the pragmatic effect of a rageful response to racial injustice. Certainly Arlene's behavior is outrageous, a violation of every American ideal. But while Baldwin sees his act as essential to his own emotional harmony, Johnson is more circumspect in depicting Matthew's behavior. Lashing out at ignorance does not bring any social change, nor (in the long run) does it make Matthew feel better. Indeed, Johnson implies that violence damages Matthew's spirit. Matthew senses the psychological damage done to him, ensnaring him more firmly in a karmic cycle of aggression and retaliation. As Matthew gazes at his skinned knuckles and scratched arm, he understands the situation's ambiguity: "I'd injured myself quite as much as I'd wasted the Pit Stop" (86). The vernacular use of "wasted" has a double meaning; unleashing violence at such an unworthy target is indeed a waste—accomplishing nothing but a momentary satisfaction, soon replaced by his gnawing dissatisfaction. Indeed, Arlene, Johnson implies, only acts out of ignorance and herself is susceptible to moral reform. Her behavior earlier toward both Chaym and Matthew confirms the reader's sense that even the most ignorant racist may change. Thinking Chaym is King, she is willing to serve them despite the restaurant's Jim Crow policy, and she even considers asking Chaym/King for his autograph.

Matthew's final test occurs when he realizes that he has failed in his efforts to reform Chaym. Matthew discovers the way to avoid his sense of loss is not through greater effort to change Chaym, but—paradoxically—through "letting go." Chaym seems willing to go along with the undisclosed FBI plot against King. When Chaym departs with the agents, Matthew's first response is clichéd: he drowns his sorrow in beer and feels betrayed, a repetition of his earlier tendency toward self-pity and self-righteous resentment. But after undergoing *his* dark night of the soul, he drives the next morning to Bethel A.M.E., the church where he and Chaym had worked earlier. While in the church, he meditates (as King does in the subsequent chapter), and (like King's) his meditation combines Christian and Buddhist practice. As Matthew sits in a pew, he focuses on two portraits of the Crucifixion story: one mirroring King's situation, of Jesus in the Garden of Gethsemane; the other, reflecting symbolically Matthew's situation—"Simon the Cyrene, an African, [who] carried to Golgotha the heavy wooden cross" (211). Finally mindful, Matthew concentrates on the image of Simon:

> A black man from the most despised tribe on earth given the priceless gift of easing the suffering of a savior. In that scene, he was an extra. On stage for but a sentence in Matthew 27:32. . . . Simon blended anonymously—invisibly—back into the wailing crowd. Outside history. I felt I knew him. Was him. (212)

Matthew's imaginative identification with Simon the Cyrene, a mere "extra" in the Passion story, releases him from the enormous responsibility that he has hitherto borne. Further, in understanding that Simon, unknown to history, also played an important part, Matthew can let go of his preconceived idea of a unique identity. He realizes that he shares qualities with one of no status, who worked humbly "in the shadows," but who went before him over two thousand years ago. Matthew can finally accept himself as an "invisible man" with equanimity.

When Chaym visits him the final time and asks Matthew for his prayers, Matthew prays, but "Not for myself as I'd always done, but instead for those I loved" (214). Significantly, he now loves Chaym, the despised one.[30] With that selfless prayer, he at last experiences his epiphany, and releases his feeble hold on the world: "I felt emptied, no longer trying to bring a distant God's grace to my finite desires as His cast-aside son, but only wishing *Thy will be done*" (214). Matthew's sensed emptiness provides the thematic counterpoint to Chaym's belief, noted earlier, that "there's nothing underneath. . . . Just emptiness" (86). The emptiness that Matthew now knows is both Buddhist (sunyata) and Christian (kenosis).

Matthew's enlightenment is highly personalized. His experience is shared by others in the novel, however. Mama Pearl, Robert Jackson, and other parishioners in the novel embody the novel's moral ideal unself-consciously. As Nash suggests, Johnson "is telling his personal history" in recounting the work of African Americans in southern Illinois. As Nash explains, Robert Jackson "closely resembles Johnson's greatuncle William, whose construction company provided the author's father, Benny Lee, the impetus to come to Chicago."[31] Beyond autobiographical significance, Matthew's liberation is also reflected in millions of unknown African Americans, all "proud, quietly pious, good people" (130). Matthew's enlightenment is a microcosm of the wider world of African Americans. Johnson's theme moves beyond his personal self-reflection to the origins of political activism in America: the Black Church. This point is conveyed in the name of Reverend Littlewood's church, Bethel A.M.E.—the name of the first African Methodist Episcopal denomination, established in 1816 by Richard Allen. Johnson emphasizes that the civil rights movement was shaped not only by famous people like King, but also by ordinary African Americans, whose unheralded commitment Johnson enshrines in the novel, now lying in shadows, in unmarked and forgotten graves throughout the South. Their courage and self-sacrifice began in the Black Church. They had the faith that "their political and racial struggles were but the backdrop against which a far greater spiritual odyssey was unfolding" (134). Although Johnson does not evade the sometimes petty, squalid competition King occasionally confronted in the church's ministers, "prayer and racial politics inseparably melded" in the Black Church. King himself was rooted there in a faith that sustained his profound love. During the 1960s, the Black Church alone offered to King and others safety "from the ravages, the irreality, the racial stupidities of the world outside" (133).

CHAPTER 7

Soulcatcher and Other Stories

As a child, I never doubted—not *once*—the crucial role my people have played since the seventeenth-century colonies in the building of America on *all* levels—the physical, cultural, economic, and political.

Charles Johnson, *Turning the Wheel*

Soulcatcher and Other Stories (2001) results from Johnson's collaboration with Patricia Smith and the WGBH Series Research Team to create the television series *Africans in America: America's Journey through Slavery*. The book companion, published in 1998, includes Johnson's twelve stories, written to accompany Smith's history, which dramatize historical events recounted in the series. Since the history covers the period from the Middle Passage up until the beginning of the Civil War, Johnson was able, as he writes in the preface, to fictionalize the "facts and historical figures essential for deepening our understanding of America's past and present."[1] The stories in *Africans in America* comprise the separately published volume *Soulcatcher*. Johnson did not change the stories, nor did he add to their number.

Johnson's stories disclose highly specific historical facts that give greater authority to the volume's historical discourse. Johnson's thorough research for the project makes vivid in precise details the oft-forgotten history of African Americans. For example, Johnson describes his African characters in "The

Transmission," about the Middle Passage, as "forced to lie on their right sides to lessen the pressure on their hearts" (8). Johnson also explains that African captives had their fingernails clipped to prevent them clawing each other in the excruciatingly tight ship's hold. However, he is not completely restrained by historical fact, and sometimes Johnson imaginatively recreates the historical events to reinforce the historical point being made in the accompanying history. In "The Mayor's Tale," for example, Johnson writes a parable, imagining the chaotic effect on America's economy if all escaped slaves, to avoid recapture after the passage of the Fugitive Slave Act in 1850, had left for Canada. If African Americans were really outside of American history as a racist may claim, the story implies, disaster would be the result. The necessity of fictionally illuminating a history text, however, has its disadvantages for Johnson's independently published volume. Occasionally the dialogue, always Johnson's strength, seems contrived, designed to illustrate a fact propounded in the history text; the narratives themselves, sometimes too short to support his complex and meditative themes fully, often seem unnecessarily truncated.

Nevertheless, this project once again demonstrates Johnson's innovative technique. As he writes, *Africans in America* "is the only history text that features fictions commissioned from a contemporary writer" (xiv–xv). The collection consists of twelve short stories that dramatize, primarily with a focus on individual contemplation and action, the events chronicled in the history text—the imagined conversation of Phillis Wheatley with her mistress; the thoughts of Frederick Douglass after his beating by racist whites in Pendleton, Indiana; Richard Allen's meditation on racism as African Americans assist Philadelphians during the yellow fever plague of 1793. Even the placement of the stories in the history text is strikingly original. They are usually featured as interchapters, but occasionally they are interpolated within the chapter itself. And in the case of "A Soldier for the Crown," which recounts the story of a cross-dressing African American fighting for the British during the Revolutionary War, Johnson's story interrupts Patricia Smith's single paragraph. In several stories, Johnson chooses as his subject the consciousness of ordinary African Americans forgotten by history, such as the terror felt by an African child during the Middle Passage, or the desolation of a captured slave rebel about to be executed after Jemmy's slave rebellion in 1739.

In the history volume, Johnson's primary purpose is to provide a sense of dramatic immediacy to the moments of American past too often omitted by mainstream historians. *Soulcatcher* also reiterates many of Johnson's themes, especially the African American artist's incommensurable purpose in the contemporary United States. Many of these stories provide a justification for Johnson's own literary career thus far: his resolute commitment to artistic originality, his repudiation of polemical art, his confidence in expressing in art an ineffable religious vision, and his sense of the divinity of the artistic mission.

"The Transmission," the collection's first story, introduces the griot who sings his own race's story—clearly a surrogate for Johnson himself, and his artistic project in *Soulcatcher*. Malawi, the story's protagonist, is a member of Johnson's Allmuseri tribe who suffers the horrors of the Middle Passage, as the Africans are "transmitted" to America for enslavement. As in the novel *Middle Passage,* Johnson frankly presents the Africans' suffering without didactic comment. Malawi is chained to the decomposing corpse of his brother, Oboto, who was the village's original griot. As Oboto died, he whispered the village's history to

Malawi, and the story ends with Malawi's "transmission" of the song to an uncomprehending but presumably receptive white crewman.

Malawi's acceptance of his new role as griot links him to his author, who has also shouldered the burden of communicating the history of African Americans to a sometimes uncomprehending audience. In the worst of circumstances, Malawi nevertheless shares his author's fundamental optimism, gained through his newfound artistic work. Malawi's recognition that he had "no time to dwell on his despair" (9) is the key to his narrative. By taking up his new vocation, he is released from his personalized suffering, for he knows that he alone is responsible for communicating the story of his race to America. But like Johnson in accentuating his own innovations, Malawi also knows that he cannot simply repeat in rote fashion the stories of the past; he understands that the African "people's chronicle was unfinished. New songs were needed. And these *he* must do" (11). African identity in America will be entirely different, Malawi seems intuitively to realize, calling for new forms and new narratives, but he understands that his heritage, though transformed, was not "wiped from the face of the world" (8). Malawi's song, then, is a symbol for Johnson's own aesthetic purpose in his career: to create a new vision of race in America, to sing an entirely new song for the hope of renewed interracial understanding and compassion.

Johnson's concern for the appreciation of the artist is repeated in his imaginary dialogue between Phillis Wheatley and her mistress, Mrs. Wheatley. Once again, the story conveys important historical information about African American history (Phillis's dialogue contains numerous allusions to her poetry), while simultaneously voicing Johnson's theories about art and politics. The story's narrative hinges on Phillis's vocational anxiety, her doubts about her own poetry that is devoid of explicit political messages. In her conversation, Phillis ruminates on her art's utility. Specifically, Phillis worries that her apolitical literary production will do "nothing to further our cause" (28): "Sometimes I wonder if my people see me—my work—as useless" (29). Phillis cannot, she admits, write convincingly about racism because she lacks emotional detachment in dealing with racism; she is more effective in composing "a hymn to morning" —a self-reflective cynosure of Johnson's "singing the world" in his own work.[2]

Mrs. Wheatley assures Phillis that explicit political commentary in a literary text is not essential, nor even in most cases praiseworthy, since what is needed most is artists who have "enriched others through their deeds" (30). Mrs. Wheatley expresses Johnson's own disdain for polemical literature:

> While a pamphlet can be valuable and stir people to action, a hundred years hence it may be forgotten—as the injustice it assails is forgotten—or it will be preserved only as a historical document, interesting for what it reveals about a moment long past, but *never* appreciated as art. I'm speaking of writing *poems* about oppression. (28)

As if to corroborate Mrs. Wheatley's scorn for "poems about oppression," Johnson ends the story with a compliment to Phillis actually sent to her by George Washington, written in response to Phillis's occasional poem on Washington's taking command of the Continental Army. The letter's conventional valediction, making Washington Phillis's "obedient, humble servant," justifies Phillis and allays her fears of inadequacy. Johnson uses

Washington's historical reputation to confirm Mrs. Wheatley's assessment of Phillis's art: "It is a noble calling, Phillis, this creating of beauty, and it is sufficient unto itself " (29).

The "noble calling" of the artist does not necessarily conflict with the historian's undertaking, and this point is made in several stories where Johnson changes the literal events of the past or imagines possible repercussions of actual events in order to convey the emotional experience of African American history. The story makes clear Johnson's idea that "history" and "fiction" are yet another false dualism, since a fiction may endow a historical moment with greater meaning than would a mere recitation of facts. In a footnote to "The People Speak," Johnson acknowledges that he has fictionalized history "in order to conjure a moment in time with feeling" (67). "The People Speak" concerns a crucial moment in African American history, "a debate on two equally powerful yet antithetical dreams within the black American soul" (68). In January 1817, African Americans gathered at A.M.E. Bethel Church in Philadelphia to debate whether people of color should emigrate to Africa. In the story, Johnson includes historical figures who were absent (for example, Paul Cuffe), and women, who were not allowed to participate. The purpose of his revision, however, is to provide to the reader a greater sense of inclusiveness in this pivotal event. The story is, to use Johnson's phrase from *Middle Passage*, a "useful fiction." The unanimous decision of ordinary African Americans to remain in America, despite the nation's racism and slavery, represents an epochal rejection of defeatism as articulated by Paul Cuffe: "No, methinks it is asking too much for both sides, theirs and ours, to live peacefully as one people" (71). If, as Reverend Allen claims, the unanimous vote indicates "which direction *all* our people will take in the future"

(72), Johnson's faith in the gradual but irresistible amelioration of race relations through American history is expressed dramatically.

"The Mayor's Tale" is written in the form of a parable that elaborates on the possible but not actual consequences of the Fugitive Slave Act of 1850. Because this legislation (as explained in *Africans in America*) provided legally for the forcible return of escaped slaves to the South, Johnson poses a theoretical question: What if, to escape southern "soulcatchers" (that is, bounty hunters), all African Americans emigrated to Canada? What would America be like without an African American presence?

In Johnson's comic tale, the mayor goes to bed one night thinking that "all was well in the world" (93), especially since his narrow, self-centered, materialistic concerns seemed satisfied. He has African American servants and employees, a big house, a well-fed family, and a good job. The mayor's complacency is a result of his misunderstanding of the world's interrelatedness, essentially based on the invisibility of African Americans who labor in his house and town: "It wasn't as if he looked for them every day. No, most of the time they blended into the background of his day" (96). Because, he believes, he is not materially affected by the passage of the Fugitive Slave Act, he need not consider its calamitous consequences for his village or his nation. But he awakens to his city where all African Americans have fled to Canada to escape their re-enslavement. Without servants and support at every level of life, "he saw chaos" (97). His chaotic situation is humorously brought home by his cold house and his angry wife, who refuses to leave her bed. At his office, he realizes his insufficiency, for his work "had taken two—perhaps three—times longer to do" (97). The tale points to a moral Johnson continually repeats: African Americans were integral to the making of American history—and, of course, still are.

"The Mayor's Tale" also reiterates Johnson's theme of mindful labor as critical for gaining enlightenment. The mayor's and his wife's incapacity relates to a Hegelian master-slave relationship. In Hegel's view, the master is ultimately reduced because his continuing dependence on his slave has denied him the moral and spiritual education inherent in labor. The slaves, in contrast, achieve individuality through their work. Work, then, serves as the indispensable condition for achieving a sense of one's place in the world, a condition that the mayor and his wife have denied themselves. The story's ending focuses on the mayor's despair, not simply because he lacks coal or the service of African American waiters, but because he has failed fundamentally to understand his world: "Hizzoner broke down and wept in the snow" (101).

Racism and its accompanying epistemological failure is also the theme of "Martha's Dilemma." Once again, Johnson employs a Hegelian depiction of the reversal of slavery, as the mother of our country feels herself imprisoned by the peculiar institution. Martha Washington must adjust to living with her slaves after George posthumously manumitted them in his will, to be effected at Martha's death. She suddenly finds herself in their lifelong predicament, her very life depending on their continued goodwill. Like the mayor, Martha has depended on her slaves obsessively throughout her life, to her own detriment: "Ironically, we were enslaved to *them,* shackled to their industry, the knowledge they'd acquired because we were too busy running the country to develop it ourselves!" (46). Martha's proclaimed self-importance is rendered comically in the story, and Johnson depicts her as a shrew bawling out her famously austere husband as a "big oaf" (43), a mere politician who was "a slow reader. A poor speller. He was a man of deeds, not ideas" (45). Through Martha's diatribe, Johnson debunks the "well meaning mythmakers who began enlarging his legend before we could properly bury him" (44). The mythmakers' stories (as opposed to Johnson's own) are "balderdash" (45).

Johnson's dismissal of phony myths as kitsch in "Martha's Dilemma" repeats his celebration of common, ordinary people working deliberately and routinely in everyday life. Although he dramatizes the lives of a few famous African Americans, such as Frederick Douglass and Reverend Richard Allen, Johnson primarily demonstrates their fame achieved through their daily labor, usually performed in mundane, ordinary circumstances. "A Lion at Pendleton" describes Douglass's charisma and his beating by a white mob in Pendleton, Indiana. But the primary focus of the story is Douglass's commitment to his work to end slavery, his willingness to labor unstintingly for the cause: "he had not rested. Nor had he wanted to. How could his spirit sleep as long as a single black man or woman was in chains?" (89). The story's climax is not a famous speech by Douglass, but Douglass climbing back on his horse, off to yet another meeting. Johnson's celebration of work is repeated in "The Plague," where Reverend Allen works steadily for months to relieve the suffering in Philadelphia, preaches five sermons per day, but is rewarded only by "lily-white faces glaring . . . through the windows, twisted lips drawn down in distrust" (57). Neither Douglass nor Allen can realistically envisage an earthly reward—the abolition of slavery—and instead they must see themselves as working for the future, themselves as "a conduit, an anonymous instrument through which the music of our Lord and Savior bursts forth" (52).

Work at mundane tasks, as is typical in his fiction, carries a supreme thematic importance for Johnson. The ordinary work of unknown, unheralded people—like the African Americans the history book immortalizes—choosing moment by moment, day by day, may lead America to a more socially just nation. Johnson demonstrates that he plays a part in that vision. Like Tiberius, the captured slave rebel in "Confession," Johnson's readers may awaken to a new, enlightened reality—one that they too may help create:

> Everythin' looked *changed* after he spoke. Like I'd lived alla my life in a cave, believin' the shadows I seen were real. . . . I felt like a sleeper. A man who'd been dreamin' his whole life. But Jemmy woke me hup. (19)

It is Johnson's task as a literary bodhisattva to wake us "hup."

Notes

Chapter 1—Understanding Charles Johnson

1. Ken McCullough, "Reflections on Film, Philosophy, and Fiction: An Interview with Charles Johnson," *Callaloo* 1, no. 4 (1978): 127.

2. Stanley Cavell, *In Quest of the Ordinary: Lines of Skepticism and Romanticism* (Chicago: University of Chicago Press, 1988), 6, 71.

3. Johnson, "I Call Myself an Artist," in *I Call Myself an Artist: Writings by and about Charles Johnson,* ed. Rudolph P. Byrd (Bloomington: Indiana University Press, 1999), 5.

4. Johnson, "I Call Myself an Artist," 4.

5. William R. Nash, "A Conversation with Charles Johnson," *New England Review* 19, no. 2 (1998): 50.

6. Johnson and John McCluskey Jr., *Black Men Speaking* (Bloomington: Indiana University Press), 179–80.

7. Nash, "A Conversation with Charles Johnson," 49.

8. Charles H. Rowell, "An Interview with Charles Johnson," *Callaloo* 20, no. 3 (1998): 533.

9. Johnson, "I Call Myself an Artist," 23.

10. Johnson, *Being and Race: Black Writing since 1970* (Bloomington: Indiana University Press, 1988), 50.

11. I wish to thank John Whalen-Bridge for biographical information on Johnson.

12. In the last half-century, English-language books on Buddhism have burgeoned. If the reader wishes to consult references on Buddhism, he or she might begin with Heinrich Dumoulin's magisterial *Zen Buddhism: A History* (New York: Macmillan, 1988); *The Three Pillars of Zen: Teaching, Practice, and Enlightenment,* ed. Philip Kapleau (New York: Doubleday, 1989); and *Zen Flesh, Zen Bones: A Collection of Zen and Pre-Zen Writings,* comp. Paul Reps

(Rutland, Vt.: Charles E. Tuttle, 1998). See also Johnson's discussion of Buddhism in *Turning the Wheel: Essays on Buddhism and Writing* (New York: Scribner, 2003), especially 3–79. A recent discussion of Buddhism employing a postmodernist perspective is Dale S. Wright's excellent *Philosophical Meditations on Zen Buddhism* (New York: Cambridge University Press, 1998). Both Dumoulin's and Wright's books have been essential to me. For ease of reading, Buddhist terms will not be italicized.

13. This tension between criticizing social institutions as determinative while simultaneously arguing for the freedom of the individual has led Ashraf H. A. Rushdy to describe Johnson as a "novelist who has exhibited persistent tensions in his work, who treads on the borders of a conservative and an oppositional aesthetic" (*Neoslave Narratives* [New York: Oxford University Press, 1999], 184).

14. Thich Nhat Hanh, *Living Buddha, Living Christ* (New York: Riverhead Books, 1995), 89, 11, 194, 197, 106.

15. Johnson, *Being and Race,* 32, 4.

16. Nash, "A Conversation with Charles Johnson," 58.

17. Ralph Waldo Emerson, "Nature," *The Portable Emerson,* ed. Carl Bode (New York: Penguin Books, 1983), 11.

18. Emerson, "The American Scholar," *The Portable Emerson,* 69.

19. Alfred North Whitehead, *Religion in the Making* (New York: Macmillan, 1926), 140.

20. Johnson, *Being and Race,* 123.

21. Johnson, *Dreamer: A Novel* (New York: Scribner, 1998), 133.

22. I take these two terms from John B. Cobb, "The Meaning of Pluralism for Christian Self-Understanding," in *Religious Pluralism,* ed. Leroy S. Rouner (Notre Dame, Ind.: University of Notre Dame Press, 1984), 177.

23. Johnson's approach to ethics resembles virtue-based ethics, which argues that the proper domain for ethicists is the evaluation of whole persons (as opposed to specific acts, called act-based ethics).

24. Translation from Nhat Hanh, *Living Buddha, Living Christ,* 22.

25. Johnson, *Faith and the Good Thing* (New York: Atheneum, 1987), 5.

26. Wright, *Philosophical Meditations on Zen Buddhism,* 51. For perhaps the definitive treatment of Buddhist "emptiness," see Frederick J. Streng, *Emptiness: A Study in Religious Meaning* (New York: Abingdon Press, 1967).

27. Johnson, *Middle Passage* (New York: Plume, 1990), 171; Molly Abel Travis, *Reading Cultures: The Construction of Readers in the Twentieth Century* (Carbondale: Southern Illinois University Press, 1998), 77.

28. Johnson, *Being and Race,* 14.

29. *The Dhammapada,* trans. Irving Babbitt (New York: New Directions, 1965), 6.

Chapter 2—*Faith and the Good Thing*

1. Johnson, "Introduction," in *Oxherding Tale* (New York: Plume, 1995), xiii. *Oxherding Tale* was originally published without the introduction by Plume in 1982. All parenthetical notes in this chapter refer to Johnson, *Faith and the Good Thing* (New York: Viking, 1974).

2. In contrast to my reading, see Peter Hallward, who argues, "The *best* philosophy of the Good Thing must come from a figure properly beyond relationality altogether" (*Absolutely Postcolonial: Writing between the Singular and the Specific* [New York: Manchester University Press, 2001], 145).

3. William R. Nash, *Charles Johnson's Fiction* (Urbana: University of Illinois Press, 2003), 66. For a different analysis of this passage, see 66–67.

4. Rob Trucks, "A Conversation with Charles Johnson," *Tri-Quarterly* 107/108 (Winter–Summer 2000), 2.

5. Emerson, "Nature," 11.

6. Rowell, "An Interview with Charles Johnson," 543.

7. Dumoulin, *Zen Buddhism: A History,* 19.

8. Ibid., 25.

9. Jonathan Little, *Charles Johnson's Spiritual Imagination* (Columbia: University of Missouri Press, 1997), 72.

10. For a contrasting view of Alpha Omega Holmes as artist, see John McCumber, "Philosophy and Hydrology: Situating Discourse in Charles Johnson's *Faith and the Good Thing,*" in *I Call Myself an Artist,* 259–61.

11. Perhaps Alice Walker's cultivation of the folk tradition is one reason Johnson disapproves of her novel *The Color Purple.* See *Being and Race,* 106–7.

12. Rowell, "An Interview with Charles Johnson," 542. Johnson also tells Rob Trucks that "none of [his writing] is about ego. None of this is about career for me. It never has been. I have no interest in that" ("A Conversation with Charles Johnson," 1).

13. For a discussion of the novel's naturalism, see both Little, *Charles Johnson's Spiritual Imagination,* 77–79, and Nash, *Charles Johnson's Fiction,* 76–78.

14. Magic realism, a mode of writing often associated with marginalized writers, implies (as the oxymoron suggests) that fantasy and magic coexist in the text with their antithesis, realism; yet magical elements are not textually subordinate to a realistic scene but are organically connected to the whole work, neither more nor less privileged than the novel's realistic components. The boundaries between reality and fantasy, then, are erased, defeating a reader's presumption that a commonsense, rationalist interpretation of events can be easily discovered. In effect, the reader must revise his or her traditional, Western distinction between a Cartesian epistemology of a rationally knowable world governed by natural law and a spiritual vision of world controlled by the imagination.

Chapter 3—*Oxherding Tale*

1. Kapleau, *The Three Pillars of Zen,* 23; see also Dumoulin, *Zen Buddhism,* 123–54.

2. Dumoulin, *Zen Buddhism*, 132.

3. Wright, *Philosophical Meditations on Zen Buddhism*, 130.

4. Johnson, *Turning the Wheel*, 150.

5. Jennifer Levasseur and Kevin Rabalais, "An Interview with Charles Johnson," *Brick* 69 (Spring 2002): 141.

6. Johnson, however, does not limit himself to the two most famous slave narratives; Vera Kutzinski demonstrates how Charles Johnson "rewrites" James W. Johnson's *The Autobiography of an Ex-Colored Man* in "Johnson Revises Johnson: *Oxherding Tale* and *The Autobiography of an Ex-Colored Man*," in *I Call Myself an Artist*, 279–87. Johnson also loosely patterns his narrative after William and Ellen Craft's escape from slavery, related in their *Running a Thousand Miles for Freedom*.

7. John Sekora, "Slave Narrative," in *The Oxford Companion to African American Literature* (New York: Oxford University Press, 1997), 667.

8. John Haynes quoted in S. X. Goudie, "'Leavin' a Mark on the Wor(l)d': Marksmen and Marked Men in *Middle Passage*," *African American Review* 29, no. 1 (1995): 109; Linda Hutcheon, *A Theory of Parody: The Teachings of Twentieth-Century Artforms* (New York: Methuen, 1985), 33, 101, 43, 41.

9. James W. Coleman also calls attention to these textual interruptions, arguing that Johnson's purpose is to undermine the reader's stereotypical preconceptions about the nature of African American fiction ("Charles Johnson's Quest for Black Freedom in *Oxherding Tale*," *African American Review* 29, no. 4 [1995]: 632).

10. William Gleason, "The Liberation of Perception: Charles Johnson's *Oxherding Tale*," *Black American Literature Forum* 25, no. 4 (1991): 705–28.

11. Jeremy Bentham, "An Introduction to the Principles of Morals and Legislation," in *A Bentham Reader*, ed. Mary Peter Mack (New York: Pegasus, 1969), 85.

12. Ibid., 85, 86–87.

13. Denis de Rougement, *Love in the Western World*, trans. Montgomery Belgion (New York: Harper and Row, 1974), 15.

14. The reference to Minty's eyes may also be an allusion to the idealistic narrator of Jean Toomer's *Cane;* Johnson refers to *Cane* as an ancestral text for his work.

15. De Rougement, *Love in the Western World,* 285.

16. Though almost unmentioned in *Narrative,* Douglass's wife (a freewoman herself) was instrumental in his escape. It was her idea that Douglass dress as a sailor, and she altered his clothing so he could play the part. She also sold her feather bed to help finance his escape. See William S. McFeely, *Frederick Douglass* (New York: Norton, 1991), 70.

17. This point is also made by A. T. Spaulding, "Finding the Way: Karl Marx and the Transcendence of Discourse in Charles Johnson's *Oxherding Tale,*" *Sycamore* 1, no. 1 (1997); originally available on line at http://www.unc.edu/sycamore/97.1/oxherd.html (accessed June 2002).

18. For a different interpretation of this scene, see Ashraf H. A. Rushdy, who explains that "Marx did write about the ideas Johnson has the fictional Marx articulate" (*Neo-slave Narratives,* 210). Rushdy explains that Marx did recommend "love" as the ideal condition for achieving "human actualization based on communal production and not premised on the exploitation of labor and concomitant accumulation of surplus value" (211).

19. Significantly, Johnson puns on the character in his story "Alēthia" in *The Sorcerer's Apprentice,* which involves a professor (like Ezekiel) discovering the true source of joy in his student. The difference between the two characters, however, is that the professor does not begin a relationship with an image, as does Ezekiel.

20. Both Rudolph P. Byrd and Little explain that Flo is a parody of Kamala, the seductive woman who teaches Siddhartha the "games of love." See Rudolph P. Byrd, "*Oxherding Tale* and Siddhartha: Philosophy, Fiction, and the Emergence of a Hidden Tradition," *African American Review* 30, no. 4 (1996): 553; Little, *Charles Johnson's Spiritual Imagination,* 88.

21. The distinction between "act" and "rule" utilitarianism was made in the twentieth century.

22. Little, *Charles Johnson's Spiritual Imagination,* 95–96.

23. George as a parody of 1960s black nationalism is thoroughly discussed by both Little, *Charles Johnson's Spiritual Imagination,* 95–97, and Nash, *Charles Johnson's Fiction,* 109–10.

24. In this context, it would be appropriate to recall Johnson's father, who paid for Johnson's art lessons as a child, even though he had to work three jobs to maintain the family budget. His generosity was extraordinary in the circumstances, but it was the good and right thing to do—an expression of *arete.*

25. Timothy L. Parrish, "Imagining Slavery: Toni Morrison and Charles Johnson," *Studies in American Fiction* 25, no. 1 (1997): 94.

26. Little, *Charles Johnson's Spiritual Imagination,* 146.

27. For an attack on Johnson's conservatism, see Travis, *Reading Cultures,* 68–88. See also Bill Brown, "Global Bodies/Postnationalities: Charles Johnson's Consumer Culture," *Representations* 58 (Spring 1997): 24–48.

28. Gleason, "The Liberation of Perception," 724.

29. Johnson, "Black Images and Their Global Impact," in *I Call Myself an Artist,* 139, 138.

30. Nash, "A Conversation with Charles Johnson," 56. Reb's artistic inclination to dissolve his identity in favor of the work is an ideal that Johnson himself attempts to achieve as he writes. When asked by interviewer Charles H. Rowell what is the most difficult aspect of writing, Johnson replies, "The hardest part about writing for me is getting myself out of the way" ("An Interview with Charles Johnson," 542).

31. "With the perspective of dependent co-arising as its backdrop, the philosophy of debt was the center of Buddhist ethics. . . . [There were] four types of debt (to parents, ruler, sentient beings, and either heaven/earth or the three treasures [Buddha, Dharma, and Sangha])" R. Tsunoda et al., eds., *Sources of Japanese Tradition*

[New York: Columbia University Press, 1965], 1:48). In *Turning the Wheel,* Johnson writes that "'Doing' for the Dharma follower is an example of disinterested, deontological [that is, dutiful] ethics, which, like that found in Kantian philosophy is 'interested in the act, never the fruit'" (20–21).

32. Rowell, "An Interview with Charles Johnson," 544.

33. Aristotle says that *eudaimonia* is not simply a feeling or a gratification of desires (see *Nicomachean Ethics,* ed. Richard Mc-Keon [New York: Modern Library, 1947], 334–36). Significantly for Johnson, Aristotle also dismisses the slave's chance for *eudaimonia.* As Aristotle writes, "any chance person—even a slave—can enjoy the bodily pleasures . . . but no one assigns to a slave a share in happiness—unless he assigns to him also a share in human life" (531).

Chapter 4—*The Sorcerer's Apprentice*

1. M. H. Abrams, *The Mirror and the Lamp: Romantic Theory and the Critical Tradition* (1953; repr., New York: W. W. Norton, 1958), 3–29.

2. Johnson, *Turning the Wheel,* 152.

3. Levasseur and Rabalais, "An Interview with Charles Johnson," 142.

4. Johnson, *Being and Race,* 4.

5. Trucks, "A Conversation with Charles Johnson," 8.

6. Johnson, *The Sorcerer's Apprentice: Tales and Conjurations* (New York: Penguin, 1986), 117. All parenthetical notes in this chapter refer to this edition.

7. Johnson continues his allusions to Max Scheler, begun in "Alēthia." Scheler's analysis of sympathy excludes mere egotistical identification; as the narrator, a scriptwriter, says to himself about his own tears: "You yourself have been supplying the grief and satisfaction all along" (*The Sorcerer's Apprentice,* 121).

8. Matthew 6.12.

9. Johnson, "National Book Award Acceptance Speech," *Tri-Quarterly* 82 (1991): 209.

10. *The Works of George Berkeley, Bishop of Cloyne,* ed. A. A. Luce and T. E. Jessop (London: Nelson, 1967), 2:42.

11. Ibid., 1:43.

12. For Johnson's discussion of the writing process, see Little's interview, "An Interview with Charles Johnson," in *I Call Myself an Artist,* 233.

13. *The Works of George Berkeley,* 1:41–42.

14. Johnson, "A Phenomenology of the Black Body," in *I Call Myself an Artist,* 112.

15. *The Works of George Berkeley,* 2:230.

16. Ibid., 2:230–31.

17. Johnson's strategy in "Menagerie" resembles Berkeley's philosophical moves in *Principles,* in which he supposes that a person imagines "trees . . . in a park, or books existing in a closet, and nobody to perceive them" (*The Works of George Berkeley,* 1:39). Berkeley's point is that the person is imaging a world without a perceiver in the world—the activity is more analogous to the work of a creative artist than to God.

18. In replacing the Christian God with the artist as Divine Artificer, Johnson employs a strategy that is similar to that of William Butler Yeats in his essay "Bishop Berkeley," in *Essays and Introductions* (New York: Macmillan, 1961). Yeats argues that Berkeley managed to overcome one Western obstacle to self-realization (empiricism) but not the other (Christianity). To protect his Christian orthodoxy, "Berkeley deliberately refused to define personality" as reflecting "the whole act of God; his God and Man seem cut off from one another" (405–6). He dared not take the "next step"—the step taken by William Blake and Hinduism—that conceives God as embodied in humanity (408). Blake, Hinduism, and the Romantic poets, Yeats suggests, substituted for Berkeley's God the creative self as the connection between the perceiver and the perceived world.

19. Matthew 4:4.

20. *The Works of George Berkeley,* 1:219.

21. Johnson, *Being and Race,* 47.

22. Little, "An Interview with Charles Johnson," 229.

23. Johnson, *Being and Race,* 43.

24. Little, *Charles Johnson's Spiritual Imagination,* 112–14; Nash, *Charles Johnson's Fiction,* 88–92.

25. Linda Furgerson Selzer analyzes this distinction in her article on the story, "Charles Johnson's 'Exchange Value': Signifyin(g) on Marx," *Massachusetts Review* (Summer 2001): 253–68.

26. Karl Marx, "Commodities," in *Capital* (New York: International Publishers, 1987), 44.

27. Selzer, "Charles Johnson's 'Exchange Value,'" 255–56.

28. Little, *Charles Johnson's Spiritual Imagination,* 113.

29. Cornel West, *The American Evasion of Philosophy: A Genealogy of Pragmatism* (Madison: University of Wisconsin Press, 1989), 51.

30. Little, *Charles Johnson's Spiritual Imagination,* 110.

31. Johnson, *Being and Race,* 49.

32. For a discussion of Moses as artist, see Little, *Charles Johnson's Spiritual Imagination,* 109–12.

33. Linda Selzer, "Master-Slave Dialectics in Charles Johnson's 'Education of Mingo,'" *African American Review* 37, no. 1 (2003): 113.

34. W. E. B. Du Bois, "The Souls of Black Folk," *Three Negro Classics* (New York: Avon Books, 1965), 215.

35. Herbert Spiegelberg, *The Phenomenological Movement: A Historical Introduction,* 2nd ed. (The Hague: Martinus Nijhoff, 1971), 1:242.

36. Max Scheler, quoted in Spiegelberg, *The Phenomenological Movement,* 1:242.

37. Indeed, Popper's last name may be one more of Johnson's philosophical games, an allusion to the philosopher Karl Popper (1902–94). Popper's philosophy is primarily known for its refusal of authoritarian, closed, absolutist systems; he recommends instead advancing tentative solutions to problems, testing these hypotheses, and (in the context of this discussion) revising these provisional theories of reality.

38. Johnson quotes the Buddhist verses "How wonderful, how marvelous!! / I fetch wood, I carry water!" in *Turning the Wheel*, 25.

39. Getting himself "out of the way" in his work is Johnson's self-description of what he must do as a writer. See Rowell, "An Interview with Charles Johnson," 545.

40. Nash, *Charles Johnson's Fiction*, 86.

41. John 8.44.

Chapter 5—*Middle Passage*

1. Levasseur and Rabalais, "An Interview with Charles Johnson," 143.

2. Johnson, *Oxherding Tale*, 146.

3. Ibid., 176.

4. Johnson, *Middle Passage* (New York: Plume, 1990), 162. (All parenthetical notes in this chapter refer to this edition.) "Useful fiction" is a term created by Han Vaihinger in *The Philosophy of "As If"* (1913); Vaihinger's argument is that because we can never rest with ultimate truths, we create for practical purposes partial truths (that is, "useful fictions"), useful constructions of reality that help guide us in both science and day-to-day life. Johnson's anachronism in this case (Rutherford's knowing a term created almost eighty-five years after the novel takes place) subtly proves his point: the past is only truly understood through the evolving discoveries of tomorrow, which we cannot predict.

5. Little, *Charles Johnson's Spiritual Imagination*, 148.

6. Nash, *Charles Johnson's Fiction*, 144.

7. Matthew 5.30.

8. This point is made by S. X. Goudie in "'Leavin' a Mark on the Wor(l)d,'" 109–22. Goudie argues that Johnson dissolves the binary epistemology that marks human beings as either the enslaver or the enslaved.

9. Jean-Paul Sartre, *Being and Nothingness*, trans. Hazel E. Barnes (New York: Philosophical Library, 1956), 32.

10. Nash, *Charles Johnson's Fiction*, 139.

11. Goudie argues that Allmuseri is a Latin anagram: "Allmuseri/erimus, meaning 'We shall be All'" (Goudie, "'Leavin' a Mark on the Wor[l]d,'" 119n8). Travis reads it as a pun on "all misery" (*Reading Cultures*, 189).

12. Trucks, "A Conversation with Charles Johnson," 8. For a discussion that links the Allmuseri with Whitehead's process philosophy, see Ashraf H. A. Rushdy, "The Phenomenology of the Allmuseri: Charles Johnson and the Subject of the Narrative of Slavery," in *I Call Myself an Artist*, 369–96.

13. Travis calls the cannibalism scene an "intersubjective encounter" (*Reading Cultures*, 80).

Chapter 6—*Dreamer*

1. John Whalen-Bridge, "Waking Cain: The Poetics of Integration in Charles Johnson's *Dreamer*," *Callaloo* 26, no. 2 (2003): 504–21. All parenthetical notes in this chapter refer to Johnson, *Dreamer: A Novel* (New York: Scribner, 1998).

2. Nash, *Charles Johnson's Fiction*, 163.

3. Johnson, *Turning the Wheel*, xvi.

4. West, *The American Evasion of Philosophy*, 51.

5. Johnson, *Turning the Wheel*, 173.

6. West, *The American Evasion of Philosophy*, 51.

7. Johnson, *Middle Passage*, 174

8. Johnson, "The King We Left Behind," in *I Call Myself an Artist*, 194.

9. Whalen-Bridge, "Waking Cain," 504.

10. Luke 12.49.

11. Martin Luther King Jr., "Letter from Birmingham Jail," in *I Have a Dream: Writings and Speeches That Changed the World*, ed. James Melvin Washington (1986; repr., New York: HarperCollins, 1992), 91.

12. Ibid., 91.

13. Whalen-Bridge, "Waking Cain," 505.

14. Nash, *Charles Johnson's Fiction*, 186, 187.

15. Johnson, "The King We Left Behind," 195.

16. Johnson, *Turning the Wheel*, 158.

17. Whalen-Bridge, "Waking Cain," 514.

18. Ibid., 513.

19. Compare Nash, who writes about this incident: "with his volunteering himself and Bishop to serve at Bethel A.M.E., he puts his newly formed self into action. As during his other time of retreat, Smith finds every action to be holy, all of a piece in his sacrifice of self" (*Charles Johnson's Fiction*, 174).

20. Wright, *Philosophical Meditations on Zen Buddhism*, 129.

21. Johnson, "The King We Left Behind," in *I Call Myself an Artist*, 194.

22. Michael Eric Dyson summarizes how neoconservatives have coopted King's speeches for their political use in his book *I May Not Get There with You: The True Martin Luther King, Jr.* (New York: Free Press, 2000), especially 11–29 and 234–48. Johnson also discusses misuse of King's speeches in "The King We Left Behind," in *I Call Myself an Artist*, 194.

23. Johnson's principal source for *Dreamer* is Stephen B. Oates's *Let the Trumpet Sound: A Life of Martin Luther King, Jr.* (New York: HarperPerennial, 1982). Oates reports King's deep depression and that "he was beginning to lose faith" (457).

24. Johnson, "A Sangha by Another Name," in *Turning the Wheel*, 54.

25. Significantly, Johnson in an essay on Buddhist political action also warns against unrealistic utopian expectations. Despite the necessity of political engagement for all people, especially Buddhists, Johnson warns that "suffering will continue, despite our best efforts, until all of us experience—like Shakyamuni Buddha—enlightenment and liberation" (*Turning the Wheel*, 64). Instead, he urges the seemingly mundane action of registering to vote in the coming presidential elections (45).

26. King urges Matthew to "[g]et the Nietzsche out of your system," and to read Edgar Sheffield Brightman instead (*Dreamer*, 27). Brightman is one of the proponents of personalism, which emphasizes the real personhood of God. However, Matthew discovers personalism is philosophically inadequate for his needs, "as dead as Neoplatonism" (110).

27. Johnson discusses the Ware attack in Johnson et al., eds., *King: The Photobiography of Martin Luther King, Jr.* (New York: Viking Studio), 55.

28. Nash, *Charles Johnson's Fiction*, 169.

29. James Baldwin, *Notes of a Native Son* (1955; repr., Boston: Beacon Press, 1984), 94, 97, 94.

30. Whalen-Bridge, "Waking Cain," 516.

31. Nash, *Charles Johnson's Fiction*, 172.

Chapter 7—*Soulcatcher and Other Stories*

1. Johnson, *Soulcatcher and Other Stories* (New York: Harcourt, 2001), xii.

2. Johnson, *Being and Race*, 123.

Bibliography

Selected Works by Charles Johnson

Black Humor. Chicago: Johnson, 1970.

Half-Past Nation Time. Chicago: Aware, 1972.

Faith and the Good Thing. New York: Viking, 1974.

Oxherding Tale. New York: Grove, 1982.

The Sorcerer's Apprentice: Tales and Conjurations. New York: Penguin Books, 1986.

Being and Race: Black Writing since 1970. Bloomington: Indiana University Press, 1988.

Middle Passage. New York: Atheneum, 1990.

Black Men Speaking. Edited by Johnson and John McCluskey Jr. Bloomington: Indiana University Press, 1997.

Dreamer: A Novel. New York: Scribner, 1998.

Africans in America: America's Journey through Slavery. By Johnson, Patricia Smith, and the WGBH Research Team. New York: Harcourt Brace, 1998.

King: The Photobiography of Martin Luther King, Jr. By Johnson and Bob Adelman, edited by Mary Beth Brewer, and photos edited by Robert Phelan. New York: Viking, 2000.

Soulcatcher and Other Stories. New York: Harcourt, 2001.

Turning the Wheel: Essays on Buddhism and Writing. New York: Scribner, 2003.

Selected Interviews

Boccia, Michael. "An Interview with Charles Johnson." *African American Review* 30, no. 4 (1996): 611–18.

Crouch, Stanley. "Critic, Not Cynic: Charles Johnson Talks with Stanley Crouch." 1993. In *I Call Myself an Artist: Writings by and about Charles Johnson,* edited by Rudoph P. Byrd, 245–48. Bloomington: Indiana University Press, 1999.

Levasseur, Jennifer, and Kevin Rabalais. "An Interview with Charles Johnson." *Brick* 69 (Spring 2002): 133–44.

Little, Jonathan. "An Interview with Charles Johnson." 1993. In *I Call Myself an Artist: Writings by and about Charles Johnson,* edited by Rudoph P. Byrd, 225–43. Bloomington: Indiana University Press, 1999.

McCullough, Ken. "Reflections on Film, Philosophy, and Fiction: An Interview with Charles Johnson." *Callaloo* 4, no. 1 (1978): 118–28.

Nash, William R. "A Conversation with Charles Johnson." *New England Review* 19, no. 2 (1998): 49–61.

Rowell, Charles H. "An Interview with Charles Johnson." *Callaloo* 20, no. 3 (1998): 531–47.

Trucks, Rob. "A Conversation with Charles Johnson." *TriQuarterly* 107/108 (Winter–Summer 2000): 537–60.

Selected Works about Charles Johnson

Benesch, Klaus. "Slavery as Metaphor: Charles Johnson's Cross-Cultural 'Slave Narratives.'" In *Parcours identitaires,* edited by Geneviève Fabre, 135–46. Paris: Presses de la Sorbonne Nouvelle, 1993. Argues that Johnson's theme in "The Education of Mingo" is the interconnection of all things in the universe, and a renunciation of Cartesian dualism.

Boccia, Michael, and Herman Beavers, eds. "Charles Johnson Issue." *African American Review* 30, no. 4 (1996). A special issue dedicated to Johnson's work that includes several unpublished cartoons by Johnson, his essay on John Gardner, a screenplay, and an "apprentice" story. Also includes eight important critical essays on his work and a bibliography.

Brown, Bill. "Global Bodies / Postnationalities: Charles Johnson's Consumer Culture." *Representations* 58 (Spring 1997): 24–48.

Asserts that the story "China" is an uncritical celebration of American consumerism; also decries Johnson's depiction of women in the story.

Butler, Robert. "Charles Johnson's *Faith and the Good Thing:* The Open Journey as Metaphysical Quest." In *Contemporary African American Fiction: The Open Journey,* 88–102. Madison, N.J.: Fairleigh Dickinson University Press, 1998. A study of Johnson's innovations of picaresque conventions, emphasizing the unending nature of Faith's picaresque journey.

Byrd, Rudolph P., ed. *I Call Myself an Artist: Writings by and about Charles Johnson.* Bloomington: Indiana University Press, 1999. An indispensable work for Johnson scholars. Combines many of Johnson's most important essays, reviews, interviews, and short stories with nine groundbreaking critical discussions of Johnson's work.

Coleman, James W. "Charles Johnson's Quest for Black Freedom in *Oxherding Tale.*" *African American Review* 29, no. 4 (1995): 631–44. Asserts that Andrew and Johnson both find freedom: Andrew, from socially constricting boundaries; Johnson, from "non-black texts."

———. "Charles Johnson's Response to 'Caliban's Dilemma.'" In *Black Male Fiction and the Legacy of Caliban,* 81–99. Lexington: University Press of Kentucky, 2001. A provocative study of *Oxherding Tale* and *Middle Passage* that presents Andrew and Rutherford escaping through intersubjectivity "Caliban's dilemma" (that is, racist gestures, stereotypes, and discourse that begin in Shakespeare's *The Tempest*).

Cox, Timothy J. "Caricature of a Non-Existent Essence (A True Philosophical Conundrum) in *Middle Passage.*" In *Postmodern Tales of Slavery in the Americas: From Alejo Carpentier to Charles Johnson,* 93–105. New York: Garland Publishing, 2001. Concerned that Johnson is not sympathetic to the victims of slavery, and asserts that Johnson conservatively affirms the status quo by undercutting "subversive" attitudes.

Gleason, William. "The Liberation of Perception: Charles Johnson's *Oxherding Tale*." *Black American Literature Forum* 25, no. 4 (1991): 705–28. Explains the novel in terms of Johnson's Buddhist source, the "Ten Oxherding Pictures."

Goudie, S. X. "'Leavin' a Mark on the Wor(l)d': Marksmen and Marked Men in *Middle Passage*." *African American Review* 29, no. 1 (1995): 109–22. An imaginative analysis of the "mark image," showing how the characters learn to negotiate stigma.

Hallward, Peter. "Charles Johnson and the Transcendence of Place." In *Absolutely Postcolonial: Writing between the Singular and the Specific*, 133–75. New York: Manchester University Press, 2001. An overview of Johnson's works; asserts that to "describe the ultimate truth of the world, you first have to escape it."

Jablon, Madelyn. "Mimesis of Process: The Thematization of Art." In *Black Metafiction: Self-Consciousness in African American Literature*, 29–45. Iowa City: University of Iowa Press, 1997. A reading of *Middle Passage* that identifies Falcon as a postmodernist (rejected by Johnson) and Rutherford as the "new realist" who experiences the subjectivity of all experience.

Lenz, Günter H. "Middle Passages: Histories, Re-Memories, and Black Diasporas in Novels by Toni Morrison, Charles Johnson, and Caryl Phillips." In *Crabtracks: Progress and Process in Teaching the New Literatures in English; Essays in Honour of Dieter Riemenschneider*, edited by Gordon Collier and Frank Schulze-Engler, 235–52. Amsterdam: Rodopi, 2002. Emphasizes the processual nature of history in individuals, races, and nations in *Middle Passage*.

Little, Jonathan. *Charles Johnson's Spiritual Imagination*. Columbia: University of Missouri Press, 1997. First book-length publication on Johnson. Little provides an insightful explication of Johnson's works, demonstrating Johnson's "integrative impulse" in the fusing of Buddhist, African, and Asian modes of thought in stories that point out the illusory nature of race.

Nash, William R. *Charles Johnson's Fiction*. Urbana: University of Illinois Press, 2003. A thorough, insightful, and carefully argued discussion arguing that Johnson's career evinces "whole sight," fusing mainstream white literature and philosophy to effect a holistic vision of experience.

Ouimet, Lorraine. "Freedom through Contamination: Collapsed Boundaries in Charles Johnson's *Oxherding Tale* and *Middle Passage*." *Canadian Review of American Studies* 30, no. 1 (2000): 33–51. Positions Johnson as critiquing both white and African American historiographies of slavery; finds that imagery of "contamination" serves to dissolve the body/soul, self/other dichotomies.

Page, Philip. "'As Within, So It Is Without': The Composite Self in Charles Johnson's *Oxherding Tale* and *Middle Passage*." In *Reclaiming Community in Contemporary African American Fiction,* 116–56. Jackson: University Press of Mississippi, 1999. A close reading of both novels; argues that Johnson dramatizes the effort to achieve intersubjectivity and community, depending upon the development of a composite self.

Parrish, Timothy. "Imagining Slavery: Toni Morrison and Charles Johnson." *Studies in American Fiction* 25, no. 1 (1997): 81–100. Attempts to reconcile the differing visions of Morrison and Johnson by asserting that both writers imagine a protagonist undertaking an ongoing revision of the past.

Reichardt, Ulfried. "Writing the Past: History, Fiction, and Subjectivity in Two Recent Novels about Slavery." *Yearbook of Research in English and American Literature* 11 (1995): 283–98. Discusses the problem of narrating history in *The Chaneysville Incident* and *Oxherding Tale,* arguing that Johnson understands history as a "multi-layered web of relationships."

Retman, Sonnet. "'Nothing Was Lost in the Masquerade': The Protean Performance of Genre and Identity in Charles Johnson's *Oxherding Tale*." *African American Review* 33, no. 3 (1999): 417–37. A close reading that asserts Andrew's liberation from slavery and the reader's freedom from a naive realist understanding; expresses concern about Johnson's depiction of women.

Rushdy, Ashraf H. A. "Serving the Form, Conserving the Order: Charles Johnson's *Oxherding Tale*," 169–200; and "Revising the Form, Misserving the Order: Charles Johnson's *Middle Passage*," 201–26. In *Neo-slave Narratives: Studies in the Social Logic of a Literary Form.* New York: Oxford University Press, 1999. Two important, complexly argued discussions of Johnson's work using postmodernist theory; argues that *Oxherding Tale* equivocates in its attack on antiessentialism, while *Middle Passage* has a more revolutionary potential, as it turns reactionary institutional form (for example, the slaver's log) against itself.

Selzer, Linda. "Master-Slave Dialectics in Charles Johnson's 'The Education of Mingo.'" *African American Review* 37, no. 1 (2003): 105–14. Employing Hegel's theory of the master-slave relationship, shows that Johnson revises the simple notion that slaves were reduced to objects; instead, the slave and the master mutually transform themselves in their relationship.

Selzer, Linda Furgerson. "Charles Johnson's 'Exchange Value': Signifyin(g) on Marx." *Massachusetts Review* 42 (Summer 2001): 253–68. A sophisticated analysis of Johnson's use of Marxist theoretics used in the short story; demonstrates that Johnson links Marxist theory to racial discrimination.

Spaulding, A. T. "Finding the Way: Karl Marx and the Transcendence of Discourse in Charles Johnson's *Oxherding Tale*." *Sycamore* 1, no. 1 (1997), http://www.unc.edu/sycamore/97.1/oxherd.html (accessed June 2002). Analyzes Marx's visit to Ezekiel, placing in Marx's self-identification as "householder" the novel's theme.

Thaden, Barbara Z. "Charles Johnson's *Middle Passage* as Historiographic Metafiction." *College English* 59 (November 1997): 753–66. A persuasive analysis of the novel that identifies Johnson's "metafictional" use of the historical novel, arguing that Johnson concerns himself primarily with contemporary American social problems affecting African Americans, not the issue of slavery.

Travis, Molly Abel. "*Beloved* and *Middle Passage:* Race, Narrative, and the Critic's Essentialism." In *Reading Cultures: The Construction of Readers in the Twentieth Century,* 68–88. Carbondale: Southern Illinois University Press, 1998. Attacks Johnson's "transcendence" of race as an evasion of contemporary social problems and criticizes his "masculinist" plots; prefers Toni Morrison's *Beloved* to Johnson's *Middle Passage.*

Walby, Celestin. "The African Sacrificial Kingship Ritual and Johnson's Middle Passage." *African American Review* 29, no. 4 (1995): 657–69. Discusses the novel as an amalgamation of various African mythologies, especially the African kingship ritual.

Whalen-Bridge, John. "Waking Cain: The Poetics of Integration in Charles Johnson's *Dreamer.*" *Callaloo* 26, no. 2 (2003): 504–21. An excellent discussion that traces the Buddhist and Christian influences in the novel; argues that the novel recommends healing through integration in King's character.

Wyrick, Deborah Baker. "Charles Johnson's Battle of the Books." *Postscript* 11 (1994): 1–9. A comparison of Johnson's *Middle Passage* with Melville's *Benito Cereno,* Defoe's *Robinson Crusoe,* and Swift's *Gulliver's Travels.*

Index